THE *Creole* REBELLION

The *Creole* Rebellion

〜〜〜〜

THE MOST SUCCESSFUL

SLAVE REVOLT IN

AMERICAN HISTORY

〜〜〜〜

Bruce Chadwick

〜〜〜〜

University of New Mexico Press / Albuquerque

ISBN 978-0-8263-6347-3 (cloth)
ISBN 978-0-8263-6348-0 (e-book)

Library of Congress Control Number: 2021948224

Founded in 1889, the University of New Mexico sits on the traditional homelands of the Pueblo of Sandia. The original peoples of New Mexico—Pueblo, Navajo, and Apache—since time immemorial have deep connections to the land and have made significant contributions to the broader community statewide. We honor the land itself and those who remain stewards of this land throughout the generations and also acknowledge our committed relationship to Indigenous peoples. We gratefully recognize our history.

PHOTOGRAPHY EDITOR: Timothy Stuckey

COVER ILLUSTRATION

Slave ships on the ocean. Wood engraving by Smyth. Wellcome Library, London. Wellcome Images. Copyrighted work available under Creative Commons Attribution only licence CC BY 4.0 http://creativecommons.org/licenses/by/4.0/

Vintage engraving shows a crowd of African men, women, and children who had been rescued by the British navy from a slaving vessel in 1884. istockphoto.com

DESIGNED BY Mindy Basinger Hill

COMPOSED IN 10.75 / 14.8pt Fanwood

FOR MY LATE WIFE,

Marjorie,

THE INSPIRATION

OF MY LIFE

CONTENTS

Illustrations follow page 112

PREFACE

❖❖❖❖❖❖

A Slave Ship in
Uncharted Waters

I STUMBLED ACROSS THE STORY of the slave ship *Creole* and its mutiny while researching another book. I was immediately transfixed by the sea saga of the 135 people aboard in bondage and how they rose up to take over their ship, killing one man and injuring several others, including the captain, while it sailed down the coast of Florida on its way to New Orleans in the early winter of 1841. The slaves were led by a huge, muscular Virginian, Madison Washington, named after two US presidents, who had been captured while trying to spirit his wife away from his old plantation, from which he had escaped a year earlier. The rebel slaves took control of the *Creole* after a bloody scuffle and forced the crew to sail to the Bahamas, a group of islands in the Caribbean where African Americans, and all people of color, were free. The crew knew how to get there and so did thousands of white mariners who sailed the waters of the Atlantic. But the slaves were headed into uncharted waters, toward islands where their fate, as either mutineers and murderers or as heroes, would be sealed.

The tale of the *Creole* had been overshadowed in history by that of the *Amistad*, a slave ship that was taken on the high seas by its African prisoners in 1839 and whose case wound up in the United States Supreme Court and was made famous in song, story, and a successful movie. The *Creole* was just a faint footnote to the drama of the *Amistad*, but today it is considered the most successful slave revolt in American history. Washington and the eighteen men who were directly involved in the mutiny managed not only to take over a large vessel but also to sail it to the Bahamas, where they were put on trial on charges of mutiny, murder, and seizure of the ship. They were up against the president of the United States himself, John Tyler, and his legendary secretary of state, Daniel Webster. The fight was so heated that diplomats in the United States and Great Britain, which had jurisdiction over the Bahamas, feared that it would lead to a war. American public officials were pressured heavily by slave-owning southerners, who feared that the success of the mutineers would lead thousands of other slaves to stage similar revolts and perhaps overturn slavery altogether in the American South.

As I plunged into research on the story, the tale assumed great depth because this was not just the drama of a mutiny. A group of prisoners did not just seize a ship and sail off, free men, into the mist. Innumerable questions began to arise.

For instance, how did Madison Washington, an enslaved African American whose only known skill was being a cook, stage and carry off a successful armed mutiny? How did he know that the islands of the Bahamas were British territory and that African Americans lived freely there? How did he know that the British courts had freed numerous slaves whose ships had washed ashore in the Bahamas?

The mutiny went smoothly, but Washington never thought anyone would be hurt, much less killed. The mutineers' problem now was not just that they had taken a ship; they were also guilty of assault and battery and murder. Would that change the complexion of British justice in the Bahamas? A mutiny was one thing, but a murder was something else.

And as I followed the story, I wondered, as many people in that era did, what exactly was the legal definition murder? Was the killing of slave trader John Hewell on board the ship premeditated? Was it self-defense because Hewell was armed? Was Hewell just an accidental victim of a fight on the ship?

Was Hewell's death murder under American law because the *Creole* was an American-owned ship or was it not? Was it murder under British law because the murderers surrendered themselves in Nassau and admitted that a man had been killed? Could a Nassau court try American citizens? What about murder on the high seas? Was it different than murder on land? In whose jurisdiction was it? Or, since the ship traveled through international waters, was it a murder that could not be adjudicated by anyone?

I also explore the intricate slave trade up and down the Eastern Seaboard in the period between 1820 and 1842, shedding new light on why it was instituted and how it worked. Why were thousands of slaves, including Washington and the other prisoners aboard the *Creole*, taken from Richmond, Virginia, south along the coast, around the tip of Florida, and on to New Orleans? It was because Virginia had too many slaves and Louisiana too few. The solution seemed simple to slavers back them: haul the slaves from Virginia, where they were not needed, down to New Orleans, where they would be sold to planters in Louisiana who did need them.

And speaking of slaves, what about the 116 slaves not charged with any crimes who were released in Nassau? There is evidence that some boarded ships to Jamaica. Others boarded ships for other islands in the Caribbean or moved to other islands in the Bahamas. Not one remained in Nassau to await the outcome of the mutiny trial of their fellow passengers. Why? Did they lack confidence in British justice? American justice? Did every one of them believe the American sailors' talk that the US Navy would arrive, capture them, and put them back into slavery in the United States?

And why did none of those 116 people help the nineteen men who staged the mutiny? Well, they were scared. The penalty for participating in a mutiny is usually death. Slave mutineers on other ships in the Caribbean and on the oceans had been executed for taking part in a mutiny. The nonparticipating slaves on the *Creole* probably reasoned that if they refused to join the mutiny and it failed, they would not be legally responsible. They may have reasoned, too, that if the mutiny succeeded, they could gain freedom without taking any risk. If someone else was willing to carry off the mutiny—well, let them.

The search for the *Creole* story led me to a distinguished, admirable, and hearty British governor, Francis Cockburn, a veteran administrator who had worked for the British for years in Canada and enjoyed his work in the Bahamas as its governor. Cockburn had one big skeleton in his diplomatic closet, though: his older brother, Sir George Cockburn. Americans remembered that he was the British admiral who, during the War of 1812, had burned the White House and US Capitol, as well as some other governmental buildings, infuriating not only Americans but also his British superiors back home.

Francis Cockburn saw his decision as very simple and at the same time very complex. Slaves who landed on his islands, no matter how they arrived, were free under British law. This was the case with three recent ships—the *Comet*

(1830), *Hermosa* (1840), and *Encomium* (1831)—that had not experienced mutinies but had simply foundered at sea and washed up close to shore. Slaves fled these ships and found safety on shore. Cockburn oversaw the freedom of the slaves aboard the *Hermosa* during his time as governor. With the *Creole*, though, he had a murder to deal with. Should he free the killers on the dock when they arrived, put them on trial for murder in Nassau, or send them to England for justice?

AND WHAT WAS THE BRITISH GOVERNOR do with the *Creole* itself? Did he have to tell its crew to sail on to New Orleans or was the ship, somehow, now an impounded British vessel, since it was anchored in a British harbor and was also the scene of a murder?

What about battered Captain Robert Ensor? What was British or American law concerning him and all other sea captains in that terribly unique situation? He now had no ship, just wounds. What would happen to Ensor when he returned to the United States?

AND WHAT OF AMERICAN REACTION, which was swift, harsh, and well publicized. If the British governor took a misstep, would the US Navy invade the Bahamas and start shelling the town of Nassau in an effort to get the slaves back?

Slaveowners in the United States were terrified of slave revolts. The United States had experienced a number of them over the years, including the Stono Rebellion in 1739; one led by Gabriel Prosser in Richmond, Virginia, in 1800; one led by Denmark Vesey in 1822; and the revolt led by Nat Turner in 1831. Here was another, and it involved not only 135 slaves who fled to freedom but also the British government and its antislavery policies. The southern states pressured Tyler and his savvy secretary of state, Webster, to get the ship and all the slaves back. They were the property of their owners, not freedmen and certainly not freedmen who now believed they were British citizens, no less. At the same time, many northerners wanted the slaves to be free but also wanted Tyler to stand up to the British. Who were they to seize an American ship and its slaves? This seizure of men at sea was the same thing that had caused a war in 1812. Cannons had answered their impressment of American sailors then and should answer it once again, some thought. The pressure on Tyler was enormous.

And what about Tyler? He was the "accidental president" because he was the first president to take office upon the death of a former chief executive. In office just a few months and already battered by politicians in Washington, he now faced the *Creole* crisis, which could either sink his presidency or, he knew, make his presidency a great success.

The *Creole* story also involved three of the most important political figures in early American history—John Quincy Adams, Henry Clay, and Daniel Webster. The three would battle each other, and at times President Tyler, to solve the mutiny ship's puzzle—legally, morally, and politically. The bombastic Adams was the sixth president of the United States and the son of the second president, John Adams. He was a staunch abolitionist and had plenty of friends for that antislavery stand, and plenty of enemies too. Webster, who uttered so many memorable quotes ("Liberty and Union, now and forever, one and inseparable"), was a former Massachusetts senator and secretary of state for William H. Harrison and then John Tyler. He had an enormous reputation, power, and influence. Last but certainly not least was Henry Clay of Kentucky, a charismatic senator at the time of the mutiny and a former congressman who had been elected Speaker of the House at the tender age of twenty-nine. Clay was the great puppeteer of the Senate, using his many political skills, and a lot of arm-twisting, to get his way on issues. He also desperately wanted to be president and would come within a handful of votes for the prize in three different elections.

The three would pull out their political swords and duel over the *Creole* and its slave mutineers, and duel with the British too. The dispute would change American politics.

And what of the abolitionists, those intrepid antislavery champions who wanted the "peculiar institution" abolished? They had won a great victory with the Supreme Court decision in the *Amistad* trial, but the slaves on the *Amistad* were Africans. The slaves on the *Creole*, though, were Americans, all born and raised in the United States. They were far, far better symbols of slavery than the *Amistad* captives, who did not even speak English. The abolitionists hoped that the *Creole* incident would help their case and make their ranks grow. They needed something, because the movement had landed on hard times. The number of abolitionists was dwindling. Their support had stagnated, their funds had just about run out, they had much trouble gaining newspaper attention, and their new abolitionist journals, except for the *Liberator*, had foundered. The abolitionist senators and congressmen were few, too, and never enough to get antislavery bills passed. They knew the *Creole* dispute might change all that.

And what about the British, seen as haughty bullies by most Americans, who still felt the wounds of both the War of 1812 and the American Revolution? Were these not the dogs, most Americans believed, who not only killed more than ten thousand American soldiers in the Revolution but burned the White House in the War of 1812? Burned the White House!

How could Tyler and Webster deal with them? Their antislavery laws, which had been passed by Parliament from 1807 through 1833, seemed to protect the slaves from the *Creole*. The US government, led by and Tyler and Webster, had to get around those laws somehow, some way. Could they? Should they?

And, finally, there was Texas. James K. Polk received, and deserved, much of the credit for getting the Lone Star Republic annexed as a US state, but it was John Tyler who started the annexation process. Why did he do it, starting just after he took over the White House following President Harrison's funeral? Was it just because he saw Texas joining the Union as a way to get elected president in 1844, riding into the White House on a wave of Texas elation, especially in slave states? Or was there something else? Was there a feeling on Tyler's part that the United States would be incomplete without Texas?

You could say that this is yet another book about slavery, but it's not. You could say it is yet another book about high seas adventures, but it's not. You could say that this is a book about a man's undaunted desire to be with his wife, but it's not. You could say that this is yet another book about politics but it's not.

No. This is a book about a great nation, the United States, that came face to face with a dark, ugly issue that was and still is tearing it up—slavery, on the waters of the Atlantic Ocean in 1841—and won. And lost.

It is also a book about 135 enslaved men and women in chains who, unwilling to take their oppression any longer, rose up and freed themselves in a bloody fight. It is a theme heralded in American streets recently under the flags of Black Lives Matter and other social justice movements. It is a theme, too, that others will march for in the future, again and again, until the United States becomes the nation Madison Washington and his mutineers dreamed about on the high seas so long ago.

THE *Creole* REBELLION

CHAPTER ONE

ɞɞɞɞɞɞ

Cruising down
the Atlantic Coast

ɞɞɞɞɞɞ

November 7, 1841
On board the Creole, Atlantic Ocean,
130 miles northeast of the Bahamas, 9:00 p.m.

ENSLAVED BONDSMAN MADISON WASHINGTON, age twenty-five, was a huge
man who towered over just about everybody. He had thick arms, thick legs,
a large head, a strong torso, and a barrel chest. He was "of manly form, tall,
symmetrical, round and strong. In his movements he seemed to combine . . . a
lion's elasticity. His torn sleeves disclosed arms like polished iron. . . . [He had]
Herculean strength," wrote one observer. Another said he had high integrity
and intelligence and was determined to succeed at whatever he did, and a third
called him "one of the handsomest of his race."[1]

In addition to his physical size, he had numerous leadership skills, all hinted
at in the way he carried himself. People followed him, one newspaper editor
wrote, because of his "commanding attitude and daring orders when he stood
a freeman on the slaver's deck."[2]

Washington leaned against a thick wooden pillar in the darkened hold of
the *Creole*, a slave ship carrying him and 134 other enslaved men and women
from northern Virginia, where they had worked at plantations and factories, to a
busy slave market in New Orleans. There they would all be sold to the highest

bidder or delivered to men who had already purchased them from agents. Washington did not want to go to New Orleans; he wanted freedom. He had been a free man for a year, living in a free black community in Canada, where slavery had been outlawed, and enjoying all the benefits of freedom. He had given up that life to return to America to stage a daring raid to free his wife at the Virginia plantation where she was enslaved.[3] The attempt failed.

His big body moved from side to side as the *Creole*, a 157-ton, two-masted brig—with two large square sails that billowed in the breeze plus a trysail at the rear and a jib in front—moved south. The ship was just a year old, owned by the Johnson & Eperson Company of Richmond. It slid gently through the quiet waters of the Atlantic on its voyage off the coast of Florida to New Orleans. Brigs such as this, designed by the navy for warfare in the Mediterranean in the early 1800s, later became popular cargo ships. They had large, wide, and deep holds that could carry tons of tobacco, hemp, flax, corn, and other merchandise. Smaller than most ships, they could move in and out of harbors, large and small, with ease. The navy and merchant shippers built a second wave of brigs in the late 1830s. Ironically, one of the best was the *Washington*, a naval vessel that was in service when the *Creole* sailed off Florida with Madison Washington. Many such ships were built with forced labor, as Washington and the others knew.[4]

Shipping merchants engaged in the very profitable slave trade found the brigs to be the best possible ships to transport African Americans up and down the East Coast. The brigs had large, open holds that could serve as simple quarters for substantial numbers of slaves (generally apportioned at one slave per ton of ship's weight). The captives required nothing more than a floor and a blanket for sleeping. Brigs easily accommodated deck-side cooking pots to feed slaves. The hatches and deck doors on brigs led African Americans down wooden stairs to their quarters in the hold. Some brigs, including the *Creole*, painted black with a white ring around the top perimeter of its hull, could be sectioned off, so that part of the hold carried slaves and another part cargo. On the *Creole*, tobacco was packed into the middle of the hold and exuded a sweet smell. The *Creole*'s voyage, with its interior full of slaves, was routine. Many slave ships had made the trip down the Floridian coast before it, and many more would do so in the next twenty years.

What the slave traders did not realize, though, was that the same hatches that permitted crews to go in and out of the hold to check on cargo also permitted

African Americans to run out of the same hold, rapidly, during any attack on the ship, which is exactly what happened on the *Creole* on that still November night.[5]

A crew of just a few mates and six men ran the ship, under Captain Robert Ensor, who was at the time of the mutiny in the captain's quarters with his wife, four-year-old daughter, and niece, age fifteen, whom he had brought along so they could take a vacation with him when the ship docked. New Orleans was a colorful and exciting city, jammed with visitors who meandered up and down its noisy streets at night and populated its enormous shopping emporiums in the daytime.

Ships from all over the world traveled to the Crescent City. It was flooded with fine restaurants, bars, clubs, and theaters. One could find music from the Caribbean, South America, and Central America in the clubs there, played loudly by pianists in saloons. The lanterns that lit the city looked like long strings of fireflies in the night. The clubs were generally open until the wee hours of the morning. Captain Ensor had visited the city several times and wanted his family to see the sights there. Brassy and bold New Orleans had become one of the world's most fabled cities, a magnet for travelers from around the globe.[6]

Very few ships' masters brought their families with them on slave transports because the cargo holds were full of produce and African Americans. Captains usually did not like to subject their loved ones to several weeks of travel on the oceans, which were subject to turbulent weather conditions and sometimes fatal sinkings. And there was always the possibility, although small, of a slave uprising on board the vessel. But Captain Ensor had no worries about any of those problems as he talked quietly with his wife in his quarters that night. This was just another voyage of a ship carrying a large number of captive African Americans. The weather had been good, the seas relatively calm, and the crew hardworking. His wife, daughter, and niece had been successful at entertaining each other over the nearly two weeks of travel, so that social problem had been solved rather easily. They were sailing several miles off the coast of the United States and had seen no other ships on their voyage. Another reason Ensor had invited his family to join him on the trip, such an unusual practice on slave transports, was because he did not expect any trouble from his captives, even though they were unhappy about their relocation to New Orleans. Slaves were always unhappy.

Ensor thought little of the recent Supreme Court decision that upheld a lower court ruling that the captives on board the slave ship *Amistad*, traveling through the Caribbean in 1839, in international waters, were free men and could not be incarcerated in America for their role in a shipboard mutiny that resulted in the deaths of several crewmen. This was the only slave insurrection at sea that Ensor had ever heard about, and it did not bother him at all. His ship was different; his crew was different; his slaves were different. They were Americans; the *Amistad* captives had been foreigners.[7]

Ensor did not connect the *Amistad* to the *Creole*. To him, the *Amistad's* seizure was an isolated incident. Other captains involved in the slave trade did care, though. They were always worried about something. Most of all, they feared slave rebellions. To take control, enslaved men and women on ships had far less territory to conquer than those on a plantation, and they had easy access to ship tools that could be used as weapons.[8] Oppressively hot weather on the sea was just as uncomfortable as weather on land, but on a ship there was nowhere to go for breezes when you were kept prisoner in a steamy, hot hold. Tensions grew in hot weather. So ships' captains used a great deal of caution with their captives. During the daytime, they routinely chained the hands and/ or feet of the slaves and at night fastened those chains to the floor of the hold to prevent any possibility of a mutiny. Doors and hatches to the hold were locked tight and armed guards were posted in front of them.

Ensor was not like the other captains. He was so certain that the enslaved men and women would not trouble him that he decided not to restrain them at all. They moved freely about the hold, the men on one end and the women on the other, separated by a large wall made of the thousands of pounds of bundled tobacco the vessel was carrying to the Crescent City. He knew all about the harsh conditions on slave ships that carried Africans across three thousand miles of water in the Atlantic from Africa to America. But those men and women were foreigners, angry about their capture and unable to speak English. The slaves on the *Creole* had been born in America, spoke English, and posed far less threat of trouble than the Africans. He had no fears, but he should have known that letting his captives roam the ship unbound increased the chances for a rebellion.[9]

November 7 was the eleventh day of the voyage down the coast, and there had been no hint of trouble. The *Creole*, its sails full of wind and its wooden beams creaking as it sailed through the waves, was making good time. All was well. The ship was more than halfway to New Orleans. The voyage was routine and much like the more than one hundred other slave transport trips made from southern cities to New Orleans.[10] The *Amistad* mutiny was far from Captain Ensor's mind.[11]

On deck that night, it was dark except for a single lantern that hung near the wheel, so that the man sailing the ship, the first mate, could see. It was quiet. Waves lapped gently against the side of the ship, which rolled easily in the water. A gentle breeze drifted through the night and was caught by the large sails of the vessel, helping it to travel southward and stay on schedule. The ship creaked a bit as it moved gently through the water.

Washington, the leader, had spent the previous ten days privately organizing a large-scale insurrection on board the slave ship; he hoped it would result in a quick and bloodless takeover of the vessel and freedom for all. When the ship was his, he planned to order the captain, at gunpoint, to sail the *Creole* to the nearby Bahamas, where slavery had ended in 1833. There, he and the rest of the slaves would disembark, never to return to the United States. They would be free people, free from everybody. "The fundamental principles of the Republic . . . are inapplicable to us," wrote Frederick Douglass later about slave insurrectionists at sea and in international waters. They lived in a no-man's-land, separated from everybody.[12] "Slaves [at sea] were neither criminals nor citizens," historian James Kettner agreed.[13]

The plan to sail to an island in the Bahamas was a good one because, over the previous few years, the British government there had freed all the enslaved men and women who had arrived there after shipwrecks. Abolitionist William Wells Brown shrugged his shoulders later when he heard about the *Creole* mutiny. "The slaves were, of course, free as soon as they stepped foot on British soil. Thus were 134 persons made free by the intrepidity of one slave [Washington]," he wrote.[14]

The Bahamas was probably the best port Washington could have chosen. The tropical island chain, which enjoyed pleasant weather all year and sported elegant, palm-tree-lined beaches, had a long history of cordiality to freed and runaway slaves. It was one of the many islands in the Caribbean taken by the Spanish in 1782, during the American Revolution. When that war ended, fearing retribution, thousands of British loyalists fled the United States. Most headed for Canada, but thousands, mostly southern slaveholders, went to the

Bahamas or Bermuda after pleading with the British for help. The crown established and armed a joint British–loyalist army that attacked and captured the islands in 1783 after a short battle. More than seven thousand loyalists took part in the invasion. Loyalists from slave states such as North and South Carolina did not sell or free their African Americans back home at the end of the war; they brought them to the islands and started farming. Then they began importing more slaves from Africa to establish cotton plantations. Within a few years, the island population tripled, mostly through the arrival of slaves in bondage.

American planters stopped importing slaves to the Bahamas in 1807, when England passed the first in a series of laws designed to eliminate the ocean slave trade. In 1818 the crown ruled that any African American who arrived in the Bahamas, by any means, was automatically free. In 1833 an act of Parliament freed all slaves in the British Empire and all its Caribbean possessions. The Bahamas became a mecca for slaves yearning to be free. In the 1820s, hundreds of imported Africans living in Florida, plus hundreds of enslaved Seminole Indians, fled their plantations. As part of the complex escape plot, black Bahamians sailed to the coast of Florida in twenty-seven large schooners loaded with clothing and food. The Bahamians and the slaves they rescued braved treacherous storms, rough waters, and oppressive heat to make the unprecedented journey across the ocean to the island chain. They landed on lightly populated Andros Island. It was far from the capital of the Bahamas, bustling Nassau, and they established a free colony there and thrived. Later, in the 1830s and 1840s, Nassau became a stop on American slave trade routes from southern ports down the Florida coast to New Orleans. Several vessels were wrecked in storms. The *Hermosa* was one of those ships, as were the *Comet* and the *Encomium*. They all found help in the Bahamas, and the African Americans on them all found freedom. There was a dual purpose to the British policy. First, and foremost, it was a humanitarian effort to end slavery. There was a second motive, though, and that was to strengthen ties between the all-powerful and all-white British government with the primarily all-black population. Freeing blacks from slavery made white British leaders very popular with black Bahamians and Bermudians, whom they ruled, and that made all government, social, and cultural relationships between the residents of the islands much better.

The Bahamas also had about six thousand newly arrived Africans freed from foreign slave ships the British navy had stopped at sea after implementation of the 1807 law. None of the slave ships risked a sea battle with the heavily armed warships. The crown needed a central place to put the newly freed slaves, and it chose the warm-weather Bahamas, where freed slaves already lived. In 1834 alone, the British liberated nine hundred Africans discovered on Spanish ships near Cuba and took them to the Bahamas and freedom. This infusion of newly free people from Africa gave the islands a large free black population. Some of the freed Africans joined the Bahamian army, others worked in shops in brightly painted buildings, and others labored on farms.

Their children and grandchildren grew up as free men and women. Some of them established plantations or went into the fishing business. Some Nassau residents visited the freedmen and freedwomen on Andros and helped them to assimilate and to move to Nassau.

By the time the *Creole* sailed into the waters of the Bahamas, the blacks there had enjoyed freedom for nearly a decade and were eager to help any African Americans who arrived on their islands. There were approximately thirteen thousand free blacks in the Nassau area and just three or four thousand whites. The crown employed five hundred soldiers, almost all of them black. British officials, badly outnumbered, were eager to maintain good relations with the residents. The black residents were overjoyed to see new, and freed, faces in their midst. The newly freed men and women reflected their own dreams about the elimination of slavery. These dreams were not only coming true but were being made true by the navy and army of a major world power, the British. Their success over the previous few decades in freeing thousands of slaves on ships at sea might encourage other nations, even the United States, to do the same thing. So the Bahamians blacks not only welcomed runaways also but cheered them on.[15]

Madison Washington thought about the Bahamas as he waited in the hold. The giant slave needed to succeed in his plan of mutiny because rebels who tried to gain control of slave ships were always executed, often right on the deck of the boat. In 1829, 197 slaves held in bondage aboard another slave transport sailing down the Atlantic coast, the *Lafayette*, had attempted a mutiny too. The crew put it down after a violent encounter on deck. There was an aborted revolt on another ship, the *Ajax*, right after that. In 1844, following a failed mutiny on the slave ship *Kentucky*, forty-five male slaves and one woman involved in a failed takeover were hanged from the yardarm of their ship. The captain then lowered their dead bodies to the deck and had crewmen shoot each in the chest as a show to the remaining slaves on board. The bodies were then dumped into the ocean.[16]

Washington had to know, too, that while there had been successful mutinies, the overwhelming majority had failed and that many of their leaders and participants had been killed in the fight to grab control of the vessel. A good example was a failed revolt on a ship out of Newport, Rhode Island, commanded by Captain T. Rogers in 1758. He led his crew in a pitched battle against slave mutineers who tried to seize the ship on the high seas. In the skirmish, eleven Africans were killed, thirteen jumped overboard to their deaths, and several were wounded by pistol and rifle fire.

Revolts on land also met with harsh opposition and severe punishment. Southern reaction to Nat Turner's revolt in 1831 was swift. After the revolt, Harriet Jacobs, an enslaved woman living in Edenton, North Carolina, wrote that news of Turner's rebellion "threw our town into great commotion" and that she was surprised that whites were so perturbed by blacks, whom they always claimed were happy bondsmen and bondswomen. "Strange that they should be so alarmed when their slaves were so contented and happy," she commented.

Jacobs added that whites roamed through the town and nearby plantations, looking for any evidence of local plots, and punished any slaves they could find for Turner's actions. "Everywhere men, women and children were whipped until the blood stood in puddles at their feet," she said.[17]

Many African Americans did not rise up but revolted on plantations by acts of arson, poisoning, and work slowdowns. The *Liberator* reported that a ten-year-old girl in Georgia accused of arson was tied to a tree and burned to death. Whites closely monitored areas of the South that were well-known for slave resistance. One of them was the area of northern Virginia where Madison Washington resided. That's where the notorious rebel Gabriel Prosser launched his failed 1802 revolt. Black leader Robert Purvis acknowledged Prosser's work in his writings. Slave populations would continue to "raise up Gabriels and Nats," he wrote, and that included Richmond and northern Virginia, where Madison Washington had been held in bondage.[18]

Slaveholders in New Orleans, where the *Creole* was headed, fretted over the shipboard mutinies. They said slaves involved in them were criminals and agitators whom the Virginians wanted to get rid of, therefore sending them to

Louisiana and elsewhere in New Orleans. This was, said the editor of the *New Orleans Courier*, "among many of the evil consequences attendant upon the system followed by our northern neighbors of sending the most worthless and abandoned portion of their population to this place."[19]

Slave revolts troubled southerners because they worked. World history is full of them. Small-scale revolts on farms in various countries in different centuries often resulted in freedom for a family or a small number of slaves, who fled following the uprising. Larger revolts, such as one in ancient Troy, often succeeded as well. Several revolts freed slaves in different parts of the Roman Empire. One of the largest, led by Spartacus, nearly toppled the empire itself.[20]

Slaveowners and local proslavery farmers did not know how to assess the attitude of their slaves. Should they worry about the quiet ones or the angry ones? Planters constantly talked about irritated slaves and their troublesome nature, which they saw as a perpetual threat. "There is scarce a day passes without some robbery or insolence committed by them in part or other of this province," complained James Wright, governor of the colony of Georgia, as early as 1774.[21]

Madison Washington had no fear of dying. He was dead already, he believed. He had escaped from his Virginia plantation a year earlier but was unable to free his wife, Susan. Moving about stealthily and traveling at night, he made it to Canada, where he lived for a year with white abolitionist Hiram Wilson at a freed-slave colony in Dawn, a village near Toronto. There he became friendly with other abolitionists, such as Joseph John Gurney from Great Britain. Part of the British Empire, Canada had outlawed slavery too, and slave catchers could not touch slaves there. Washington was safe and would have stayed there, safe and free, if he had not missed his wife so desperately. He saved his money and sneaked back to Virginia to rescue his wife and bring her back to Canada with him. His plan backfired, and he was captured. A few weeks later he was sold to Thomas McCargo, a slave agent in Richmond who routinely took slaves to New Orleans for resale. He put Washington in a slave pen in Richmond. A few days later he added him to a slave gang and led them all to the dock area of the Virginia capital, where they were ushered up the gangway of a vessel. They were headed for Louisiana. That region desperately needed slaves for its booming sugar plantations, and Virginia had too many of them. So Virginians were eager to sell excess slaves, dispatch troublemakers like Washington, and even ban former slaves who had won their freedom from the state.[22]

Washington never expected to be put on a slave ship. He knew that if the ship made it to New Orleans and he was sold to an owner of a sugar plantation, he would never see his wife again. So he knew he had to take the ship on the high seas and be free.[23]

Washington also knew that plantation insurrection leaders had been hanged too. They might not have been successful, but they rattled the slaveocracy of the South. Most Americans knew of the rebellions of Denmark Vesey, Gabriel Prosser, and Nat Turner. Numerous people had been killed in Turner's rebellion. During his abortive rebellion in Richmond, Prosser had planned to kidnap Virginia governor James Monroe, a future president, and hold him hostage. Washington was aware of dozens of other rebellions that had been put down brutally or discovered and crushed in their planning stages.[24]

The *Creole* slaves knew, too, that the severe retaliation against slaves all over the South because of Nat Turner did not deter others from planning takeovers, even if they failed. The Turner retaliation had been quick and massive. Following it, the editor of the *Messenger* of Macon, Georgia, described "dismay and terror" in people "of all ages and sizes." Vigilante committees and "regulators" in different states murdered blacks they suspected of planning rebellions like Turner's. One group of slaves was tied to a cluster of trees, admonished for the Turner uprising, and then hacked to death by men with long swords. People in New Orleans were gripped by rumors of security forces that had brought in weapons to put down any slave uprising. The fear of more uprisings was so great in Southampton County, Virginia, where Turner lived, that a security force of more than one thousand armed white men was raised.[25]

In Madison County, Mississippi, in June 1835, a number of slaves were determined to rise up against their owner, Ruel Blake, and kill him. They would be aided by several white men in the area. The plot failed and local authorities hanged fifteen slaves and six white men. That same summer and fall, failed slave uprising plots were reported in Georgia, South Carolina, North Carolina, Virginia, Alabama, Louisiana, and Texas.[26] People in Charlestown, Maryland, were certain that a rebellion was about to begin. A newspaper reported, "The community was guarded every night by respectable white men."[27]

That autumn, white "agitators" who had tried to help slaves rebel were hanged in Lynchburg, Virginia; Lumpkin County, Georgia; Aiken, South Carolina; and Jefferson County, Georgia. Many blacks connected to those rebellions were killed too. In other southern counties, cities, and villages, residents panicked over every rumor of a slave uprising.[28]

Southerners feared blacks because it was easy for them to get real weapons or to turn hoes and rakes into weapons. Slaves also had vast information-gathering networks, and news flew easily from plantation to plantation. The biggest reason for worry, though, was that there were so many slaves. Some states had nearly as many slaves as white citizens. In Mississippi in 1835, for example, slaves represented 39.6 percent of the state's population. As the years went by, the percentage of slaves grew higher in all southern states. Whites went to sleep worrying about what that army of blacks was preparing to do to them.

As early as 1713, Virginia's chief executive, William Gooch, had written that just a few troublemaker slaves could bring about a mass insurrection: "And in case there should arise a man of desperate courage amongst us, exasperated by a desperate fortune, he might with more advantage than Cataline kindle a servile war. Such a man might be dreadfully mischievous before any opposition could be formed against him, and tinge our rivers, wide as they are, with blood." A contemporary, Colonel William Byrd, had agreed with Gooch, deplored the rising number of blacks in Virginia. He told friends that blacks not only dominated the workforce but also destroyed white residents' desire to work.[29]

Many prominent Americans, including future president Thomas Jefferson, said that slaves felt they had to revolt—and probably should. This was the theme of the antislavery abolitionists. The words of Jefferson on slave revolts echoed through the valleys of Virginia, other southern states, and the decks of slave ships: "And can the liberties of a nation be thought secure when we have removed their only firm basis, a conviction in the minds of the people that these liberties are the gift of God? That they are not to be violated without his wrath? I tremble for my country when I reflect that God is just; that his justice cannot sleep forever."[30]

In small enclaves of the South, planters also trembled when they read the writings of John Parrish and others. Parrish wrote that during the previous few decades, crops had been infested by weevils and worms and the growing season had been curtailed by endless rain because of an angry God. Parrish and others also argued that the nation was not going to stay half slave and half free. "A house divided against itself cannot stand; neither can a government or a constitution," he said, taking lines from the Bible in language repeated, with more thunder, by Abraham Lincoln in 1858.[31] Others, such as Luther Martin, had suggested that there would be a terrible price to pay for slavery in America. "National crimes can only be, and frequently are, punished in this world by national punishments," he warned.[32]

For decades, long before Denmark Vesey, some had preached for violent slave revolts. "And so all the black men now in our plantations, who are by unjust force deprived of their liberty, and held in slavery, as they have none upon earth to appeal to, may lawfully repel that force with force and, to recover their liberty destroy their oppressors," wrote a pamphleteer in 1760.[33] In 1816 a pamphleteer wrote that "no human law must be obeyed when it contravenes the divine command; but slavery is the combination of all iniquity and therefor every man is obligated not to participate in its corruption."[34] A man in Darien, Georgia, wrote that it was upsetting "to human nature that any race of mankind . . . should be sentenced to perpetual slavery; nor, in justice can we think otherwise of it, that they are thrown amongst us to be our scourge one day and another day our sins; and as freedom to them must be as dear as to us, what a sense of horror must it bring about."[35]

The antislavery speeches and writings of Jefferson and others in Virginia had been made at the turn of the century. By 1820, when the Missouri Compromise was being argued in Congress, Virginia's leaders had set aside the antislavery trumpet and warmly embraced slavery. Forty years had passed since the end of the Revolution. Eli Whitney had invented the cotton gin, making farming more profitable (increasing production by a factor of three hundred times)—with slave labor. Southerners were making a fortune off cotton and their bondsmen and -women slaves. Why abandon the system? Madison Washington shook his head from side to side whenever he thought about the plantation slave system, more determined than ever to flee.[36]

A slave revolution? Many, North and South, had advocated that. They all said that once a small band of slaves had successfully taken a village, millions of other slaves would rise up, obtain arms, and overthrow the governments in each slave state. That idea gained strength in the early 1800s when armed slaves overthrew the government of Haiti and defeated a large French army in the process. (The army was not beaten by armed slaves, though. It was beaten by illness. Almost twenty-six thousand French soldiers in Haiti died of yellow fever.) Numerous Haitian slaves later moved to Virginia and told that heroic story often. Washington, who was captive on a plantation near Richmond, where many Haitians had settled, probably heard the story, but he and others realized that such a revolt could not happen in Virginia. None of the militias in that state would be incapacitated by disease since these solders had grown up in the state and were likely immune to any epidemic. A rebellion would not work. The one major effort, led by Prosser in 1802, had failed and its leaders were all hanged.

The bill that ended the slave trade, passed in 1807, had accomplished little good. The total number of slave ships violating the ban was unknown, but dozens were captured in different waters. In Pensacola, Florida, in 1818, soldiers under General Andrew Jackson captured three slave transports. These captures spurred President James Monroe to sign a bill that permitted payments to slave smugglers who turned in their employers. Monroe also dispatched a small fleet of US Navy warships to intercept slave ships off the coast of West Africa.

In the late 1830s, President Martin Van Buren sent another fleet of ships to West Africa to stop slave traffickers. The fleet was successful and brought back captured slavers. Some of the slaves on seized ships were freed or escaped when the vessels docked in American ports. In most of these cases, though, the owners of the ships were foreigners and could not be prosecuted, so the ships were seized but the owners were let go. Some cities, such as New York, were lenient on captured slavers. Others, such as Baltimore, were harsh. In some cases, a judges confiscated one of an owner's ships and let the other go. Some slavers sued the United States in those instances. All this made naval captains reluctant to do anything. Many simply anchored at an island off the coast of Africa and did nothing, regularly sending home reports that they had found no transgressors in that part of the ocean. The US Navy seized an average of just two or three ships each year in the 1840s.[37]

Politics was involved too. Slavers knew there were bad relations between the United States and Britain and that the United States fiercely opposed the crew of any English ship boarding an American vessel looking for "deserters" from the British navy. Worried that in that effort the British would find their slaves, slave ships simply brought down their own flags, no matter what nationality, and hoisted an American flag to prevent seizure by British ships. Any British captain who righteously seized a slave ship flying an American flag found himself mired in the middle of controversy and castigated by American diplomats, even though he was, in fact, right to seize the ship. Such an action "would seem to want nothing to give it the character of a most flagrant and daring outrage and very little to sink it in to an act of open and direct piracy," argued Andrew Stevenson, US minister to London, concerning the Spanish ship *Mary*, which had struck its American flag when it observed a British cruiser approaching.[38]

The illegal slave trade flourished in direct proportion to the increasing need for slaves in the southern states as the cotton industry boomed. The success of cotton spurred farmers in other states and territories, such as Texas, to grow it too and to use new seaports, such as Galveston, to get the cotton to European markets.

Dozens of slave ships traveled from Africa to Brazil and the southern US states, their holds loaded with thousands of slaves. As long as they kept away from sea traffic on the Atlantic, or continued to switch flags, they were able to avoid being stopped and, if discovered to be slave ships, sailed into northern US ports. Their captains, often paid ten times the normal merchant captain's pay, were successful at evading detection most of the time.[39]

Most nations that permitted slavery simply ignored US efforts to stop it on the high seas or in foreign ports. In 1845 Henry Wise, US minister to Brazil, tried to get the Brazilian government to seize US slave ships entering its waters, and failed. Exasperated, he wrote the State Department," I beseech—I implore the President—to take a decided stand on this subject. You have no idea of the effrontery and the flagrant outrages of the African slave trade and of the shameless manner in which its worst crimes are licensed here. . . . Every patriot . . . would blush for our country did he know and see how our citizens sail and sell our flag to the uses and abuses of that accursed traffic."

The State Department's response to his fervent plea? Wise was reprimanded for exceeding his instructions.[40] Ironically, the very political Wise became a proslavery governor of Virginia in the late 1850s and was the executive who signed John Brown's death certificate after his Harper's Ferry raid in 1859.

The only resolution Washington could think about was mutiny. The knowledge of uprisings made it easier for him to recruit men on board to seize the slave ship. He had convinced the slaves that takeovers were easier on sea than on land and that the unshackled slaves had enough freedom to serve as an unstoppable force. The men on the *Creole* believed that despite the odds, they just might succeed. They were not chained, were overseen by a very small crew, and had, in Madison Washington, a strong leader.

As the balmy night of November 7 continued on the *Creole*, Washington, in the darkness of the hold, made fists with his hands again and again and whispered to the eighteen men he had recruited for the takeover. He kept thinking about his plan. If everything worked, it would get him and the other slaves out of the United States and to some safe haven, hopefully in either British-occupied Bermuda or the Bahamas, where Great Britain would, he hoped, accord him and his fellow slaves legal protection. However, they had sailed well past Bermuda by that time, so the target now had to be the Bahamas.[41]

He had met American abolitionists when he was free and discussed his plan to return to Virginia to rescue his wife. They opposed it, warning him that in a journey that long, he might be captured and tossed back into slavery. He did not pay attention. Among the things he learned from them, and remembered, was that if a slave ship was liberated on the high seas, or in the territorial waters of another country, the slaves were usually ruled free. He knew of the *Hermosa* case. He had probably heard of the 1772 case of the *Somerset*, in which a slave who had lived in England as a freeman was captured on a ship in the Caribbean, pressed back into slavery, and then freed by British courts. And from Underground Railroad leaders, he likely heard that British ships that captured slave transports had been freeing the slaves and sending them to the Bahamas.[42]

Most of all, he learned all about the 1839 *Amistad* mutiny. He visited abolitionist Robert Purvis, who had just received a portrait of Cinque, the leader of the *Amistad* uprising. Purvis told him the story of the insurrection on the ship, the trial in American courts, and the verdict that set all the mutineers free. Fifty years later, recalling the visit, Purvis said that "he drank in every word and greatly admired the hero's courage and intelligence."[43]

That night, Washington also knew, from earlier conversation with several of the ship's mates, that the *Creole* was out of US waters and near the Bahamas. At that moment, far from the state of Florida, he and his companions were legally free. He was certain of that because when he was put on the boat, he shrewdly asked to be made the cook for the slaves. He made food on the deck of the ship and, with assistants, served it to his 134 fellow men and women in bondage. As the cook he also struck up numerous conversations with the mates and other members of the crew, with whom he had become friendly. They good-naturedly kept him apprised of where the brig was as it moved down the Florida coast. They had great confidence in him as a cook and saw him as a reliable person on deck. They never suspected his real motive. In the same way, plantation owners on land often overlooked the motives of slaves entrusted with important jobs.[44]

During all those hours as a cook, he also learned how many crew members were on deck in each shift, where they stood, who actually sailed the ship, when their shifts began and ended, what time the captain retired, and where the few guns on the *Creole* were stored. He kept all this information in his head.

Washington may have met some of the slaves on the ship prior to its sailing, when he was kept in the dank, dirty slave pens. He had not known the other slaves held there with him; they were from other plantations in Virginia or had been dock or factory workers in the city. On board the *Creole*, he had a chance to scrutinize different slaves, and he picked out those he thought could help him in the mutiny. These were men who were strong, worked hard, were agile, could move rapidly, fought well, and, most importantly, wanted to break free, risking their lives if need be, to accomplish that goal. Washington could not have done all that if he were down below in the hold. Many of the men he recruited for the takeover were eager to participate. By November 7, Washington had formulated a strategy.[45]

What he and his recruits had to do that evening was burst through the door of the hold and, as quickly as possible, disarm and disable the crew on deck, seize the wheel, get the captain to set sail for the Bahamas, and then confine the captain to his quarters, guarded by armed men. If the mutineers moved fast enough, and boldly enough, they could succeed. They had only one chance though, and they had to make the best of it. Captain Ensor's crew consisted of cook William Devereux, acting mate Lucius Stevens, Henry Speak, John Silvy, Jacque LaCombe, Frances Foxwell, Jacob Leitner, and Blinn "Jim" Curtis. There was also a French cook named Lewis. The mates were Zephaniah Gifford and William Merritt.

Everything Washington knew about ship seizures and international law he had learned in casual conversations and readings; he had never studied any of it, since back in Canada, he never envisioned himself as a slave on a slave transport on the ocean. That night he was hopeful of freedom in another country, if he and his men could seize the vessel, but he was not sure he could succeed. Was he tough enough to do it? Could the men he had recruited summon up not just strength but the courage to face musket fire, knives, and clubs and take over the vessel?

His confidence had grown day by day on the voyage from Richmond, though, and he was sure of himself by the night of the revolt. That evening, as the ship drifted lazily through the ocean, everything went according to plan. The hatch to the hold was not locked, and Washington sent a slave to the deck to find first mate Zephaniah Gifford, who was steering the ship. The slave told Gifford that another slave had crept into the women's section of the hold and was annoying them. Gifford and mate William Merritt, who was working for the captain in return for passage to New Orleans, went down to the hold to remove the slave. Merritt opened the hatch but did not lock it behind him. Gifford stood at the top of the hatch and held a lit match to illuminate the stairs as Merritt slowly descended into the hold where the slaves were kept. As soon as Merritt reached the bottom of the stairs, he saw that the intruder in the female section of the hold was Madison Washington.

Merritt was startled. "Madison, is it possible that you are down here? You are the last man on board the brig I expected to find here," he said, worried.

"Yes sir, it is me," replied Washington softly.

Washington moved behind Merritt quietly and, with another man, suddenly overpowered him. Merritt was pushed against the wall. Gifford was grabbed and pushed down to the bottom of the stairs. Adrenaline flowed fast for Washington and his mutineers, who were all waiting for the capture of the first crewman to begin the battle. At Washington's signal, Elijah Morris and Washington's seventeen other co-conspirators, all eager for a fight, ran up the wooden stairs from the hold as fast as they could, barreled their way onto the deck of the ship, and raced toward the crewmen, who were walking about just where Washington knew they would be. Washington charged after them, his eyes watching every part of the deck for resistance.

"We have commenced and must go through," shouted Washington. "Rush boys. Rush off, we have got them now," he shouted to his fellow mutineers as they scrambled onto the deck in the night.

Washington then ran to the large hold where the slaves were kept and told them what was going on. He urged them to join the mutiny. "Come up every damned one of you. If you don't lend a hand, I will kill you all and throw you overboard," he yelled over the din of the squabbling on deck.

The mates on the boat were eyewitnesses to his exhortations. "Some of the Negroes refused to join in the fray, [and] they were threatened by Washington that they would be killed," said Gifford. One slave, Andrew Jackson, was dragged out of the hold and told to join the mutineers. As soon as he reached the deck and saw the fighting, he decided he did not want to participate in the mutiny, fearful of its consequences. He shouted to mate Frances Foxwell, "Where can I go to save my life?" Foxwell, watching the fighting on the deck, pointed to one of the masts and told him to climb it and hide. Jackson did, and he remained there until the fighting was over.[46]

Suddenly, everyone on the ship heard the sound of a single shot. Gifford, trying to get up from his position at the foot of the staircase in the dark, felt a bullet crash into the back of his head, knocking him back down and injuring him severely. Bleeding, Gifford turned around to see who fired the shot, but the assailant was gone.[47]

When he got on deck, Washington ran toward the helmsmen and shouted "Liberty!"[48] Frederick Douglass later said that Washington "leapt from beneath the hatchway, gave a cry like an eagle to his comrades beneath, saying we must go through."[49]

Within seconds, the captain was alerted to the mutiny. Ensor bolted from his cabin, telling his wife to lock the door behind him, and ran to one of the cabins that housed his crew. "The Negroes have risen. Get on deck," he said. They ran out the door, down the hallway, and up the stairs to the deck. Blinn Curtis was one of them. On his way, he grabbed a handspike for his protection and use in the battle against the mutineers. He encountered some of the rebellious slaves in the hallway. He slashed out with his handspike, knocking one of them to the ground. The others tried to grab him, but he escaped their grasp. Curtis ran into Lucius Stevens's cabin, where he encountered more slaves, all armed with spikes or knives. He and Stevens were beaten. Stevens burst through the crowd of blacks and made it into the hallway. One of the mutineers aimed a gun at him and fired, but missed. Stevens ran to the deck. Curtis followed him but was hit on the head by a bludgeon and knocked to the floor. Holding his head, he rose and stumbled up the stairs to the deck. There he saw slaves all over the ship, battling with the crew. Curtis ran to the rigging in an effort to hide from the slaves but was spotted.

"Who is that?" yelled one slave.

"It is Jim," said another.

"Come down. You shall not be hurt," a slave yelled at him, and he did.

All around, Curtis could hear the sounds of people battling with each other and frequent exhortations from the mutineers. He feared for the lives of all. The scene on the deck of the Creole was a frenzy. Stevens heard several slaves yelling, "Kill him! Kill the Captain!"

At this point, a group of mutineers was intent on finding the second mate, William Merritt, who had escaped. "We will have that long, tall son of a bitch, the second mate," yelled one slave as they trotted about the main deck, all eyes peeled for Merritt. They ran through the already crowded hall, looking for him, shouting his name every few seconds. They ran to his cabin, where several blacks were beating crewmen. The bloodied men were crying out for mercy. Merritt was not there. They continued their search and burst into another stateroom.[50]

Washington had told the mutineers that they had to capture the captain, Ensor; first mate Gifford; and second mate Stevens. They were the three authority figures on the ship, the men in control, men who knew where the weapons were and who would be needed after the takeover to sail the ship to a friendly port where the slaves could be freed. None of the slaves knew enough about sailing or navigation to get them anywhere; the crew had to be forced to do that.

The deck was dark except for a lone lantern at the helm. It shed little light on the surrounding areas. The mutineers had only one gun between the nineteen of them, and that was kept by Morris, one of Washington's lieutenants, who had smuggled it on board.[51]

"There's a mutiny on deck! I've been shot!" bellowed Gifford, bleeding, as he stumbled across the hall and into the crew cabin. The rest of the travelers tried to emerge from their rooms and get to the deck, but the slave insurrectionists, with handspikes and clubs, stopped them and kept them prisoners in their rooms. They were slave trader John Hewell, slave agent Thomas McCargo's nephew Theophilus McCargo, guard Merritt, and Jacob Leitner, working as a steward in return for passage to Louisiana. Several of them did get out of their cabins amid the shouts and sounds of the melee.

It was a critical moment for Washington, who worried over the entire enterprise and wondered if it would work. The rebellion was the culmination of his life. "The whole world seemed on fire and it appeared to me that the day of judgment had come, that the burning bowels of the earth had burst forth and that the end of all things was at hand." he said of that night.[52]

He was grateful that the ship's crew was small, and happier still that the insurrection was taking place on a warm night with gentle waters and "a fresh breeze" blowing across the deck. The sky was "hazy," passengers said later, "with track clouds flying." Staging the mutiny in rain or amid ocean squalls would have been more difficult.[53]

There was rough hand-to-hand fighting on deck between the slaves and the crew. Both sides used whatever weapons they could find or simply grabbed clubs and hard, blunt objects. Some had knives they had stolen from the ship's kitchen. The slaves, who outnumbered the crew nineteen to six, battered most of them, shoved many down on the hardwood deck, stabbed some, and forced the rest into submission as rapidly as they could. The slaves then went hunting for Hewell, whose boss, McCargo, owned thirty-nine of them. Hewell, sleeping when the commotion started, was scared. The first thing he saw was a gang of four or five slaves brandishing knives and handspikes at his door. He ran out of his cabin and headed upstairs to seek protection from the mates. On the way, he stopped at Merritt's now vacant cabin to grab the only musket on board the vessel. He nervously walked out of the room and went up to the deck. There he spotted a pack of mutineers, silhouetted in the darkness. He pulled the musket up to his shoulder, aimed at the middle of the crowd of men, and fired. The gun went off as the powder ignited, but there was no ball in the chamber.[54]

The slave agent was shortly confronted by mutineers, who grabbed his musket. He found a handspike and swung it at them. Frightened and thinking he was loading up another musket, they backed off.

A few minutes later, slave Ben Johnstone, also known as Ben Blacksmith, ran up behind Hewell, unseen, and grabbed his arm. At the same time Morris, who had lost his gun, joined Blacksmith. Hewell could not wriggle free from Blacksmith's grip because of the slave's strength. He was "the Vulcan of the plantation, a fellow of Herculean strength and dauntless courage," said one man. Blacksmith pulled out his large bowie knife and stabbed the slave agent, who fell to the deck. Witnesses said the two mutineers then got down on their knees and took turns stabbing Hewell in the stomach and chest as he tried to wrestle with them. They stabbed him more than twenty times; he bled profusely.[55]

The mutineers incorrectly assumed that Hewell was dead and left him on the deck; he was not. The slave trader managed to stagger to his feet. Weak in the knees, he slowly found his way to the doorway to the crew cabins and went down the short flight of steps. Leaning against the walls of the hallway for support, because he was badly wounded and blood was pouring through his shirt, he made his way to the cabin of McCargo. Hewell lurched past him. "The Negroes have risen. I am a dead man. The damned slaves have killed me," he told McCargo.

The bloodied Hewell slowly climbed into McCargo's sleeping berth. He died there thirty minutes later. Slaves took his lifeless body and pushed it out of a porthole into the sea.[56]

Crewman Jacob Leitner was shocked at the sight of Hewell when he stumbled through the door. "He was weak from loss of blood and, with some difficulty, got into the stateroom. He climbed into his berth . . . and I saw the blood running down from his berth. He asked me for water but by that time the cabin was full of slaves and I was afraid to assist Hewell."

"Here I am, you may kill me if you like," said a weary, very frazzled Jacob Leitner, his arms outstretched in surrender to the slaves as they piled into the cabin.

"No, you shan't be hurt. Come out here," said one of the slaves, who gently grabbed his arm, took him up to the deck, and had him surrounded by three slaves for his protection.

A few minutes later Elijah Morris, full of power, stood in front of Leitner and yelled as loudly as he could to the other mutineers, "Kill every God damned white person aboard the vessel. If none else will, I will."

Leitner, who had become slightly friendly with Morris during the voyage, looked him straight in the eye. "Will you kill me, Morris?" he asked.

Morris paused and his tone quieted. "No, you shall not be killed. Get down to the hatch," he answered. He walked away.

A few minutes later, Leitner, now in the hold, was called back up to the deck by one of the slaves and brought to the captain's cabin, now occupied by Washington and a few others.

"Do you know where the liquor is?" he was asked.

He nodded that he did and was ordered to get it. He returned with four bottles of brandy, a jug of whiskey, and a demijohn of Madeira wine. The men began to drink it and later distributed glasses of wine to the others. They also called for food, and Leitner brought out loaves of bread and barrels of apples, which were apportioned among the slaves.

There was a moment of quiet. Leitner, the only white man in the crowded room, then watched as Ben Blacksmith, his body covered in sweat and his eyes wide, pulled out his huge bowie knife, still drenched in blood, and flashed it in front of all.

"I sent some men to hell with this tonight," he said quietly. He then put the knife back in his belt.[57]

As Leitner looked at Blacksmith, McCargo, still in his cabin, was trying to figure out what to do. He had two pistols in a box in his room. He took them out and went up to the deck to help the crew put down the uprising. He saw a group of slaves running across the deck. Aiming both pistols at the same time, he pulled the triggers. The guns misfired. McCargo was then captured. Several men wanted to kill him, but the French steward, Lewis, intervened. He explained that McCargo was now unarmed and harmless. He would put McCargo into his cabin and keep an eye on him so that he could not interfere with the ship's takeover. He did, locking the door behind him and saving McCargo's life.[58]

About this time, he headstrong Elijah Morris, pistol in hand, walked through the hall in the hold, shouting as loudly as he could, "Merritt shan't live! Merritt shan't live, by God."

A few minutes later, Madison Washington arrived. Washington talked to the steward and had McCargo removed from his cabin. He told the slaves to tie McCargo up and put him in the hold. A few minutes later, the slaves grabbed Lewis and wanted to execute him, but Washington talked them out of their plan. "Don't hurt the steward. Do not hurt Jacob [Leitner] or Mrs. Ensor," he yelled above the noise of the fighting. Washington also talked other slaves out an assault on the French navigator, Jacque LaCombe, defending him as a Frenchman and not a slaver. Washington at this point had seen much bloodshed in his rebellion and was worried about the casualties. The rebel leader wanted only to take the ship; he did not want further deaths, stabbings, or beatings. LaCombe was tied up and put in the hold next to McCargo.[59]

At about the same time, slaves forced open the door to the captain's cabin, where a trembling Mrs. Ensor held her niece and daughter close to her. She backed away from the door as the slaves burst into the room. She pleaded with the slaves: "Please do not kill us!" The slaves told the trio to sit on chairs or the bed and that they would not be harmed. Then they left them. "We will not hurt you, but that damned Captain and mate we will have, by God!" sad Morris as he closed the door behind him.[60]

The next captured was William Merritt, the guard, whom the slaves hated. "Kill him! Kill him!" they yelled. A gang of three slaves had been looking for Merritt. One had a gun, one a knife, and the third a wooden club. They marched through the hallways of the ship and ran into the captain's cabin in search of him, but they found only Mrs. Ensor, huddled with the children.

"There's his cabin!" shouted a slave, and the trio burst through door to the cabin Merritt shared with others. They saw Merritt, and the mutineer with the pistol fired at him, but the shot hit a slave grappling with another member of the crew that the mutineers had not spotted at first. Merritt took advantage of the shooting of the slave and ran onto the deck, looking for a place to hide.[61]

A half dozen mutineers surrounded Merritt on the deck. They waved knives, handspikes, and a musket at him and kept shouting as loud as they could. Merritt thought he was going to die.

One slave, wielding a large, sharp meat cleaver he had taken in the kitchen, slashed at Merritt, cutting open his shirt and grazing his chest. His blood seeped into the shirt.[62] Another slave found a heavy handspike on the deck, picked it up, and swung it at Merritt. He missed Merritt but sunk the spike into the chest of a mutineer standing behind Merritt, causing him to slump to the deck. The slaves stood over him. Then, when their attention was diverted by a noise, Merritt stood up and ran. He fled to the hold and into the women's quarters. He told two women to hide him under a mattress and sit on top of him to save his life. They did, but they became very nervous when they heard the mutineers rummaging through the two holds looking for crew members.

Several mutineers entered the women's quarters and saw Merritt under the mattress. "Come out here, damn you!" one said. The shaken Merritt emerged.

Merritt, his body shaking and his eyes darting from side to side, very quickly realized that the slaves were going to take over the ship and could kill him, as they were threatening to do at that moment. There was noise all over the vessel, chaos, and Merritt felt that his life was in danger. The group of slaves formed a circle around him. Some were armed with pistols and some with knives. One motioned to the others to back up, to form a space when Merritt's body could fall to the floor after he was shot. The mate was terrified. One of the two women in the cabin, seeing what was about to happen, ran into the hall and found Washington. She told him how the slaves had surrounded Merritt. She tugged on his arm, asking him to save Merritt's life.

A moment later, with the woman next to him, the hulking Washington entered the room.

Speaking quickly, Merritt told Washington that he knew how to navigate and also sail the ship. He could take them wherever they wanted to go, he pleaded. Washington listened to his story and told the men to put him in a mate's room, where Washington interrogated him further about his navigation and sailing skills. Several other mutineers, including Blacksmith, were with him. Blacksmith agreed with Washington's analysis of the British policy of freedom for escaped slaves who made it to the Bahamas. He, too, had heard details of the *Hermosa* incident. Washington told the others, once again, that they were close enough to make it to the Bahamas in a day or two. Merritt said he had been to the Bahamas before, knew the waters, and could take them there. Washington nodded his head in agreement and put Merritt temporarily in charge of sailing the ship to the Bahamas.[63]

The only missing officers were Gifford and Ensor, who had been stabbed several times. They were found hiding inside the ship's topsail, rolled up in the rigging.[64] The captain and Gifford had arrived at the rolled-up topsail at the same time. Each had a hand covering his wounds. "Mr. Gifford, I am stabbed and believe I am dying," the wounded captain said to the first mate. Gifford saw him bleeding badly. Then Ensor, pale and weak, fainted from the loss of blood. Gifford wrapped him in rope from the rigging to prevent his body from slipping out of the sail enclosure and falling to the deck.

Washington and his men had been looking for them on the darkened ship for more than thirty minutes, moving through the deck areas and the downstairs hull. Washington led the searchers and held up a lantern to see better in the night. They had Stevens. It was now 11:00 p.m.

Gifford said later that while the two men were rolled up in the large sail, they heard various voices threatening them and the entire crew. "Kill him!" shouted one man. "Kill the son of a bitch!" yelled another. "Kill every white person on board; don't save one," intoned another.

The captain and first mate were ordered out of the sail and back down to the deck of the ship. Gifford slowly came down. When he was ten feet above the deck, he asked Morris why he wanted to kill him. Morris shouted at him, "Come down you damn son of a bitch and receive your message."

Gifford continued down to the deck, where Morris, Washington, and the others waited. Gifford asked Morris why he wanted to kill him. Morris pointed his gun at Stevens and told him that the slaves wanted him and the captain to take them to "any English island" in a three-day sail. "This is what Mr. Merritt says," he added. It became known that the slaves at first wanted to execute Gifford and the captain but were talked out of that by Washington.[65]

Leaving Washington, Blacksmith, armed with his bowie knife, and Morris, a pistol in his hand, walked to where McCargo was being held, intending to kill him. Several shipmates, talking quickly, clung to McCargo for his protection and convinced the two slaves to spare his life. McCargo, relieved, was ordered down into the hold with his shipmates.

At this point Gifford spotted Merritt near the wheel of the ship and walked over to him; the slaves followed. The two men said they could take the ship to the Bahamas and needed the slaves to raise the sails to begin the journey. They all agreed to head for Nassau. Gifford gave Stevens a bottle of water and told him to bring it to the captain, who was still in the main sail, bleeding, guarded by some of the mutineers. He did, and Ensor came down. He told the slaves he was too badly wounded to aid in the sailing of the ship but that Gifford and Merritt could do it. They took him into the hold to be with his wife.[66]

Stevens encountered Blacksmith, who was then carrying a gun. "You had better go below and stay there, or you will be thrown overboard," said Blacksmith. "There are a number of bad Negroes on board."

Stevens went below, and a few minutes later Morris found him there. "Stevens, I do not want to see you hurt, but they talk strong of heaving you overboard tonight," he told the crewman. Morris too warned Stevens to stay in the hold and not to wander onto the deck.

Stevens asked Morris to intercede for him with Washington, who by now was in total command of the vessel. He did. A few minutes later several slaves asked Stevens to come up to the deck and resume his duties as first mate. He thought he was safe. He asked permission to have his dinner and received it. Stevens walked down to the room where he dined, opened the door, and stopped short. There, seated at the table, facing him directly, was a slave holding a pistol. Stevens looked at the slave's face, down at the weapon, and then up at his face again. The two men stared at each other. Stevens backed up, closed the door, and went back to the deck.[67]

Stevens walked back across the deck, shaking from the encounter. Suddenly, someone fired a shot at him and missed. Stevens shuddered and thought they were all going to be killed. The single shot caught everyone's attention. Gifford turned away from the wheel and saw the slave who had fired on Stevens trying to reload his gun.

"Go up to the top [of the mast] and try to spot something," Gifford said to Stevens. He did, hurriedly, in an effort to get himself away from a second shot. The slave lowered his gun and went away as he saw Stevens scamper up the mast. Stevens waited for a few minutes and then went back down to the deck of the ship. No one talked to him, and he went back to his duties as a crew member. It was 2:00 a.m.[68]

During the night, Washington took several steps to ease the tension on the ship. He disarmed the mutineers to make certain there was no gunplay when the vessel reached the Bahamas. He permitted Mrs. Ensor to do all she could to take care of her husband and provided pans of water and sheets to bandage up his wounds. He assisted Mrs. Ensor because the captain had lost a considerable amount of blood, and the leader of the mutineers did not want him to die. Washington did all he could to make Mrs. Ensor and the children comfortable and then posted two armed guards at the door to the room in the hold where he was keeping them. The leader of the mutiny then went into the hold to find the mates who had been wounded. He arrived with another pan of water and bandages. With assistance from other mutineers, he cared for their wounds and made them as comfortable as he could. He told the captain and his wife and the mates that they would be taken to a hospital as soon as they anchored in Nassau. He allowed the mutineers to rummage through the trunks of the passengers and crew. They cavorted about the deck in the passengers' finest clothes, including expensive stockings. Washington talked to Gifford and Stevens at length about what they needed to do next as they steered the ship to the Bahamas.[69]

As the liquor and wine party on board the *Creole* was going on, the captain, after being bandaged, was taken, with his family, to sleep in the forward hold of the ship, where the male slaves had lived. The rest of the crew was allowed to roam throughout the ship and do whatever they wanted. They ate with the slaves on deck and slept wherever they could find a bunk or blanket that night.

The slave ship headed toward Nassau, making good time on calm seas under the direction of Merritt and Gifford.

Washington, in his first ocean voyage, maintained calm and order on board the vessel all night. He instructed the slaves who had not participated in the revolt not to come to the aid and comfort of the mates and crew. He allowed them to do whatever they wanted on the ship, even if they had not sided with the rebellion. He kept the mutineers separate from the rest of the slaves at all times. The non-mutineers ate separately, on deck, and remained in their quarters during the night. Meanwhile, the shipmates wrote down the names of the nineteen mutineers and made notes to explain that none of the others had participated in the takeover of the ship or threatened anyone.[70]

The following day, November 8, was full of tension. It followed an incredibly tense night in which Washington and other slaves monitored the sailing of the ship by the white mates. They were due to arrive in Nassau on the ninth and worried about their reception. Would they be seen as the heroic slaves aboard the *Amistad* and *Hermosa* had, or would they be seen as criminals because of Hewell's death? Would they be viewed as butchers because of what had happened to the captain? Sent back to America in chains? Hanged in America? Hanged right there at the dock in Nassau? "If we are murderers, so were they," scoffed Washington about the death of Hewell.[71]

And the slaves who had taken no part in the mutiny worried that if the mutineers were punished, they would be also.

Arguments raged over the treatment of the captured ship's officers. Tempers flared. Both Morris and Blacksmith threatened to murder Stevens and throw his body overboard to eliminate him as a witness to the homicide of Hewell. Other mutineers harassed the second mate, Merritt.

Several slaves knew how to read a compass. With Washington, they constantly watched it to make sure Gifford and Merritt were not taking them somewhere other than the Bahamas. Washington told Merritt and Gifford that if they attempted to sail the ship to some other port, he would shoot them dead right on the deck. He also forbade them to talk to each other, fearful of a conspiracy.

It was an overly warm day, with the temperature at sea close to ninety degrees. The ship moved along slowly in the light wind. The mutineers took up various duties in sailing the ship, instructed from time to time by Gifford. The rest of the slaves stayed on deck, lounging and keeping a distance from the mutineers to protect themselves from charges that they had taken part in the seizure of the ship. Breakfast was served around 8:00 a.m. and lunch around noon. Groups of the free slaves sat on deck, ate their food, and drank water. Some constructed crude awnings to block out the intense rays of the sun. The ship plowed on, its bow cutting through the waves, ever eastward toward the Bahamas.

That night, Washington and others took turns watching the helmsmen. The two men, who needed to reach Nassau to save their lives, kept the slaves abreast of where they were on the water and told them how much distance they had to go. The night went by slowly.

CHAPTER TWO

✦✦✦✦✦✦

Sandy Beaches, Swaying Palm Trees, and Hoped-for Freedom in Nassau Town

✦✦✦✦✦✦

November 9, 1841
On board the *Creole*, off Nassau, 8:00 a.m.

THE FIRST SIGN OF POSSIBLE LEGAL RELIEF for the mutineers came at 8:00 a.m. on November 9, when the ship tentatively anchored opposite Hog Island, a long, thin island about a mile north of the town of Nassau. The mutineers waited for the harbor's pilot to arrive on his small ship to accompany the *Creole* into the port, using detailed maps of the waters and reefs, a common practice.[1] Washington was surprised to find that the pilot and all the members of his crew were black Bahamians. He explained the mutiny situation to them, and the pilot, who knew British law on slaves, shrugged. He said "they were freemen; they could go on shore and never be carried away from there."

One man in the pilot's crew told the men on the *Creole* that he had lived as a slave in Baltimore but had managed to get to Nassau when a slave transport he was on was wrecked in the Bahamas. Locals had carried all the slaves off the wrecked brig and set them free.[2]

One of the *Creole* slaves grabbed him, hugged him, and kissed him on the cheek out of sheer joy at hearing the news. "You are my brother," he said.

"The Negroes of the Creole laughed," said one of the white passengers. "[They] appeared much rejoiced, particularly those who heard the Negro say that he had got free in that way."[3]

Another thought that ran through the minds of the rebels was that if they had taken the *Creole* to Massachusetts, for example, where slavery was illegal, they would be free men and women. Their owners might have tried to pursue them as runaways through the Fugitive Slave Act, but their fate would be decided by a liberal court in the Bay State. And they could flee Massachusetts and get to slave-free Canada rather quickly. Washington had plenty of friends in the Toronto area who would house all of them and find them jobs. What was the difference, then, between slaveless Massachusetts and the slaveless Bahamas? None. Even so, they all were worried about the murder of Hewell, which might give them trouble no matter where they landed.[4]

When the ship arrived in the harbor at Nassau itself, first mate Gifford, taken aback by the pilot's remarks, jumped onto the dock and walked quickly to the office of US consul John Bacon, more than one mile away, to report the mutiny. Bacon, who frequently met with ships' mates and captains as part of his job, saw Gifford right away, at 10:00 a.m. or so, and listened to his frantic story of the seizure. They sat in his office on the first floor of a two-story building. It was painted a turquoise blue and had numerous windows, all with shutters, to catch the breeze coming in off the sea. Visitors to the well-appointed office could hear the faint sounds of water lapping at the stone walls of the seaport and smell the sea. Bacon raised his eyebrows when Gifford began to tell the harrowing tale of the ship's capture by the slaves, the murder of Hewell, and the attempted murder of Captain Ensor. This was exactly the sort of thing he had been warning State Department superiors about for years, ever since the British ended slavery and refused to recognize it in the Caribbean.[5]

Bacon had arrived in Nassau a year earlier, when the governor there had freed the captives aboard the *Hermosa*. This case was very different, Gifford argued. The slaves on the *Creole* had taken the ship violently, killing one man and nearly killing the captain. In the *Hermosa* case, the ship had been wrecked on a reef. The slaves were liberated by licensed "wreckers" from Nassau and then freed by the Nassau government.

Governor Francis Cockburn did not agree with Gifford. He once again cited the 1833 British law on slavery, which stated that any captive who arrived on British shores, no matter what the circumstances, was free. Cockburn argued, too, that the *Hermosa* case was the perfect precedent for the *Creole* debates because the *Hermosa* had followed the same cruising route down the Atlantic coast. Both were slave ships; both sailed from Richmond, Virginia; and both had been headed for New Orleans.

The *Hermosa* hit a reef in October 1840 and began to take on water. Wreckers arrived and got all the cargo and slaves off the ship, put them on a schooner, and sailed them to Nassau. The slaves were taken off the ship under heavy police guard and brought to a magistrate's office. "[They were] examined as to their age and occupation and told that they were free to remain on the island, and were then questioned as to their wishes on the subject," testified the master aboard the *Hermosa* at a hearing in Nassau.

The arrival of the *Hermosa* escapees in Nassau was greeted by a huge celebration of the residents there. Several thousand greeted them as they arrived on the schooner and sailed to town in launches. A crowd of some two thousand to three thousand people joined them on shore and followed them, and their police guard, to the courthouse. The townspeople surrounded the courthouse, and many inside were forced outside by the surge of the crowd. Those who remained inside said there was so much noise that they could not hear what was being said. The men and women of the *Hermosa* were detained overnight and interviewed in the morning by the governor, who freed them under British law.[6]

Bacon took Gifford to the governor's mansion, which overlooked the harbor. Cockburn, age sixty, was wary of both men as he listened to their stories. Bacon could see that. So instead of asking the governor to jail all the slaves, he just asked for a squad of police to get the wounded off the ship, which was anchored in the water a hundred yards or so from shore. Cockburn did, dispatching a guard of black Bahamian soldiers, led by a white officer, to accompany Bacon to the ship. They took Ensor and the wounded crewmen off the boat and to an island hospital.

Bacon was certain, given the governor's decision to send armed soldiers to the ship, that the British authorities would detain all the slaves and, after a day or so, permit Gifford to take the ship and its remaining passengers to its destination, the city of New Orleans. When he boarded the ship, Bacon "found the slaves very quiet About twelve o'clock at noon twenty African soldiers, an African sergeant and corporal, commanded by white officers, came on board . . . I returned to the shore."

He seemed content, but the next time he boarded the *Creole*, the air was tense with passion. "I was informed by respectable persons that an attempt would be made to liberate the slaves by force. I saw a large collection of boats near the brig and was also informed that there was a great concourse of people collected on the shore," he said.[7]

Bacon assumed the *Creole* passengers would now be told that they had to remain in bondage on the ship and sail on to New Orleans. He was wrong.

Bacon had completely underestimated Cockburn, who was not only a veteran military officer but had been a distinguished administrator at several posts in the British Empire's colonies in Canada, the Caribbean, and Central America. Cockburn was a tall, thin, handsome man with a head of thick gray hair that was always carefully combed. He liked to wear his numerous glistening military medals on his coat to remind people of his experience and to impress them.

He had started his military service in the Dragoon Guards at the age of nineteen and become a captain at twenty-four. He served with distinction against the Americans in Canada in the War of 1812 and remained in Canada at various administrative posts. He worked in the quartermaster corps for several years and then helped fifteen hundred British immigrants found several towns and villages in Upper Canada.

His administrative skills were recognized in 1830 when he was made superintendent of the colony of Honduras in Central America. He was transferred to the Bahamas, where he was named both governor and commander in chief. He had been made a knight earlier in 1841. So when Bacon tried to strong-arm Cockburn, he found himself dealing with a man with enormous military and administrative skills, a man with good political connections who did not back down under pressure, especially under pressure from an official of the country he and his men had fought against in 1812.

His brother was George Cockburn, who had gained notoriety in the War of 1812 when his troops occupied Washington, DC, and burned the US Capitol and the White House to the ground. Both the Americans and the British were furious with him for such a crude tactic, and he fell into disgrace. George Cockburn's days in the military and diplomatic doghouse ended, though, and in 1840, a year before the *Creole* incident, he was elected to Parliament in Great Britain and named the naval lord. His fortunes had turned around completely; he was a powerful and popular man. He was a strong ally of his brother, who in 1841 used George's position to solidify his own political strength in the Caribbean.

When he got back to his office, Bacon was told by his secretary that he could have an immediate audience with Cockburn and his entire council. He went into the large, airy council room with its open windows and felt optimistic, but that hope was dashed right away. Cockburn told him that Nassau could not punish anyone on the ship for the death of Hewell and near murder of the captain. The best they could do, and would do, was detain the nineteen mutineers and exchange notes with the US secretary of state, Daniel Webster, to see what legal steps would follow.

This was a blow to Bacon, who hoped Cockburn would see the situation as he did, but a worse decision was yet to come. Cockburn told the American consul that the 116 non-mutineers were within his jurisdiction, on British soil, where slavery was not tolerated. They were to be freed immediately, no hearing required, and were free to live in Nassau or anywhere else in the Bahamas and were free to leave and sail off anywhere they chose. Cockburn, in a careful choice of words, also told Bacon that all "persons" on board (the captives) were to be released. He did not say "slaves" in order to strengthen the claim of his government that forced labor would not be accepted anywhere in the British Empire. The judge who signed the freedom order referred to "135 black passengers," not slaves.[8]

Edward Everett, US minister to England, was unhappy with the decision. In a note to the parliamentary authorities in London, he charged that that the removal of the slaves from the *Creole*, "so far from resting on any sound legal basis, is contrary to every principal of maritime law applicable to the case."[9]

Bacon was rebuffed again the next day when he reported to Cockburn that hundreds of very noisy and ebullient Bahamians had gathered on shore near the slave ship and that he feared they would attack the ship and take the mutineers and others to shore and safety. First mate Gifford, watching them gather, had described a scene of a "threatening nature."

The enormous crowd of black Bahamians, said to number more than two thousand, should not have surprised Bacon. When each of the two previous slave ships had been wrecked on the islands, large gangs of Bahamians had surrounded the African Americans getting off the ships, greeting them with wild cheers and making certain their slavers did not put them back on the ship or confine them in a Nassau warehouse. The black Bahamians were there to protect their black "brothers." It was a color bond, a kinsman's bond that no colonial nation could shake. The size of the crowds and their wildly celebratory nature always intimidated the Bahamian police officers or soldiers ordered to watch them. The governing powers of the island worried a bit about the legal details of freeing slaves from wrecked ships, but they worried a lot about the possibility of a riot or even a revolution brought on by poor treatment of the African Americans who had just arrived on the island.[10]

The Bahamians were there to protect and to rescue the people of the *Creole*, and they did not care what crimes they were accused of. One black American, on hearing news of the mutiny, muttered, "Those who have given us blood to drink for wages, may expect that their turn will come one day."[11]

Governor Cockburn was aware of the rapid gathering of people near the ship. When Bacon brought this latest, and largest, mass to his attention and again said, nervously, that he feared an attack, the governor sneered. "I beg to state that I cannot think it possible that any of Her Majesty's subjects would act so improperly as to attempt to board by force," he wrote, adding that if the mob did surge onto the ship, he would order soldiers to disperse them.[12]

While Bacon argued with the governor, the Bahamian soldiers back on the *Creole*, delighted that the slaves had taken the ship, became very friendly with them. Over the course of the next few days, the soldiers conversed with the slaves frequently, some flirting with the women, and told them all about previous court decisions concerning seized slave ships. That news cheered the slaves considerably. The commander of the soldiers noted glumly, though, that if the mutineers had taken the ship without killing or wounding anybody, they would have had a much better chance at freedom. The murder of Hewell and wounding of several others, and near murder of the captain, would present a challenge to the courts in the Bahamas.[13]

Bacon was rebuffed once more when he received word that H. S. Fox, a British diplomat, was furious with him, Everett, and their American colleagues for assuming that they would get their way with the prisoners and with Everett's defiant statement that "the courts of law here [the Bahamas] have no jurisdiction over the alleged offenses."

Fox wrote, "An impression prevails here that the 19 Negroes detained at Nassau charged with the murder on board the *Creole* of one of the American slave-owners will be delivered up for trial in the United States. I conclude that this will not be the case."

Fox added that the US Supreme Court had ruled that the United States did not have to surrender any criminal prisoners to Great Britain, and so the British, likewise, would not have to surrender the blacks on board the *Creole*. He also insinuated that US officials were tricky. Fox said that if the African Americans were sent back to America to stand trial and were acquitted of murder, they would immediately be put back into captivity and not freed at all. The Americans turned that argument on its head by charging that the British might, in fact, sell the men and women from the *Creole* at a huge profit, in addition to stealing them from their rightful American owners. Everett mused: Would American authorities seize a British ship forced into a US port by a storm, grab all the opium on board, and toss it into the sea? That was what the British were doing with those on the *Creole*, Everett said.[14]

British officials were also upset with the demeaning and accusatory language of the Americans in memos to the crown. For example, in describing the arrival of the *Creole* in Nassau, Everett wrote,

> The vessel was thus taken into a British port, not voluntarily by those in command of her, but forcibly and violently against the master's will and with the consent of no one but the mutineers and murderers. . . . It would seem to have been the obvious duty of the authorities in Nassau, the port of a friendly power, to assist the American counsel to put an end to the captivity of master and crew, restoring to them the control if the vessel enabling them to resume their voyage and take the mutineers and murderers to their own country.

He added that British officials in Nassau had to "remove all impediments" to the landing of passengers from a ship, and they did not do that for the captain and crew.[15]

Everett further asserted that British officials should have boarded the *Creole* to arrest the mutineers, but that was not the reason for their presence on the deck of the ship. "Their presence for any different purpose, especially for any opposite purpose, was not asked and therefore not lawful," he wrote. He added that the British officials might as well have discharged all the crew while they were visiting. He said too that the attorney general had permitted fifty boats full of Bahamian protestors to remain at the side of the ship, armed with clubs and making considerable noise, in order to give himself tremendous leverage over the crew of the ship, and that was illegal too. Everett said there was "a well-founded fear inspired by the concourse assembled in boats around the vessel, and the reasonable doubt of the protection that would be afforded in case of assault." He also charged that the magistrates did not conduct themselves properly but urged an insurrection in the boats if the crew did not permit the African Americans to disembark.[16]

The Bahamian boats that surrounded the *Creole* created quite a scene. There were two large schooners filled with shouting men brandishing long, thick wooden clubs. Around the *Creole* in a large and full circle were the remaining fifty or so boats. They were of all sizes. Some were fishing boats, some transport launches to take people from ship to shore, and many just small rowboats that bobbed gently in the water. There were some four hundred people in the boats, most of them armed. If you looked at the ship from the shore in Nassau, you saw the boats circling the ship in a flotilla and Hog Island in the background. If you stood on Hog Island and looked the other way, you saw all the boats plus a huge crowd of residents on shore, with people spilling off the dock into several adjoining roadways. Many of them were armed and all were making noise of some kind. The slaves on the ship felt very comfortable surrounded by hundreds of blacks in those boats, and the white crew felt very scared.

Everett parsed his words and phrases. He charged the governor with malfeasance in failing to categorize the "cargo" of the *Creole*. Everett said that if the ship carried a variety of furniture or fruit, an inventory would have been requested and checked, but Cockburn did not do that. He assumed that all the men and women on the ship were slaves. The minister said that some of them might not have been captives but instead free people. Some might have been soldiers. Some criminals. How could the governor know the nature of the "cargo" when he did not conduct a human inventory?[17]

The British thought that Everett fumed too much. He charged that under "comity," a term that described how friendly powers helped each other outside the law, the British should have sent the mutineers back to America and that "the interference of the authorities was exerted only in a manner which has already resulted in setting the mutineers free and murderers at liberty without punishment and without trial and which had the immediate effect of preventing the captain from resuming command of his vessel."

Bacon insisted that the slaves could not be tried in Nassau but had to be taken to a court in the United States. "If they were to be tried here, it would therefore be impossible to obtain the attendance of all witnesses without which the persons implicated could not be convicted, though guilty," he said.[18]

Americans asked for this political friendship. "The great communities of the world are regarded as wholly independent, each entitled to maintain its own system of laws and government while all in their mutual intercourse are understood to submit to the established rules and principals governing each intercourse. This system . . . requires non-intervention of any with domestic concerns of others," argued Everett with great fervor. But British officials said there was no comity to recognize. "The [Americans'] comity is appealed to on behalf only of the pretended owners of the Negroes, while no mention is made of what is due, not to 'comity,' but in justice and by absolute right, towards the Negroes themselves," wrote Fox.[19]

Everett argued that if a US ship was blown off course during a storm and anchored in a British port, or was wrecked on a British island, the British would of course return the ship to the United States, ignoring a half dozen cases in which slaves on wrecked ships were freed in the British-governed Bahamas. He even attached Senate resolutions demanding that any American ship taken into a British port by bad weather or an "other unavoidable cause" would be returned to the United States.

One of the people Everett wrote was George Gordon, the Fourth Lord of Aberdeen, who was Great Britain's foreign secretary. Lord Aberdeen was a veteran diplomat. He had served as foreign secretary before, from 1828 to 1830. His current term would last until 1846. Later, in 1852, he would become England's prime minister and serve until 1855.

At the end of one letter to Lord Aberdeen, an angry Everett said that "an American vessel, lawfully navigating the sea, and brought temporarily into a foreign jurisdiction by violence, is to be regarded, as far as her national character is concerned, as still pursuing her voyage." He said that "the conduct of the authorities of Nassau will be viewed by the American government in no other light than that of an outrage," adding that the actions of England sanctioned "mutiny and murder."[20]

These were resolutions that the British routinely ignored and countered with citations from several acts of Parliament. One said that it was "just and expedient that all persons held in slavery in Her Majesty's colonies should be manumitted and set free."[21]

DURING THE FIRST DAY the ship was anchored in the harbor, the two dozen black troops on the ship, guarding both the crew and the mutineers, obeyed the rules set down by their commander and Governor Cockburn. They were to prevent anyone from leaving the ship, maintain order, and especially avoid any fraternization with the slaves. On the second day the black soldiers began to chat with the male captives and flirt with the females. The socializing between the Bahamian soldiers and the ship's women was pretty obvious. Men and women stood very close to each other as they talked. Some of the soldiers put their arms around the women. "The soldiers were in constant contact with the slaves," said mate William Merritt. In the evening there was no guard over the prisoners at all. "[I was told] that if you tell the sergeant, it will be attended to," said the mate. Merritt went looking throughout the brig for the sergeant, intent on getting him to pull the black soldiers away from the women. He found the sergeant, who was chatting quietly with one of the slave women himself. He was smiling down at her and had wrapped his cloak around her, pulling her close to him. Merritt then walked away, certain that the Bahamian soldiers were not going to observe much discipline and certain too that all the slaves might soon be taken off the ship.[22]

That next morning Merritt and another mate talked to numerous slaves and tried to get them to stay on the ship and continue the passage to New Orleans. But British officials who boarded the ship over the next few days told slaves to get off the *Creole* if they could. They warned that the slaves could all be charged with murder, or at least conspiracy to commit murder, once the vessel landed in New Orleans.[23]

Several days of tension passed. On the fourth day, the surging crowd returned, this time bigger and louder than previously. Early in the morning, several thousand jammed the docks closest to the *Creole*. Hundreds left work to do so. Mothers brought their small children with them. Hundreds piled onto balconies of homes in the dock area, using spyglasses to see what was transpiring on the ship. Others flooded the shore to the north and south to get a better view of the activities on the ship. Rumors flew through Nassau. They said the crowd was planning to obtain weapons, attack the *Creole*, free all the blacks, and escort them to freedom on shore, helping them vanish on the island, as crowds had done for other slave arrivals over the previous few years. All anyone discussed was the slave ship. Black servants told their employers that they had heard graphic rumors of an assault on the ship and that they planned to take weapons and clubs from their homes and use them to help free the blacks on the *Creole*. They did not care what their employers thought of their plans. The entire city was filled with tension. Bacon was terrified. This was not just a crowd of onlookers anymore; it was an angry crowd intent on freeing those they considered to be heroes being held hostage by the Bahamian government.[24]

The governor, sensing trouble from the unruly group on the docks, sent his attorney general, G. C. Anderson, to the ship to have the mutineers removed and placed in a Nassau jail, while the argument about who had jurisdiction over the murder charges commenced. However, Cockburn added hastily that the other 116 prisoners would be freed on the spot and permitted to go ashore. They were free men and women. All of this was going to be accomplished in a few hours, Cockburn decided, and neither Bacon, Gifford, nor anybody else was going to hold it up.[25]

All this was witnessed by William Woodside, the master of the *Louisa*, another US ship in the harbor. Bacon had asked Woodside to go with him to the *Creole* to make certain that Anderson did not break any law. Bacon feared Anderson would try to liberate the slaves.

The first thing that struck Woodside was the fast gathering of boats full of Bahamian protestors. They scared him, because this did not appear to be an ad hoc protest. It seemed to be organized. "A sloop and other boats came along the starboard side of the vessel and anchored within about two rods. A number of small boats were at the same time around the other side of the vessel, all filled with black people, and no attempt was made to keep them away, except not to board the vessel," he said.[26]

The crafty Bacon then began his final, wildest scheme. He knew that another US ship, the *Congress*, was in the harbor. He convinced Woodside to take arms from the *Congress*, board the *Creole* with a dozen or so crewmen, seize the ship, and sail it to the harbor of Indian Key, a Bahamian port about four hundred miles away, where a US warship was anchored. The men on that ship would take command of the *Creole* and get it out of British supervision.

Woodside tried to help Bacon. Members of the crowd saw Woodside hide weapons in a rolled-up American flag before sailing out to the *Creole* in a large launch. He and his men were followed by a suspicious Bahamian in a single boat. He reached the side of the *Creole* before Woodside did and told the commander of the twenty-four soldiers protecting it that this was an armed attack party.

Woodside and his men sailed up to the edge of the *Creole*, their boat rocking gently on the water as the huge crowd seemed to get larger and fill up with tension. After Woodside boarded the *Creole*, a British officer on the brig ordered his twenty-four soldiers to fire on the Americans if they did not retreat. He said he would give that signal within moments. The soldiers, lined up on the edge of the ship's deck, cocked their rifles, aimed carefully at the Americans, each targeting one, and waited.

The situation was tense. Everyone wondered if there would be a battle. Then a second officer appeared and ordered Woodside to leave. He told him his business had been concluded and that the commander wanted him off the ship right away. Woodside turned, walked to the side of the ship, slowly climbed down the ship's ladder, got into his boat, and sailed back to shore, feeling very much alone and vulnerable. The Bahamian throng let out a huge roar.

After he docked, Woodside, agitated and scared, told Bacon that he had no chance of success, and neither did anyone else. "The brig was literally surrounded with boats full of black people armed with clubs," he told Bacon, adding that two large ships had arrived next to the *Creole* and that their crews had supplied the men on the smaller boats, hundreds of them, with clubs and bludgeons. Gifford said that the Americans were certain that a mass attack on the ship was imminent. He feared that members of the crew would be hurt.[27]

THE WHITE CREW MEMBERS on the *Creole* were also scared at the sight of the boats and the navy of Bahamians. "Soon after breakfast [I] discovered boats coming 'round the vessel and black and white people collecting on shore opposite the brig. . . . During the morning I [saw] a number of clubs in many of the boats and that [the men] showed fight with them by swinging them about in a threatening manner at us, at the same time using insulting language," said mate Lucius Stevens. He noticed that the pilot boat and its captain had returned and sailed up right next to the *Creole*. The black captain, an angry look on his face, asked one of the magistrates on the *Creole* when he would finish his business. He was told they would conclude shortly. "Come, get through your business on board; we want to commence ours," the captain said. A British official warned Stevens that if he or any crew member resisted the removal of the slaves from the ship, "there would be some blood spilt." Dozens of men in the small boats that bobbed in the harbor kept up conversations with the Bahamian soldiers and the captives standing on the deck of the brig. Stevens and the other mates on the ship were very apprehensive and had to rely on protection from the armada of all-black protestors by an all-black military force.[28]

Anderson arrived in his boat and was greeted warmly by the soldiers. Prior to his arrival, he had sailed throughout the harbor and assured the Bahamians in the fifty or so small boats, many armed with clubs and sticks, that the black passengers were going to be freed. He also warned them against any action to assist in their release. Anderson was rowed over to a large sloop holding several dozen angry men carrying clubs. He told them the same thing. Some of the men threw their clubs into the water, on his advice, but others clenched them in their fists, ready for a full-scale brawl with the white crew of the *Creole*.[29]

Gifford made his way through the black troops and confronted Anderson. He told him that he and the other whites on board were very concerned about the flotilla of black Bahamians that surrounded them. Many appeared to be armed with not only clubs but also guns. They all looked menacing. The whites on board the *Creole* needed official protection. Anderson shocked Gifford when he said that as soon as the soldiers disembarked, the Bahamians would probably attack the white crew and that "there would be bloodshed." Two magistrates who had accompanied Anderson on board warned Gifford that he and his friends should guard their money hidden in their cabins. They said that if Gifford interfered with the release of the African Americans, there was nothing they could do to protect him and his mates from an assault on the ship by the hundreds of Bahamans in the nearby boats. The attack would likely include the robbery of every cabin, in addition to physical harm. They also said, Gifford stated in testimony, that the armada in the boats would attack the *Creole* and injure its white crewmen just as soon as the passengers were released and arrived in the town of Nassau.[30]

As the nineteen mutineers were being put near the side of the brig before stepping down into a launch, Anderson addressed the other slaves. He asked Gifford to assemble them on the deck under a warm, sunny sky, and he did so "cheerfully." Anderson told Gifford that "it was not his desire to detain on board his vessel any of the persons shipped as slaves who did not wish to remain and they had his free permission to quit her if they thought proper to do so." He did not note that as Gifford heartily agreed, he kept an eye on the hundreds of men with clubs glowering at him from their boats.[31]

Anderson carefully explained to the other slaves that the mutineers were being held because they were accused of committing serious crimes during the ship's takeover, but there was no evidence that any of the others had broken any laws during the mutiny. Therefore, he said, "all restrictions on your movements were removed." He paused for a moment and then said, with finality, "Men, you are all free. You can go where you please."[32]

Suddenly, Merritt walked up next to Anderson and looked out at the deck, jammed with the mass of captives, two dozen soldiers, and various magistrates. He needed to say something for the moment and for history. He told the captives that "they were at perfect liberty to go on shore if they pleased."

"They received this with great pleasure," added Anderson in a note later.

Anderson also noted that neither he nor any other Bahamian official urged the African Americans to leave the ship. "The departure of the Negroes in question from the *Creole* was their own, free and voluntary act, sanctioned by the express consent of the mate and neither myself or any other of the authorities of the colony on board interfered," he said, putting the situation on the official record in accordance with international law.[33]

A jittery Gifford expressed concern about the armed Bahamians in the boats, but Anderson assured him that the two dozen soldiers on board would protect him and the other crewmen. Anderson climbed off the *Creole* into his launch and asked the launch driver to take him to the large schooner, bobbing in the water with its dozens of armed Bahamians. He told the captain that the men and women on the *Creole* were now free. He did want any violence. He wanted the schooner and other, smaller boats to transport the now freed slaves to shore and the crew of the ship and the American diplomats left unharmed. As he finished his request, several of the men on the schooner, all smiling, tossed their clubs into the sea. Men in nearby small boats who heard the conversation threw their clubs into the water too.

Merritt got into an argument with Anderson, pointing out that it would be horrific for them to be injured by black attackers while black Bahamian soldiers stood by the did nothing. Anderson nodded toward the men and women standing on deck and then looked back at Merritt and Gifford. The crewman understood, right away, what the situation was.

"Let them go," Merritt said to the crew. Anderson nodded his agreement.[34] He told the slaves that they were officially free and that nobody would stop them from leaving the ship and going anywhere they wanted to.

"What would you like to do?" he asked loudly, so that all would hear him.

"Leave the boat!" they roared back together.[35]

Anderson turned toward the harbor, filled with the armada of small boats. "Boats, you can come alongside," he said, sweeping his arm toward the side of the Creole.[36]

The commander of the Bahamian soldiers then turned and yelled out to the captains of the rowboats, fishing vessels, and sloops to pull up to the side of the ship so that all of the 116 freed captives could get on the vessels and sail to shore.

With the exception of the nineteen mutineers and five women who chose to remain on the ship, the slaves slowly started to leave the Creole. After a last look, they boarded the small ships, making themselves as comfortable as they could be. When all the freed captives were in the boats, which rocked slightly in the port's waters, someone on the deck of the Creole, perhaps Anderson, signaled with his arm that they should move away from the brig and head for shore. As he did so, Lucius Stevens recalled later, all the freed men and women, in unison, delivered up a five separate roars, cheering that they were free of the Creole and free of slavery.[37]

The boats left the side of the Creole and headed for the town of Nassau while Merritt and the other crewmen leaned on the rail of the Creole and watched the drama unfold. The shipmates later told a New Orleans court that none of the African Americans would have left the ship and gone to Nassau if the British had not coerced them into doing so. They would have stayed on the Creole, traveled to New Orleans, and remained in captivity. No one believed them.

None of the boats, or their occupants, returned later to harass the crew of the Creole. The small boats and sloops that had surrounded the brig earlier, with their cacophony of noise, had all sailed away within thirty minutes of the slaves' departure, leaving the Creole very isolated. An hour or so later, soldiers returned and told the crew to help them retrieve and pack up the clothing and other belongings that the captives had left behind. The crew did so but said it would be illegal for them to take the supplies to shore in the *Creole*'s launches. So Governor Cockburn sent British launches to the vessel and had the soldiers put all the belongings on these boats. By late afternoon, the hold of the ship was cleared and clean, except for the clothing of the five women who opted to remain. By nightfall, all was quiet on the ship.[38]

The departing African Americans huddled together on the small boats were startled to see more than two thousand cheering Bahamians at the docks and in the streets to greet them. The enormous, surging crowd, now also full of shopkeepers, soldiers, and police, all smiling and yelling encouragement, surrounded them like a huge phalanx. Making loud noises, the crowd accompanied them for their protection, ready to battle anyone if need be to make sure they reached the police station. There, law enforcement officials, happy for them, had the ship's escapees all register legally as free men and women who were visiting the Bahamas. Then they left, again to the cheers of the crowd, which was growing larger and larger, and louder and louder, as the minutes went by.[39]

It was at this point, American officials later said, that the British had illegally interfered with the *Creole*. "The civil and military officers of Nassau had entire command of the vessel," said one. "A corps of colored troops was on board, and the vessel was surrounded by a fleet of boats filled with colored people armed with bludgeons and impatiently awaiting the signal to rescue the liberated slaves."[40]

In the harbor, Anderson told Madison Washington and his mutineers that they could not walk away because of the murder and assault charges. The government had to decide whether or not to send them back to the United States for trial, try them in Nassau, or free them. They all knew this was the legal process. "They expressed themselves to be satisfied," said Anderson. With their hands tied, they were put into a boat, sailed to Nassau, and placed in jail, just a block from the waterfront.[41]

WASHINGTON AND HIS MEN vowed to each other that they would stick to the same story, Washington's story, and swear they did not intend to hurt anyone and that those harmed had all been hurt by accident. They were honoring a slave code to stick together. "We must unite together . . . never to betray one another, and to die before we would tell upon one another," Denmark Vesey had said at his trial.[42] A day after being jailed, two of Washington's men died of injuries suffered when they had seized the ship.

The chief executive of the Bahamas, Cockburn, was rapidly losing his patience with Bacon. The fiery consul had tried to get US ships to seize the *Creole*, anchored peacefully in a Bahamas harbor, against orders from Cockburn. He had then tried to get the captain of one of those ships to talk the *Creole*'s captives into surrendering, without telling Cockburn about the plan. Bacon had told Cockburn, several times, angrily, that the blacks on the ship were not free Americans but people whom somebody owned and that they had to be returned. In a letter sent the day after the mutineers were incarcerated, Bacon told Cockburn that the ship's passengers "were as much a portion of the cargo of the said brig, as the tobacco and other articles on board . . . while they were under the American flag."

Cockburn was livid. American southerners, and their elected officials, repeatedly refused to call their slaves "people," "Americans," or "freed blacks' but instead always referred to them as "property" or "cargo." This galled the governor. And here was Bacon calling the slaves "cargo" yet again.

In a letter to Daniel Webster, Bacon said directly that Cockburn had violated the law. "The other slaves were liberated through the interference of the authorities of the colony," he wrote on November 17, 1841. (Surprisingly, Bacon waited a full two weeks before sending Webster his summary of the Creole incident.)[43]

A few days later, the governor's anger rose again when he learned that in a letter to his superiors, Bacon had directly charged him, Anderson, and other British and Bahamian officials with criminality. Bacon described "all illegal acts committed by His Majesty's officers and subjects and every other casualty which has occasioned liberation of . . . the slaves" in reference to men who had been careful to observe the letter of the law under not one flag but two.[44]

The day after that, as Washington and his fellow mutineers began to acclimate themselves to their jail cells, about half of the freed men and women left Nassau on a ship bound for Jamaica, where they would become paid laborers. The boat that took them to Jamaica had been advertised in the Nassau newspaper and the trip financed by the British government, causing many, led by Bacon, to charge that the British were interfering by providing an escape to Jamaica for the slaves. Cockburn vehemently denied the charge and said the ship was one of many bound for Jamaica that the government financed each year. He said that many people besides the *Creole* escapees sailed on it that day.[45]

Some said that the freed men and women left Nassau in a hurry, fearful of other tricks from Bacon that would result in their arrest and return to the United States for trial. Others said that the crafty Cockburn had ordered them onto the ship, an allegation vehemently denied by Cockburn. Once they were out of Nassau, they faced no fear of arrest. And they would be the legal problem of some other island, not his. Those people disappeared into history, never to be heard from again. (A second ship loaded with captives from the *Creole* left two weeks later.)[46]

❧❧❧❧❧❧❧

WHAT WASHINGTON AND HIS FELLOW SLAVES did not know was that back home in America, millions saw them not just as heroic mutineers but as very dashing, romantic figures. From time to time there had been violent slave uprisings, all of which were put down, but most of the time whites, and most blacks, saw slaves as sleepy, docile laborers who were unhappy but accepted their plight in life. They were, abolitionist Alvin Stewart said, "the most helpless creatures in the universe of God." The brashness of Washington and his men thrilled other blacks and abolitionists because they were certainly not docile. They had not only mutinied and taken a ship but had killed one man and injured several others in the process.[47]

A gathering of more than four hundred abolitionists meeting in Peterboro, New York, saluted Washington as a Robin Hood, liberator, and cultural star and then went beyond that in a petition practically hailing him as an American hero. They all signed it with gusto. "The insurgents on board the Creole to save themselves and their children from the untold horrors of slavery resorted to bloodshed and, whereas our fathers did so rather than submit to the comparatively trifling grievance of unjust taxation, it will be time enough for the South to charge guilt upon these insurgents, after she have charged ten thousand fold greater guilt on the heroes of the American Revolution," the resolution read.[48] Abolitionist Joshua Giddings of Ohio added that their mutiny coincidentally had taken place on the anniversary of the murder of abolitionist Elijah Lovejoy in Alton, Illinois. Washington's violent mutiny, Giddings argued, was staged on that particular day to avenge Lovejoy's death. Antislavery crusader Henry Highland Garnet said that Washington was "the bright star of freedom" and took his place "in the constellation of freedom" by leading the mutiny.[49] William Jay said that 'the sagacity, bravery and humanity of this man do honor to his name and but for his complexion, would excite universal admiration." His success propelled even the most ardent proponents of nonviolence to admire him. In the *Liberator*, one writer said that "the restraining reasons [of nonviolence] had vanished and both law and gospel justified their rising [on the *Creole*]."[50]

Later, the editor of the *New York Evangelist* would call the men and women of the slave ship, especially Washington, "hero mutineers."[51] Particularly among women there was also admiration for Washington because he had risked his freedom, and lost it, on his fifteen-hundred-mile journey to rescue his wife.[52]

The *Creole* mutineers, for a variety of reasons and timing, had aroused the feelings of US antislavery supporters, whether they lived in the chilly climate of New England or the much warmer one of the South, where a small group did feel that slavery was wrong.

Cockburn still faced complex legal problems over the ship and the imprisoned passengers. He had to continue his contentious relationship with Bacon and work with a Bahamian court and the British government's council. He had never anticipated any of this. He found himself at the center of what threatened to be an international incident involving an angry American government and enraged wealthy southerners who would hire numerous high-priced lawyers who would surely take him to court.

One very big problem that Cockburn faced, which really scared him, was an all-out war with the United States over the *Creole*. Would the American government, under enormous pressure from the southern states, launch a land–sea invasion of the Bahamas? The US Navy could sail there from the East Coast for an attack much faster than the British navy could arrive to defend the islands. With that in mind, Cockburn sat down at his desk, palm trees wafting outside his office windows, and wrote a long letter to his superior, Lord Stanley, the colonial secretary, in London. The governor was worried. He told Lord Stanley that he did not have enough men to defend the Bahamas in the event of an American invasion. The only fort on the island, Fort Charlotte, was in dilapidated condition. He also told Lord Stanley that if several American warships did assault the island, they would have no trouble reducing the fort to rubble and conquering Nassau.

Unhappy with that letter, the next morning he sent another. He started it prophetically: "I have been placed in a situation of some delicacy."

Cockburn also feared a firestorm in England. He did not want anything he said or did to lead his superiors into thinking a war with the United States was necessary.

And the mutiny aboard the *Creole* had started several firestorms in America. The incident had revitalized the antislavery movement, which despite the 1839 Supreme Court ruling freeing the *Amistad* mutineers two years earlier, had fallen on hard times. It had become difficult for abolitionist leaders to raise money, lobby in the nation's capital, and win senators and congressmen over to their cause. The mild antislavery movement in the northern states at that time was nowhere near as prominent, and its adherents nowhere near as dedicated, as antislavery leaders would have liked. The mutiny had lit a fuse, they hoped, that would eradicate bondage in America. Their great hope now was to either have the American government do nothing about the mutiny or to persuade the British to free the mutineers, as they had done previously with ships in British waters and on British islands.

The *Creole* incident captured the attention of the American press, North and South. Southern editors believed in slavery and wanted to uphold it. The mutiny threatened that institution, so they blasted the takeover in their columns as soon as they heard of it. The staunch antislavery papers wanted the African Americans freed immediately by the British government, without bloodshed, and it stuck to that claim throughout the *Creole* crisis. It became a story that readers, North and South, followed.

The mutiny also rocked the shipping community, North and South. If the mutineers got away with their action, what slave ship was next ripe for takeover? How many ships would be lost, at not only the cost of pride at lost captives but also the value of the ships themselves? Would slaves revolt elsewhere and for years? It was not just southern shippers who worried either. Hundreds of southern slave ships had been built by northern shipyards. In fact, many northern ships owned by northern companies were directly involved in slave transport.

The *Creole* crisis again shook the laws of nations and international law. Why was something legal in the South but not legal in the North? Why was something legal in America but illegal in other countries, especially England? Were slaves free on islands all over the world just because a British court said they were?

What about other islands in the Caribbean, or elsewhere, whose governments did not condone slavery? Would slaves revolt and step ashore there next? How would citizens of those islands feel about the newcomers? Would they house them, support them, arm them?

Would thousands of free but unhappy husbands charge back to their plantations armed, to get their wives? Would they charge back with a larger band of African Americans, all armed?

The incident drew ministers, priests, and rabbis into the slave ship debate. If God does not approve of murder, can he condone a murder committed in the name of freedom? If killing on a battlefield in war is not considered murder, is the deck of a slave ship not just a different kind of battlefield, and can men and women on that deck kill with impunity to obtain what they believe to be their freedom?

All these questions remained unanswered after takeover of the *Creole*. Meanwhile, the nation's government was being run by an "accidental" president, John Tyler, who became the nation's leader when President William Henry Harrison died after just a month in office. How would Tyler, a southerner who had many plantation friends and yet told people that he himself was against slavery, see the *Creole* incident? Should he fight for his country's honor and get the ship and slaves back, or fight for the antislavery cause and let them go? How would Congress, most of which detested Tyler, react? And what about several giants of American history who held the reins of power at the time: Senator Henry Clay; former president John Quincy Adams, the hero of the *Amistad* trial and an ardent antislavery champion; Secretary of State Daniel Webster, an antislavery man from Massachusetts, who in his cabinet role had to abide by the president's decisions?

The *Creole* was something that none of these leaders saw sailing their way, and now it was right in the middle of their political harbor.

The saga of the *Creole* was not over; it had just begun.

CHAPTER THREE

·⸙⸙⸙⸙⸙·

1600 *Pennsylvania Avenue*

·⸙⸙⸙⸙⸙·

Late morning, December 5, 1841
The office of the president, White House,
1600 Pennsylvania Avenue, Washington, DC

IN THE EARLY, BLUSTERY, COLD WINTER OF 1841, the newly liberated slave ship *Creole* was the best thing that could have happened to President John Tyler.

His presidency, just seven months old, was already reeling from a set of personal, political, and diplomatic miscues. He had engaged in debates, feuds, and shouting matches with some, developed jealousies of others, and generally handled intense relationships poorly. At the same time, he was caring for his ailing wife and trying to find work for his grown sons, who lived with him at the White House. Tyler was overwhelmed.

The embattled Tyler was the called the "accidental president" or often just His Accidency. Quite thin and six feet in height, he was tall for the times. He had a high forehead, oversized ears, wavy brown hair, and a large Roman nose that seemed to be the anchor of his face. Elected vice president on a Whig Party ticket in 1840, Tyler, a slave-owning plantation farmer from Virginia, seemed like a lost soul after the election. He was ignored by the new president, William Henry Harrison, and Harrison's cabinet secretaries.

A military hero of the War of 1812, Harrison had been the governor of Indiana.

During the war, he had led a militia to victory at Tippecanoe Creek against fabled Indian chief Tecumseh, gaining much fame and the nickname Tippecanoe. He had been named a general in that conflict. The presidential ticket, alliteratively named Tippecanoe and Tyler, Too, received 1.275 million popular votes, compared to incumbent president Martin Van Buren's ("the little magician") 1.13 million votes, and won handily in the Electoral College, 232 to 60.

Daniel Webster had lost that 1840 Whig Party presidential nomination but quickly became a huge supporter of Harrison and made it no secret that he was eager to serve in Harrison's cabinet. He was worried about Harrison's frail health but thought that his age was a plus—it showed wisdom. Harrison was also from the West, like Andrew Jackson, and had a lot of supporters there. "The cry of the nation is for change," Webster said of Harrison, "wafted over all the breezes, borne from every quarter."[1]

Webster campaigned hard for Harrison in different regions of the country. The general took Webster's home state of Massachusetts with 72,874 votes compared to 51,944 for Van Buren.

Men who greeted the sixty-eight-year-old Harrison when he arrived in Washington on a cold day in March 1841 commented that he looked very thin, frail, and sick. He appeared "somewhat shattered," remarked Henry Clay. The Kentucky senator had seen Harrison back in November, just after the election, and was concerned about his appearance then. He told friends that the president-elect was "much broken" and that he looked "weather beaten." This stunned those who had seen him prior to the presidential campaign, such as Joshua Giddings, who met him in January 1840 and told friends that Harrison "was in fine health and in good spirits." Henry Wise, who met him the day he arrived in the nation's capital, shook his head in disbelief at the president-elect's physical state. "He was in a high state of exaltation and agitated to a degree which could not fail to break him down physically and mentally," said Wise.[2]

Former president and current Massachusetts congressman John Quincy Adams said that although he had "come in on a hurricane," Harrison "might go out upon a wreck." A few weeks later Adams wrote, "the President's health is alarming. He was seized last Saturday with a severe chill and the next day with what his physicians called a bilious pleurisy." Yet despite Harrison's poor health, Whig leaders, more concerned about politics than their new president, insisted that he attend a long round of late-night parties and receptions in the nation's capital in the dead of a very chilly winter to herald his new administration. There were breakfasts at posh hotels, luncheons at the homes of senators, afternoon receptions, parties in the evening, and on some days lavish balls, where prominent people of the nation's capital arrived in expensive carriages, all dressed in their finest clothing. The parties had both small and large orchestras, much dancing, happy talk, and sometimes serious back corner conferences. The aging Harrison, always with a thin, wan smile on his face, grew weaker, party by party.[3]

The new president was under not only a physical strain but a psychological one as well. He was the victim of a constant political barrage by Henry Clay, the famous Whig senator from Kentucky. Clay was the most powerful figure in his party and had been a presidential nominee himself in 1824 and 1832. The man most in America assumed would be president someday had uttered the immortal line "I would rather be right than be president."

Clay was determined to prevail in all matters, using his strong majority of votes in Congress to patch up a country badly wounded by the financial panic of 1837, which lasted into the early 1840s, regardless of Harrison's ideas or plans. Clay and other Whig leaders paid little attention to Harrison because they determined he was a political neophyte. Sometimes diplomatically and just as often coarsely, Clay constantly reminded Harrison that Congress was the major power in Washington, not the president, and that Harrison would need to bend to its will. Washingtonians reminded Harrison that Clay was a very influential "dictator" and almost always got his way. He not only had a mercurial personality and years of experience at arm-twisting, but his ever-present persona as the future president persuaded legislators to do what he wanted because if they did not, he would hold up their agendas, sometimes indefinitely, and ruin their careers. Just a few months prior to the mutiny on board the *Creole*, the *New York Herald* said that Clay ran Congress like his own fiefdom: "He predominates over the Whig party with despotic sway. Old Hickory himself never lorded it over his followers with authority more undisputed. . . . Mr. Clay's wish is a paramount law of the whole party."[4]

Democrats were both amazed and incensed at his power. "Mr. Clay is carrying everything by storm," said one disheartened Democrat. "His will is the law of Congress. His Speaker in the House has made the most outrageous arrangement of committees."[5]

Clay loved to browbeat other members of the Senate and the House, badgering them for a point of information he already had just to show them, and the public, that he was the supreme being in Congress. He did it despite criticism of his style, often from his own party, and national pressure. Thomas Marshall, a Whig from Kentucky, called him a "blackguard" for his prosecutorial tone. The *New York Herald* objected to the "tyrannical insolence" of Clay. Its editor wrote that "his bullying disposition . . . causes him to forget himself sometimes."[6]

Henry Wise wrote his friend Beverley Tucker in the spring of 1841 that Clay's bad behavior had threatened the party throughout the nation: "The prospect with Clay is even worse than I had imagined. He is bent on centralism, and I shall leave him to be born down as he must be, by his accumulated power and weight of self-destruction."[7]

Wise felt his emotions rising and just four days later blasted Clay again in yet another letter to Tucker. "Clay is impractical," he said. "He is beyond conference or advice and you and I had better not approach him."[8]

Critics in both parties, and some newspaper editors, said that Clay was a marvelous politician, the broker of important compromises in 1820 and 1833, but would not make a good president. He was too concerned with politics and not the nation. He was a brilliant politician but not a good statesman. Perhaps all those years as a politician, a behind-the-scenes arm-twister, had made it impossible for him to be a statesman.[9]

Clay's "dictator" tag stuck.

Clay's power was substantial, even though he was not the president. His influence was an example of how much authority the Whig Party had gained in just ten years of existence. The wars between the Whigs and Democrats followed wars between the Democrats and others and, back in the early years of the century, the first challenge to George Washington's Federalist Party. It was a tumultuous time in American politics.

Washington had not foreseen political parties, believing that his lone party, the Federalists, would always do what was right for the nation. He was wrong. Thomas Jefferson and James Madison, believing the Federalists had too much power and that the states needed more influence, founded the Democratic-Republican Party in the early 1790s. That party, also called the Jeffersonian Republicans, became the Democratic Party and held sway in both the Senate and House of Representatives until the early 1830s, when the Whigs appeared. The

Federalists fell apart in the early 1820s. Various splinter parties and unhappy Federalists joined the Whigs, giving it an immediate power in the country. Third parties such as the Anti-Masons and Liberty Party also emerged but achieved only minor status in those years.

The Democrats and the Whigs truly created the two-party system, which became the linchpin of American democracy. The Democrats produced strong presidents, such as Jackson, and the Whigs provided the country with numerous influential leaders, such as Clay. The Whigs would eventually collapse over the slavery issue and be replaced by the Republicans in 1855.

One of those Whigs was Harrison. The tired and run-down president-elect was caught in a severe rainstorm while walking the streets of Washington one day prior to his inauguration. He was not properly dressed for the bad weather and hustled to a reception held by political colleagues. He was drenched when he got home, started to sneeze and cough the next day, and came down with a bad case of pneumonia. His health worsened, but only a few noticed. A man who was a friend to both Harrison and Tyler, James Lyons, wrote Tyler twice from Washington in late March to inform him that the president's health was quite poor and that he was sinking fast. So it was no surprise to Tyler when Harrison died on the night of April 4, exactly one month after his inauguration. His funeral procession was quite elaborate, with bells constantly ringing and loud and frequent gun salutes. Thousands of Washingtonians lined the procession route, all somber, many with their hats off or placed across their chests. This would pass for America's first state funeral upon the death of a national leader. The funeral received extensive attention in the press. Across the country, scores of people who had just voted for Harrison, and loved him, mourned his untimely passing.[10]

Several days Harrison's death, Tyler, at home in Williamsburg, Virginia, was officially informed of the chief executive's passing by a messenger arriving from Washington, DC, on horseback. He was told he would be elevated to the presidency and was asked to head for the capital in his carriage. At the same time, officials in Washington pored over copies of the Constitution, puzzled about what Tyler was supposed to do when he arrived. It was an unprecedented moment in American history, and no one seemed to know how to handle the situation.

Tyler was younger than Harrison. Just fifty-one, he was the youngest president in the nation's early history. He was not a powerful figure of the times;

nor was he well connected in the Whig Party—he had in fact been a Democrat until 1834. Assessed by many as a quiet, reserved man, he was a poor public speaker. He avoided confrontations and sophisticated plans and schemes in the political world, and with little work to do as vice president, a political tradition, he spent most of his time at home, some ninety miles away, gardening.

Many in the party thought Clay would eat Tyler alive in his quest for the presidency, just as he had done initially with Harrison. Clay had suffered a frustrating defeat at the 1840 Whig convention, when he appeared likely to win the nomination but was defeated when the Northeast faction of the party managed to change the voting rules. Now, with Harrison's death creating a monstrous succession mess, he still might have a chance to win the White House.

A friend of Abraham Lincoln's would later say that in Lincoln ambition was a little engine that knew no rest. The same could be said of Clay. Halted in his quest for the White House twice, he would pursue it again in 1844, using the *Creole* incident to win it. He would chase the Executive Mansion again in 1848 at the age of seventy. "I had reason to believe that there existed a fixed determination with the mass of the Whig Party throughout the U.S., to bring me forward again. I believe that the greater portion of that mass still clings to that wish," he said in 1847.[11]

Many shook their heads at his steely determination to win the presidency regardless of his age and political circumstances. "Is that fire of ambition never to be extinguished?" asked John Tyler.[12]

Who was John Tyler, anyway? He had been elected vice president, not president. The president's cabinet had no use for him and was quite happy that he had been spending his days in far-off Williamsburg amid his flowers and bushes. As Tyler traveled toward Washington in a carriage after Harrison's demise, he must have considered what would happen to him next. The president of the United States lived in the White House and had considerable power. The vice president stayed at home or lived in a hotel in Washington and had no power. How would Tyler's role change now? Who would support him? Who would oppose him? How would the nation's press react to the transfer of power? How would state leaders react? And the people? It was an unprecedented event in the short life of the country, and now, through no intention of his own, Tyler was the key figure in it.

In Washington, the mood toward Tyler was ugly. The cabinet had already decided that he would not be referred to as "President Tyler" but as "Vice President Tyler, acting as president." The cabinet also thought he should be put up in a home in the capital and not be permitted to live in the White House. Several cabinet members said that the Constitution was so thin on the matter of succession that in fact Tyler should be dumped as both president and vice president and sent back home. They called for a new national election for president. That option was perhaps possible due to vague language in Article II, Section 1, Paragraph 6 of the Constitution, which suggested that Congress could, in extraordinary circumstances, rule that Tyler was incompetent, declare the offices of both president and vice president vacant, and hold another national contest for the job.

Uncertain about such an interpretation, Secretary of State Daniel Webster, a former senator and a presidential candidate in 1836, asked Roger Taney, chief justice of the Supreme Court, to travel from his home in Maryland to Washington to rule on the succession crisis. Taney refused, and the uncertainty as to how to proceed remained.

On April 6, Tyler arrived in the nation's capital and went straight to the White House for a meeting with the agitated members of the cabinet. This was not the same old Tyler they all remembered, though. This was a self-confident man who knew what he wanted. He insisted that the Constitution was clear that the vice president ascended to the presidency upon the death of the president, and he demanded, with a steely-eyed look for each, to be made president. Tyler had William Cranch, a judge of the Circuit Court of the District of Columbia, certify that he could properly assume the presidency. Then to be safe he had Cranch administer him the oath of office at Brown's Indian Queen Hotel in Washington, one of the largest and poshest in the capital, where Tyler was staying.

Cranch was suspicious of Tyler's motives in being officially sworn in. "Although he deems himself qualified to perform the duties and exercise the powers and office of the President . . . without under oath that which he has taken as Vice-President, yet as doubt may arise and for greater caution [he] took and subscribed the . . . oath before me," Cranch said in an official statement that he demanded be issued and that he signed.[13]

Privately, Tyler knew he was walking on untrodden ground and that few knew who he was or really wanted him to become the head of state. The country was in just as great a convulsion as the House and Senate. "Under these circumstances, the devolvement upon me of this high office is peculiarly embarrassing," Tyler wrote to Virginia senator William Rives, a neighbor and longtime political colleague.[14]

He also knew full well that he had become the chief executive through an extraordinarily tragic accident. He told Rives, "I am under Providence made the instrument of a new test which is for the first time to be applied to our institutions. The experiment is to be made at a time when our country is agitated by conflicting views of public policy and when the spirit of faction is most likely to exist." (Rives was Tyler's attack dog in his disputes with Clay, once stating in Congress that something Clay had said was "an open and violent attack on the President of the United States.")[15]

It was not just politicians who refused to call him the president but the entire Washington governmental machinery. People at the State Department went further, awkwardly referring to him as "ex vice-president Tyler," which infuriated him.[16]

He did receive strong support from the *Richmond Whig*, a newspaper from his home state capital. Its editor wrote that the people had elected an administration in the fall of 1840, not just a president. "Nineteen states, an electoral majority of 174 the largest known in our history, have installed the existing administration," wrote the editor. "Was no deference due to the voice of so immense a majority of our countrymen? No respect to the decision of the nineteen states?" He then told readers that Tyler was part of the administration that the nation had elected. Therefore, upon the death of Harrison, he should become the president.

"Was nothing due to the old reputation of Virginia for steadiness, principle and integrity?" he added.[17]

Friends immediately warned him that this new job was different from the old and that enemies in Congress would attack him, and attack him right away. Littleton Tazewell was one of those friends. Tyler wrote Tazewell a few months later, just prior to the *Creole* mutiny. "I well remember your prediction of Gen. Harrison's death and with what emphasis you enquired of me whether I had thought of my own situation upon the happening of that contingency. You declared in advance much of the difficulty of which I have already been surrounded," he wrote.[18]

He told people during these early days of his administration that he had not sought the presidency. It came to him. He told his son Robert that people like Clay, Calhoun, and Webster had sought the presidency all their lives, doing just about everything they could to win the office, but had never gained it. He had not seek it and did win it. He said the presidency came to him because he was an honorable man who worked hard.

But even his beloved Virginians ridiculed him. Congressman John Minor Botts said of one of his messages to Congress during that first year in office, "If a boy [of mine] had written so much Tom Foolery, [I] would have taken him from school and put him to the plow."

Early in his administration, Tyler vetoed Clay's bank bill and was heavily criticized by most members of his own party. That veto, of what seemed a reasonable bill, set the stage for four years of acrimony in the national government, with Tyler always fighting, it seemed, with everybody else.[19]

The veto also began a nonstop assault on the president. "The war upon Mr. Tyler became appalling," lamented one Whig. The opposition accused the Whigs of not just wrecking the nation but wrecking the White House too, by doing all they could to gather around Clay. Congressman George Proffit sneered at the Whigs' "president-making."[20]

The veto turned Clay, a former friend, against the president. "If it had been foreseen that General Harrison would die in one short month after the commencement of his administration; that Vice President Tyler would be elevated to the Presidential chair; that a bill passed by decisive majorities in the first Whig Congress chartering a national bank would be presented for his sanctions, and that he would veto the bill, do I hazard anything when I express the conviction that he would not have received a solitary vote in the nominating convention nor one solitary electoral vote in any state in the Union?" said a bitter Clay.[21]

Friends of Tyler's saw the veto as an act the president had planned for months as part of a scheme to declaw the politically powerful Clay. Henry Wise chortled over it. "I say [Clay] is caught. It . . . was [Clay's] camp for a night only and now that the enemy occupies every height around it, he is not such a fool as to occupy it again. He desires nothing so much now as for Clay's bill to come to him, to kill it, as he certainly will, without a moment's hesitation," he wrote to Beverly Tucker in the summer of 1841.[22]

Wise and Tucker were close friends of Tyler's and had been for years.

Wise, a tall, thin man with wavy chestnut hair and high cheekbones, had been elected to Congress as a Jackson Democrat in 1832. Right after the election, the short-tempered Wise fought a duel with the man he had defeated. Two years later, he left the Democrats in a dispute with President Jackson over the Bank of the United States and joined the Whigs. His Democratic followers stayed with him though, even though he switched parties. He then established his friendship with Tyler. Wise was reelected to Congress as a Whig in 1836 and 1840. In 1840 he worked hard to secure the vice presidential nomination for Tyler. Wise was Tyler's chief political adviser, and Tyler later appointed him US minister to Brazil.

Wise was not only a shrewd politician but also a superb speaker. He gave impressive orations in the House all alone and was even better at speaking with help from friends. "He spoke slowly and with great composure," wrote Joshua Giddings, "and would frequently stop to make inquiries of those around him on matter on which he did not possess the requisite intelligence." Giddings was an antislavery crusader but always admired southern, proslavery Wise for his speaking style. Wise's friends, men like John Quincy Adams, W. J. Graves, and S. S. Prentiss, fed him information and their opinions, which he blended smoothly into his own speeches. He sometimes spoke uninterrupted for six hours or more. The House would often recess for dinner and when the members returned, Wise would continue. No one left. He enchanted all into the dark hours of the night.[23]

He had a sad private life. His wife and one of his five children were killed in a fire in 1837. He then married Sarah Sergeant, the daughter of a congressman, in 1840. That pair also had five children. He married again in 1853, three years after Sarah's death. A lifelong supporter of bondage, would later serve as a general in the Civil War.

Beverly Tucker was from one of the South's wealthiest and most influential families. His father, St. George Tucker, was one of the nation's key legal scholars in the Revolutionary War era, and his half brother was the famous John Randolph, of the prestigious and influential Randolph family of Virginia. Beverly Tucker, a graduate of William and Mary College in Williamsburg, moved to Missouri in 1816. He lived there for sixteen years, serving as a judge. He returned to Virginia in 1832 and established one of the state's most successful law practices. For decades, he served as a professor of law at the College of William and Mary. He was a fiery pro-slaver and wrote extensively in support of states' rights for various prominent southern magazines.

Ten years earlier, Tyler and Clay had been friends and admirers of each other. Tyler had once practically fawned over Clay. "Mr. Clay carries his head very loftily," Tyler told his daughter Anne in 1831. "Age has bleached it very much, but his voice is as musical as ever, and his manners as attractive."[24]

Political disagreements ruined their friendship, though. "We were once intimate, and I had a warm attachment and admiration for him, but he broke the silver cord with a reckless hand and his arm became very short to reach the golden fruit for which he gave up friendship and everything," said Tyler later.[25]

While such feuds were poisoning the House and Senate, Tyler was told by Treasury Secretary Walter Forward that by the end of 1841, the government deficit would hit $3.25 million and that it would soar to perhaps $14 million in 1842, record shortfalls. The government, in short, was broke.[26] The president knew the country needed to be on a sounder financial footing and that the bank bill provided that. Yet he had continually threatened to veto the bill, telling Clay in one of his first letters to him as president that it should not be urged prematurely. "The public mind is still in a state of disquietude" over it, the president said. He told Clay that previous bank bills had been seen as unconstitutional and that a "vast host of our own party were opposed to it."[27]

Clay knew that the senators and congressmen had to compromise with Tyler to get the bill passed, yet they did not. The president and Clay had, by this point, become steadfast enemies. Tyler would veto whatever legislation Clay proposed and Clay would disagree with whatever the chief executive suggested. Webster was caught in the middle, believing for the most part that some form of Clay's bank bill was needed and yet refusing to abandon Tyler on that and any other position. Meanwhile, the nation floundered. Webster stuck with Tyler because he saw his prominent role of secretary of state as a stepping stone to the White House.

The president was well educated, a graduate of the College of William and Mary, and had extensive professional experience as a lawyer. He had been elected to the Virginia State Legislature at the age of twenty-one and had served six years before winning a congressional seat. He became governor of Virginia in 1825. He was later elected to the US Senate and served nine years there before quitting in a heated political dispute. Tyler's problem in the winter of 1841 was that while all in Congress knew of his experience, no one gave him any credit for it. He was also a man who never dreamed of becoming president and did not know how to handle the job.

He admitted that to a friend that summer. Upon his ascension to the presidency, he said, he suddenly found an array of factions not only battling each other but also targeting him. He wrote to Tucker:

> The condition of things here is indicative of angry future contests, as likely to arise between those who were but six months ago apparently friends. When I arrived here, or within a day or two after, I became fully apprised of the angry state of the factions towards each other and set myself to work in good earnest to reconcile them. I was surrounded by Clay-men, Webster-men, Anti-Masons, original Harrisonians, old Whigs, and new Whigs, each jealous of the others and each struggling for the offices. . . . Little then did I dream that I myself was destined to be at so early a date the object of intolerant assault.[28]

He owed his vice presidential position to the tradition of selecting a vice presidential nominee from a different geographic area than the presidential nominee in order to gain regional electoral votes. It was also helpful, Whigs believed, for the politically strong South to have someone from that area to represent its interests, primarily bondage. Virginian Henry Wise said that "Tyler was put into the vice-presidency by the friends of states' rights and strict construction avowedly for the purpose of casting any tie vote in the Senate in their favor."[29]

Tyler traveled through the Midwest on Harrison's behalf during the 1840 campaign and delivered a few speeches that attracted sparse attention. In those speeches and in all his conversations, be backed up whatever Harrison had said or stood for and had no real impact on the election. The plan thereafter was to spend four years offering toasts to Harrison at dinners, having lunch with diplomats, shaking hands, and smiling to all, but spending much of his time back home in Virginia, gardening.

Then President Harrison died.

Tyler felt he needed to immediately prove that he was the nation's legitimate leader. He constantly referred to himself as the president and had friends do so as often as they could in public and private. He met with leaders of Congress as the president. He quickly moved into the White House with his invalid wife and five of his seven children, plus several house servants from his abode in Virginia. He gave two of his grown sons jobs in government. In the cleverest move of all, he made his daughter-in-law Priscilla Cooper his First Lady (since his wife was ill) and told her to seek out the assistance of the aging and beloved Dolley Madison, near eighty, America's national icon and the First Lady for sixteen years, holding the position for both Thomas Jefferson and got her husband, James Madison. She still knew everyone and was seen as the queen of Washington society. Having the effervescent Dolley Madison around the White House gave Tyler a connection to former presidents Madison and Jefferson. Tyler hosted a string of parties, balls, and receptions, which he presided over with Dolley. The gracious and admired hostess solidified his position as chief executive.

He stunned his political friends when he quickly wrote and sent to newspapers an inaugural address in which he set out his goals and tried to explain to people not only what kind of president he hoped to be but also what kind of a president the republic needed, then and in the future. That leader, he said, was a man who understood the democratic form of government, with three equally powerful branches: the executive, legislative, and judicial. He did not want to be a strong leader, he told the people, and insinuated that Andrew Jackson and his successor, Martin Van Buren, had far exceeded the boundaries of their office. Tyler thought that strong presidents like Jackson were not only out of constitutional character but also dangerous.

He argued that it was wrong for "the tendency of all human institutions . . . to concentrate power in the hands of a single man" and that that tendency led them "to their ultimate downfall." He added that an all-powerful president could name his successor, as Jackson was accused of doing with Van Buren; stack the Supreme Court; and name numerous friends and allies to key patronage jobs in the federal government. He told the people, too, that the cabinet system, invented by George Washington, was a danger because presidents controlled it. The president, he said, "should carefully abstain from all attempts to enlarge the range of powers thus granted to the several departments of the government." Tyler argued further that a strong president who controlled the cabinet departments prevented the states from having any power and that that defeated the federal–state contract the founders had envisioned. There was another demon in that mix too. The states might rebel against the presidents and departments.

"The Union might break apart or a centralized despotism might seize power," said Tyler. That would result in "a bloody scepter and an iron crown," he added.[30]

He also said that he was not the Whig president but the nation's president. "Our course is too plainly before us to be mistaken," he told Webster. "We must look to the whole country and the whole people."[31]

As a symbolic gesture in his drive to make the chief executive a president and not an ostentatious monarch, which he accused Van Buren of being, Tyler fired all the French cooks in the White House who had been hired by gourmet Van Buren and hired American cooks who would provide him and his guests with homegrown, country dishes. (Tyler's favorite dish was boiled bacon and greens.) He was applauded for this step by the Whig press.[32]

One of Tyler's problems was that he was not working with his own cabinet but with President Harrison's. Harrison, one of the oldest men ever elected president, had not envisioned himself as president for more than one term. He wanted to strengthen the Whig Party and bring stability to the country. The best way to do that, he believed, was to place the best public officials in the country in the cabinet. Those were Henry Clay and Daniel Webster. Webster had accepted, but Clay had turned him down because he saw no political gain for himself in the position and he had already served as secretary of state. So that position went to Webster. Harrison was happy with this pick, telling Webster that "since I was first a candidate for the Presidency, I had determined that, if successful, to solicit able assistance in conducting the administration."[33]

Clay was not happy that Harrison had won the presidency or with his early policies. But he told friends and party members that they had to do the best they could. "We must support this administration," he wrote friend John Clayton. "Or rather, I should say, we should not fall out with it."[34]

The American cabinet, unlike advisory groups of other nations, was understood by members of both parties, the press, and the public to be the president's think tank, his loyal collection of personal advisers. He had the power to hire and fire them and to use or abuse their views. Now suddenly president, Tyler had to confront a cabinet of men he did not know that well as a collective unit and at the same time figure out how to function as the president, and the "accidental president" at that.

Tyler's friends predicted chaos with the cabinet. Tucker said that "[Tyler] has not a sincere friend in it. Webster will adhere to him till he kills Clay, and no longer. Ewing, Bell, Crittenden and Granger will sacrifice him to Clay, Badger is too generous to betray him—but Badger is a Federalist, and will not aid him in shaking off National Republican Centralism."[35]

Tyler did not know how to handle the situation and it grew worse day by day as spring, with its colorful cherry blossoms, approached in the nation's capital. One thing that would put his own stamp on the government, friends told him, would be to fire his cabinet officers, in particular Webster, and name a brand-new cabinet.

Tucker also told Tyler that northern politicians were smothering the South. They banded together as a single regional cabal and voted down all measures that helped the southern way of life. Tucker warned that eventually the South would have to separate from the North and form its own government. This idea would gain new ground when the slave ship *Creole* crisis exploded on the international scene in early November.[36]

Tucker and others told Tyler, too, that he had to adhere to "southern honor," a code by which southern "gentlemen" stuck together on issues such as bondage and supported traditional political stances on agriculture, culture, and shipping. They could not give up their "honor" and bend to the wishes of the northerners.[37]

TALL AND THIN, WITH BLACK HAIR AND EYES, and always well dressed, Daniel Webster was a longtime and controversial political figure from Massachusetts and one of the most powerful men in the country. A crafty deal maker and dazzling orator, Webster was best remembered not for any of his planned, scripted speeches but for an accidental 1829 debate in the Senate. He found himself in a dispute over the role of the federal government with Robert Hayne of South Carolina in January 1830. Hayne argued strongly that the government was supposed to be made up of strong states overseen by a weak federal government. Webster, during a long argument that filled the afternoon, explained his view that a strong federal government was needed to oversee the states, allowing states power outside of that held by the federal government. Only in that way, he insisted, could the country survive and thrive. Finally, exhausted by Hayne's challenges, Webster bellowed with great eloquence, "Everywhere, spread all over in characters of living light, blazing on all its ample folds, as they float over the seas an over the land, and in every wind under the whole heavens [is] that other sentiment, dear to every true American heart—Liberty and Union, now and forever, one and inseparable!"[38]

He was the patriot's patriot.

The secretary of state had been a longtime supporter of any measures that strengthened the federal government. He told friends and neighbors that the government represented all the people, not just regions and individual states. The government was strong that way. It was weak, he argued, when individual states tried to assume any of the federal government's power. He was one of many, too, who warned that the endless procession of states' rights politicians would one day cause a rupture of some kind and perhaps a clash between the northern and southern states.[39]

Webster was not universally admired. He had numerous enemies.

Congressman Thomas Gilmer, of Tyler's home state of Virginia, was one of the many men who hated Webster. Earlier that year, he had written that he wanted Webster "put into some dark corner or thrown overboard entirely . . . [he was] a federalist of the worst die, a blackguard and vulgar debauchee." He said Webster was a man who "but for his splendid talents, would be in jail or on some dunghill."[40]

Henry Wise loathed Daniel Webster as well and wrote to Beverley Tucker, "With some of them we want to part friendly. We can part friendly with Webster by sending him to England. Let us, for God's sake, get rid of him."

Webster, who would soon become a key figure in the *Creole* crisis, found himself in an even more difficult spot than Tyler. Harrison had originally asked Webster to be his vice president and Webster had turned him down, saying the vice presidency was a dead-end job and would ruin his political career. Now he stood by and watched Tyler, Harrison's second choice, serve as president. (This would happen again to the luckless Webster. In 1848 General Zachary Taylor was elected president and asked Webster to be his vice president. Webster again refused, for the same reason. Taylor died sixteen months later, and his vice president, Millard Fillmore, became president.) Cheated three times, Webster could never have known that these presidents would die in office.

WEBSTER WAS A SCHEMER and had thirsted after the presidency. In 1831 he thought he had his first opportunity. The Whigs were not in existence yet, and

Webster saw numerous cracks in the existing parties. He told friends that if he befriended Jackson and stood firm with both parties on issues, he might find a way to the White House. The Democrats were firmly behind Jackson. The opposition, the National Republicans (not be confused with the Republican Party, founded in 1855), were in disarray. Perhaps, he thought, he could lead a third party and win the White House in a heated election. He became a Whig when the political organization was formed just after the 1832 elections and sought the Whig nomination for president in 1836 and 1840.[41]

Webster knew he was popular, and that was reaffirmed at every rally at which he spoke, every city he visited, and every dinner party at which he was a guest. An example of his popularity was his travel swing through the midwestern states in the summer of 1837. He gave scheduled speeches at many cities but also spoke where city officials begged to be added to his tour. Fans in Ohio gave him a cane, supporters in Buffalo organized a steamboat regatta for him, people in Louisville threw a mammoth barbecue in his honor. He received dozens of letters of support on his tour and made splashy headlines just about everywhere he stopped whether to deliver a long speech or just shake hands. He was popular, he believed, because his politics were the same as those of the typical middle-class westerner or northeasterner. He reveled in the trip, and every day it was a reminder that one day he would surely become president.[42]

He also reveled in his wealth. Webster was one of the richest men in government. He owned a large estate, Marshfield, in Massachusetts; more than twelve hundred acres of land in various states; several additional farms; thirty buildings; and numerous shares of stock in companies. He speculated in land ventures with friends. It was an era long before campaign finance laws, and he received large amounts of "campaign" money from supporters all over the United States.[43]

Webster was a loyalist to both his country and his party, and he supported Tyler as best he could in the rocky, early days of his administration. He thought that Tyler lawfully deserved to be president and that in his first weeks in office, before the Creole incident and bank dispute, he performed rather well. Webster told friends that Tyler and he had a pleasant relationship. "He behaves with much dignity and courtesy, is intelligent and appears to realize what the country expects from his administration," Webster said.

Webster's support had an underlying ulterior motive though. His thirst for the presidency was greater than Clay's. If he had turned down the cabinet post offered to him by Harrison and acknowledged by Tyler, he would be without any government job at all for four years, a long time to go without national recognition, press attention, or political strength building. It would also certainly annoy his much younger second wife, a socialite who enjoyed Washington parties. She had made hundreds of friends in the nation's capital, bought expensive dresses, filled a cellar with fine wines, and gained attention in the press. She had become a jewel in the Washington social crown and did not want to give that up.

Tyler, Webster assumed, would be a one-term president. If he remained in the cabinet, he could maintain his position of power and plot a course for the Whig nomination in 1844. There might be some international event that he could use to his political advantage.[44] So for now, Webster gave Tyler his approval.

Another loyalist, Congressman John Bell of Tennessee, who would be one of four candidates to run against Abraham Lincoln for president in 1860, approved of Tyler too. "Things look quite as fine as could be expected just now," he said of the president.[45]

And then there was Clay. The brilliant, charismatic legislator was well versed in the classics and could recite Greek plays from memory (in Greek). He was a raconteur of the first order, a skilled poker player, and a two-fisted drinker. He had long white hair, a wide face, and a receding hairline above a large forehead. He was such a consummate politician that he had been elected Speaker of the House in his very first term as a congressman, something that had never happened before and would never happen again.

At the time Clay was hard at work putting together the Bank of the United States to help end the Panic of 1837, the financial crisis that had closed many banks and crippled the nation for several years. Before Tyler arrived in Washington as the new president, Clay was already pushing legislators to support the bank system. Little did he or Tyler know that the bank would be the issue that would divide them and, along with the *Creole*, nearly bring an abrupt end to Tyler's brand-new accidental presidency and make the two men enemies.

Clay's view was that he and his colleagues had worked hard since the Panic of 1837—four long years of toil—to create a national bank that would prevent any financial crisis in the future. They were close to approval. Then along comes Tyler, out of nowhere, to call the bank plans into question. Tyler would lose the battle, Clay defiantly told his congressional allies.

Tyler's view was that the congressional ideas on banking were not substantial enough, or fair enough to different regions, to win his approval. What did he care if Clay had worked so hard for so long? The bank was not a good idea; other means of financial solvency had to be discovered. Tyler thought Clay was wrong and acting childishly.

Neither man understood the other.

Worse, Democrats said, Tyler was not completely opposed to the bank and believed that if Clay redefined it, he might approve of it. In a letter, Tyler told the Kentucky senator that he would "leave Congress to its own action" on the bank, which implied he would go along with any congressional vote. But then he asserted that his decision would depend on "the character of the measure proposed." This awkward indecision left Clay in even deeper anger. Newspapers were perplexed by Tyler's waffling statement too. The *Richmond Enquirer*'s editor wrote that his view "leaves us all in a fog."[46]

Some said the "maybe" response was wishy-washy and very timid, and showed that Tyler was not tough enough to be the nation's leader. Others said that if he caved in to Clay on the bank issue, he would become Clay's lackey and that Clay, not Tyler, would be running the country for the next four years. The *Richmond Enquirer*'s editor said that Tyler did not seem like the "high minded Virginian" his neighbors hoped he would be. Tyler was hurt by the insinuation that he was Clay's personal servant and would be his puppet for four years.[47]

Still others charged that Tyler's own actions demonstrated the conduct of a duplicitous and deceitful man. Tyler always operated that way, they said. He befriended Whigs and then betrayed them. He told people he would sign a bill and then would not. He embraced the Whig leadership but then refused to accept their advice. He talked out of both sides of his mouth. No one, regardless of party, was ever sure what he meant or what he was going to do. That poor character would lead him into immense trouble when the *Creole* crisis began.

When Harrison ran for president, he pledged that if he were elected, he would serve only one term, leaving the presidency at age seventy-two. Tyler's opponents now insisted that he make the same pledge. They were adamant that since he was an "accidental president," he had to leave his post at the conclusion of Harrison's term and go home. They all expected him to say that in his inaugural address. It would have reassured people that the constitutional system worked. But Tyler refused to do that and said that he would seek election in 1844.

This angered millions of Americans.[48] It was also bad politics, said Thomas Ewing and others. Ewing, a member of Harrison's cabinet, wrote that if Tyler had declared himself a single-term president, his succession to Harrison's job would have been considerably easier and his one term in office would be a success. "His concessions [on 1844] seemed to me to declare the idea that the Whigs, cabinet included, cared little about measures if we could clear the way for the succession," said Ewing.[49]

Another major political figure in America, John Quincy Adams, a former chief executive, simply hated the new president. "Tyler is a political sectarian of the slave-driving Virginian, Jeffersonian school . . . with all the interests and passions and vices of slavery rooted in his moral and political constitution," he said. He added that Tyler was not mentally equipped to lead the nation. Adams noted with some disdain that Tyler "styles himself" the president and that he was merely the "acting chief" and nothing more, adding that "a reading of the Constitution has placed in the executive chair a man never thought of for it by anybody."[50]

People in Washington and throughout the country formed their views of the "accidental president" right away. Many southerners saw him as a pro-bondage champion from Virginia, the South's largest slave state. "All of Mr. Tyler's associations and habits of thought are southern and states' rights," wrote William Preston of South Carolina. One Virginian went further, arguing that "*now* the abolitionists and others who would harm us are foiled—the Constitution will be preserved . . . we shall be saved."[51]

The president's friend Abel P. Upshur, from Virginia, told his colleagues to stick with the president. "I have not heard from him, nor from any one member of his cabinet, any counsel, opinion or suggestion unbecoming an honest man and true lover of his country. I do not believe we ever had an administration more truly devoted to the public good nor more free from every corrupt and improper design," he said.[52]

Upshur, one of twelve children, had been a public figure since 1807, when at just sixteen he led a student protest against rules at Princeton University, where he was a student. Upshur was kicked out of Princeton for his actions. He never finished college but passed the bar exam in Virginia and became a prominent lawyer there. He held numerous appointed and elected offices in Virginia and became friendly with John Tyler in the 1830s, by which time he was being hailed as one of the South's proslavery leaders.

Alexander Stephens, a future leader of the Confederacy, said of Tyler that "his own state papers compare favorably in point of ability with those of any of his predecessors." Henry Hilliard, the US minister to Brazil, called Tyler "one of the most fascinating men I had ever known—brilliant, eloquent."[53]

Tyler was a man who believed that the size and nature of crowds were a barometer of popularity, not the individual opinions of politicians and newspaper editors. If he drew large crowds to speeches and events, he thought, mistakenly, that meant he himself was popular, not the office of the president. Tyler luxuriated in the size of the crowd at his first annual New Year's Day party in the White House. It was mobbed. "The President's house was thronged with visitors beyond all former example—so thronged, as we heard from many of those that were there, that the crowd in the house was so great that to avert the danger of suffocation, the porter at the outer door was obliged to lock out hundreds who were rushing to it for admission," said John Quincy Adams. Thus Tyler believed he was an extraordinarily popular man.[54]

He ignored the legislators who saw him as nothing more than a caretaker, similar to the boy monarchs in Europe who sat on a throne while the men around him ran the country. Clay spread this idea, assuring many that Tyler would go along with whatever the Whigs (Clay) wanted to do. "His administration will be in the nature of a regency," Clay said. He added carefully, though, that "regencies are very apt to engender faction, intrigue etc."[55]

Tyler had no intention of being a regent, but he knew that the persuasive Clay, who could be a bully, often got his way. He had badgered Harrison and he would badger Tyler. With imperial majesty, Clay had warned the Harrison, "If the executive will cordially co-operate in carrying out the Whig measures, all will be well. Otherwise, everything is at hazard." The president-elect was startled at Clay's audacity. Looking the Kentucky senator right in the eye, Harrison told him, "Mr. Clay, you forget that I am the President."[56]

Even before Harrison arrived at the White House, Clay wrote that "notwithstanding professions of the most ardent attachment to me by Harrison circumstances have transpired which confirm opinion of which have long since formed that he is apprehensive that the new administration may not be regarded as *his*, but mine."[57]

He told Tyler the same thing on the very first day he visited him in the White House. He was wary of Tyler because the Virginian's economic policies were similar to those of Jackson, a man he had despised intensely. Tyler and Clay got into a loud shouting match that ended when Clay, red-faced in anger, stormed out of the president's office.[58]

※※※※※※

WHEN CLAY LEFT TYLER'S PRESIDENTIAL OFFICE after his shouting match, he was fuming. He walked quickly down the wide staircase, through the first floor, and out the door. Clay had had his differences with Harrison, but he saw Harrison as someone he, anybody, could work with. Not Tyler. Why didn't Tyler see himself as the "accidental President" like everyone else did? Why didn't he pledge, like Harrison, to be just a one-term president and leave the White House door open for Clay? Tyler would soon have bills on the floor, Clay knew, and he prepared to make it just about impossible for any of them to pass.

Upstairs in his office, Tyler was enraged about Clay's visit. He did not expect to get along that well with the powerful Kentucky senator, but he expected their relations to be civilized. Clearly, it would not be.

He would demolish Clay some way, somehow.

But what Tyler did not realize, and should have, was that Henry Clay was probably the most powerful man in the country. Clay had been in office for years and everybody owed him a favor. He had helped hundreds of people in Washington and throughout the nation. He truly was the "emperor of Washington." His fame was national. He drew huge crowds whenever he spoke or appeared at an event, such as a barbecue or picnic. People told their grandchildren that they had met him. Tyler did not understand how important Clay was and how influential all his friends were. As president, Tyler truly believed he was an incredibly popular man, but he was wrong. He was counting hands at a cocktail party and not votes on the floor of Congress. That's where Clay had the power and Tyler had little.

The "accidental president" would realize that soon enough, when he vetoed the bank bill that Clay was certain would stabilize the nation's rocky finances. The started a long chain of political events that would end with the *Creole*.

CHAPTER FOUR

⁂

Into the Whirlwind

⁂

April 5, 1841

TYLER DID NOT GRADUALLY TAKE UP THE WORK of the White House when
he arrived in Washington that first week of April 1841; he was pulled into it and
right away. Clay had convinced the ailing President Harrison to call for a special
session of Congress in late May to come up with a plan to end the financial
crisis. "The situation of the country is most critical," wrote Nickolas Carroll, a
New York businessman. "We have had no period resembling this at all. I could
not depict the actual amount of suffering here, the extreme destitution of our
laboring classes. Business of no kind is healthy or prosperous."[1]

Carroll had picked up on an economic truth not realized by others: although
the recession was over, it had long-lingering effects and slowed down the economy for several years.[2]

Since Tyler had just assumed the presidency, he asked Clay to postpone the
spring congressional debate on the bank question until he had a better understanding of the issue. Clay was livid. Who was this brand-new White House
interloper to tell him what to do? He told Tyler that under no circumstances
was he going to back off on the bank question and that he had the support
of the majority of senators and congressmen. The special session *would be
held.*[3]

What really annoyed Clay was how Tyler quickly moved to become a powerful chief executive and run the country. Harrison's views on the relationship

between the executive branch and Congress were quite different. Harrison ceded much more power to Congress than Tyler appeared willing to do. Writing just after Harrison's election, and before his death, Clay said that "the fact of his election alone . . . will powerfully contribute to the security and happiness of the people. The people will feel and know that, instead of their servants being occupied in devising measures for their ruin and destruction, they will be assiduously employed in promoting their welfare and prosperity." When he compared Tyler to his predecessors, he wrote, "We behold enough to sicken and sadden the hearts of true patriots."[4]

The congressional debate over the bank bill was long and raucous. In the end, with the inclusion of an amendment giving states the right to approve and support franchise banks, the bill passed. However, Tyler did not approve of the local franchise provision and vetoed it. That enraged Clay, who knew that he did not have enough votes from both parties to override the presidential veto. What Tyler was doing, Clay surmised, was using the president's constitutional ability to veto bills to make up for his overall lack of popularity and lack of power to control the nation. Andrew Jackson had vetoed some bills during his eight years in office as a way to get around the congressional approval process, and the veto gave him enormous authority. Clay detested presidents, such as Jackson, who used the veto to make themselves more powerful than the House of Representatives and more powerful than Clay. Now Tyler was doing the same thing and getting away with it. Clay was furious.[5] He stood up in the well of the Senate chamber and, waving his arms wildly and speaking loudly, criticized Tyler in a torrid, savage talk. He began by reminding all in the chamber, and the press present, that Tyler had resigned from the Senate a few years back because he said he could not conscientiously follow suggestions from the Virginia State Legislature. Now, it appeared, he could not follow suggestions from the US Senate either. Clay, a small smile of intrigue upon his face, asked rhetorically if Tyler should once again resign, this time as president.

Clay was vindictive and mean. He accused Tyler of numerous personal and political failings and assured listeners that the president carried on "the character of crimes in the conduct of public affairs. The unfortunate victim of these passions cannot see beyond the little, petty, contemptible circles of his own personal interest." One time, irate about something the president did, Clay fumed that "Tyler dares not resist! I will drive him before me!"[6]

Tyler hated Clay just as much as the Kentucky senator loathed him. "Clay is the most obnoxious man in the Union," the president wrote.[7]

In September 1841, fed up with his relationship with the president, Clay delivered a spellbinding speech to the Whig caucus and at the end, as with a rhetorical dagger in his hand, he charged that John Tyler was the new Benedict Arnold of the United States. "Tyler is on his way to the Democratic camp. They may give him lodgings in some outhouse," he said with scorn.[8]

In another speech Clay re-created a meeting between Tyler and his advisers discussing how to veto the bank bill, assuming the character, voice, and physical mannerisms of each. The portrayals drew loud roars of approval and laughter from both Democrats and Whigs, but they infuriated the president.[9]

Clay had numerous supporters in his war on the president. A Clay lieutenant, John Minor Botts, of Virginia, said that the president's weak stand against the bank bill would lose him support not only from the Whigs but from the Democrats too. He would be all alone in the political world, left to fend for himself. Botts claimed, in a letter sent to friends in Virginia and leaked to the press, that Tyler "was making a desperate effort to set himself up with the [Democrats] but he'll be headed yet . . . and, I regret to say, it will end badly."[10]

Botts and his friends amused Henry Wise. "[They] visit him at the White House, advise and counsel and teach him without being asked as to his duty, all professing the kindest friendship for the man, the warmest wish for the success of his administration and the deepest interest in the perpetuation of his fame," said Wise. That was in the daytime. At night "they were seen plotting in the lobbies and elsewhere."[11]

Congressman George Proffit agreed with him. He scoffed at the "secret whispered watchword, the maneuverings of the day, the stealthy counsels of the night, the noisy professions of fairness on the floor, the grinning and snarling in the lobby, the plotting for power." Proffit added that nothing could save the congressmen from the "withering, blighted, blasting gaze of that indignant and betrayed constituency."[12]

Clay also hated Tyler because Clay was a longtime champion of term limits (but not for him). He had told many people, written, and argued in speeches that each president should be allowed to serve only one term. If Tyler were to be elected in 1844, he would serve just about all of two terms.

Another reason Clay despised Tyler was the president's adherence to Andrew Jackson's economic policies and Jackson's desire to bring Texas into the Union as a new state. Jackson wanted Texas as a buffer against Mexico. "Texas [is] the key to our future safety," said Jackson. "We cannot bear that Great Britain have a Canedy [Canada] on our west as she has on the north."[13]

By this time, Clay's national popularity after decades in Congress and the Senate had grown to epic proportions. A man who introduced him in 1844 when he ran for president called him "an American statesman and unrivaled orator of his age, illustrious abroad, beloved at home . . . [he] saved the republic and now, like Cincinnatus and Washington, having voluntarily retired to the tranquil walks of private life [to run for president], the grateful hearts of his countrymen will do him ample justice. Kentucky will stand by him, and still continue to cherish and defend, as her own, the fame of a son who [won] immortal renown."[14]

The *Richmond Whig* called him "the savior of the nation" and asked "where or how can the people cancel the debt of gratitude which they owe that wonderful man!"[15]

Clay drew enormous crowds wherever he spoke. In 1840 he traveled to Nashville to stump for William Henry Harrison. He was met several miles before the city by a large contingent of local politicians, public officials, and townspeople, who escorted him to the city. He rode through the city in an open carriage, waving to the thousands of people who jammed the streets to see him. He was received "with the greatest enthusiasm, amidst the roar of cannon, the ringing of bells and martial music."[16]

By the winter of 1841–1842, his national standing was soaring. He received invitations to speak around the country just about every day. There was a tradition of politicians speaking at large barbecues held in their honor at parks. The crowds he drew were enormous—fifty thousand or more. In the summer of 1842, he drew eighty thousand in Indianapolis. He attracted nearly two hundred thousand people to a barbeque and speech in Dayton, Ohio. Most of his speeches lasted two hours. Clay was a natural as a speaker, whether outside or indoors. He gave long orations on the nation's problems but interspersed them with talks about the problems of the local community in which he was speaking. The speeches included plenty of thanks to local politicians, numerous funny stories, admiration of the ladies present, and exhortations to the young to help the nation.

He was such an attraction that political groups organized national tours in which he delivered dozens of speeches. Crowds of thousands flooded any town in which he stayed, often gathering in front of his hotel, hopeful of a chance to meet him or hear him speak extemporaneously for a few minutes. On a trip to New Orleans, enormous throngs lined the river and cheered for him as he went by on a steamship, waving to all. Villages he visited organized huge processions of carriages for him, taking him wherever he desired to go. In Charleston, South Carolina, he was put first into a boat parade and then into a land-based carriage procession. Throughout his route were oversized banners that read "Welcome, Bright Star of the West." Two stops later, in Raleigh, North Carolina, he was greeted by a crowd of some fifteen thousand people, all cheering madly as he was taken on a carriage ride through a city illuminated that night just for his arrival. Someone even wrote a musical work, "The Ashland March," named for his Kentucky plantation.[17]

His national tour was a great success. "His progress was one grand, unbroken triumphal civil procession, never equaled in this country," proclaimed the *Frankfort Commonwealth*. "Mr. Clay, is, undoubtedly, infinitely the most popular man in America."[18]

Like many, former mayor Philip Hone of New York called him "Harry of the West" and said he was "the spoiled child of society." Hone was one of many individuals charmed by Clay. Young Joshua Giddings, in his very first term in Congress, was startled at how likable Clay appeared. "His amiable manner and dignity of carriage, and his elevated bearing make you feel at once in the presence of one who is your superior, while you feel perfectly at ease, as much as though you were visiting with your equals or those with whom you had long been familiar," Giddings wrote in his diary.[19]

Horace Greeley, the editor of the new and already influential *New York Tribune*, called him "the hero of our country" and said that people should "behold him where he now stands—a noble and inspiring spectacle, the PILLAR of the state."[20]

Even those who did not like him praised him. Frustrated after a conversation with Clay, South Carolina senator John C. Calhoun said, "I don't like Clay. He is a bad man, an imposter, a creator of wicked schemes. I wouldn't speak to him but, by God, I love him."

And no matter where he was in those years, there was always a jab at the president. "As for Captain Tyler, he is a mere snap, a flash in the pan," he shot over a lectern in 1842.[21]

People adored Clay no matter whom he attacked. "Mr. Clay was nevertheless so fascinating in his manner when he chose to be that he held unlimited control over every member of the party," recalled a man at a social event attended by Clay.

"He is so lovely, so soothing, so unconscious of unkind intentions that it is all forgotten in a moment," said another. Someone else added that he "was the most popular man in this road nation."[22]

Tyler was shaken by his troubles with Clay. In the secretary of state's office, where he sat forlornly one afternoon after an unexpected visit, Tyler told Webster that Botts, Clay, and others in the Senate and House were using the bank dispute to wreck his fledgling presidency and get him to resign, as they had tried to do right after Harrison died. Webster described him as "full of suspicion and resentment," and Tyler told many confidants that all of Clay's attacks were premeditated.[23]

Tyler was furious with Clay. He exclaimed in anger at the conclusion of their first meeting, "Go back, Mr. Clay, to your end of the avenue where stands the Capitol, and there perform your duty to the country as you shall think proper. So, help me God, I shall do mine at this end of it as I shall think proper."[24]

The president lamented to colleagues that he was under constant attack not only by Clay but also by John Quincy Adams. "J. Q. Adams leads off a new attack shortly, in which I suppose will be a denial to the President of his right to give a reason for what he does, a privilege which J. Q. A. would readily extend to any free Negro in New England," he said.[25]

Tyler was also under heavy critical fire in the British Parliament. He retorted with insults at the wealth and age of his accusers, snapping that no one should listen to one member of Parliament because he was eighty. "Do men on that side of the Atlantic seek to gather laurels at my expense?" he wailed.[26]

Tyler saw himself as a man who was all alone. He was being attacked on one side by the Democrats and on another by his own Whigs and ridiculed in the nation's newspapers. He had no friends and many enemies. He nodded his head knowingly, though, and told colleagues that this was exactly what he expected when Harrison died. He lamented to his close friends that Congress and the press would see him as a mere stand-in and not a chief executive and would offer him no support. Anything he wanted to do would be defeated. Both sides would unite against him and either make him their puppet or, if he opposed them, destroy him. He said in the winter of 1841, just after he took office, that he would have no strength or support from any quarter. Now, after the bank veto and the subsequent congressional backlash, his prediction had come true. It was not his fault, he said, but everybody else's.

A friend, he said, had predicted trouble for him when Harrison died. "He spoke of violent assaults to be made upon me unless I yielded my conscience, judgement—everything—into the hands of the political managers. He depicted fearful combinations which I would have to encounter, and even anticipated my resignation as a measure to be forced upon me. Because I would not sanction measures . . . that would have covered me with disgrace, I was loudly denounced . . . the harshest and foulest abuse cast upon me by an affiliated press, burning effigies . . . in streets of our cities," he wrote, looking back in 1844.[27]

Four years later, in 1848, after the press had mellowed in its assessment of Tyler, he seemed relieved and gratified. "The shackles had at last been removed from the Democratic press and a kinder and more liberal course would in [the] future be pursued. . . . Future vice presidents who may succeed to the Presidency might feel some slight encouragement to pursue an independent course," he wrote to his son.[28]

The press had been brutal to Tyler, sometimes very unfairly. Later, the editor of the *Intelligencer* admitted that some statements attributed to Tyler and his sons had, in fact, been made up by his enemies and printed as the truth. "It can hardly be necessary for us to add to what we have already suggested that he have not the least idea that the President countenances in any way the base uses which are made in his name."[29]

The president received little help from his cabinet. The members of his inner circle did not like Tyler for three reasons: the cabinet members were Harrison's cabinet, with no built-in loyalty to the new president; most members saw the bank bill as the answer to the financial crisis and disagreed with his veto; and, finally, they were upset that he did not seek much advice from them but instead from friends in Virginia, the "kitchen cabinet," similar to one established by Andrew Jackson.

Wise was the leader of the kitchen cabinet. He was a longtime friend of

Tyler's and assured him that he needed that cabinet of personal friends because his political friends, the Whigs, were trying to destroy him. Tyler agreed.

The kitchen cabinet believed that the Whigs had to stick together to avoid the destruction of the nation by their political enemies. "The people felt and were convinced that they were misgoverned and power abused, that defalcations had become too common, corruption too much the order of the day, that economy and honesty were wanting and that . . . administration was despotic," said Wise of President Van Buren and his men.[30]

Wise even came up with his own battle cry: "A union of Whigs for the sake of the Union."

The problem with Wise, and the others, was that they interfered with just about everything and kept Tyler far away from his Whig political associates and real cabinet. That isolated him in Washington. The power of the friends became so great, too, that senators and congressmen saw them as a "secret society" of some kind.

Botts argued that "this very measure of compromise adopted against the wishes and judgment of every Whig in Congress, to please his [kitchen cabinet] who were generously inclined to interpose and who incurred the habit of sacrificing themselves to save him . . . turned the whole party of friends who placed him into power to ridicule."[31]

Clay saw the kitchen cabinet and the president's team of backstage advisers as grist for his sharp tongue and wicked sense of humor. He, like most Whigs, disdained the kitchen cabinet because the first had been run by political rival Jackson. He scoffed at the group and called them "the corporal's guard," the sting meant to accuse the president of not being the captain of the nation but merely a lowly corporal. Clay's constant "corporal" references made Tyler fume. (Clay aimed his sarcasm at many. In 1840, he started a speech by asking where a local lawyer, Felix Grundy, was. Some yelled from the crowd that he was in East Tennessee, stumping for Van Buren." Clay replied, "Ah! At his old occupation—defending criminals.")[32]

Despite his charms, Clay could be a difficult person. He had a hard-to-control temper and would shout at political opponents or make scurrilous remarks about them. Once he so insulted a Senate colleague, William King of Alabama, that King challenged him to a duel. Clay angrily accepted and was ready to grab his pistol. Fortunately for both men, the Senate sergeant-at-arms stepped in, arrested both men, and made Clay apologize, which he did, immediately.[33] Clay also annoyed everybody by stating something as fact and, when proven wrong, casually answering that it was "rumor only."[34]

Clay's relations with Tyler were dismal, but instead of trying to act as a diplomat, something he was very good at, he pushed, pressed, and badgered the president, insisting that everything had to be done his way and that all his bills had to be passed—and *right now*. Clay always acted like a victim of someone, somewhere, just as Tyler did. "Was there ever before a man treated as I have been and am now?" he continually moaned, the eternal target of some mysterious plot.[35]

Clay was not the only problem, Tyler's friends said. The other was his secretary of state, Webster. His friends in the kitchen cabinet and the official cabinet detested the secretary of state and did everything in their power to get Tyler to dismiss him from the national government. Wise, who had disliked Webster for years, wanted to put him three thousand miles away, he told fellow kitchen member Beverly Tucker.[36]

Webster's troubles with the official cabinet were well-known throughout the streets and neighborhoods of Washington, and people talked about the friction at boardinghouses and taverns. "We are on the eve of a cabinet rupture," said the talkative Wise, who was famous for his energy on just about everything. "In the vehemence of his defense [of the president] he [spread] terror among his enemies, his eyes beaming with the intensity of his emotions, and his lips aglow with the fires of his eloquence," said Tyler's wife Julia.[37]

At the same time, several friends of Tyler's, without his knowledge, traveled around the country, telling people that they were interviewing prospective members for a new cabinet because the president planned to fire the current one. Though this was untrue, the cabinet members and the heads of the Whig Party were incensed by the activity of these men and assumed that they had been sent on their mission by Tyler.

Rumors also said that Clay would try to get all of them to resign in protest if Tyler vetoed a fiscal corporation bill, another piece of legislation designed to alleviate the financial crisis. Another rumor was that Clay would get Congress to force Tyler to resign and call for a new national election to select another president—and that person would be Clay. Tyler was in a rage because so many had aligned themselves against him. "My back is to the wall," he roared. "[I shall] beat back the assailants."[38]

Tyler's cabinet sat by while these fires burned, excepting Webster, who was mocked by the other secretaries for his support of the president. In the days prior to the sailing of the *Creole*, Tyler was very alone in the White House. "Tyler does not have a sincere friend in the cabinet," Abel Upshur, from a longtime farming and political family and an ardent proslavery advocate, told a friend. He added that just about all the cabinet members were supporters of Clay.

Clay, like Upshur, was a slavery champion. "The right to slave property, being guaranteed by the Constitution, and recognized as one of the compromises in that instrument, should be left where the Constitution has placed it, undisturbed and unagitated by Congress," Clay said, even though he tried to appease all with his compromises.[39]

Upshur was famous for his height. He stood about six feet, as tall as Tyler. "[Upshur] was physically a much larger man than Mr. Webster, though there was a striking sameness about the brow of each, as if the brain forced it forward. He usually wore upon his shoulders a handsome cloak with tassels which lent dignity to his appearance," said Tyler's wife, Julia, many years later. She added that he had "a glistening eye, his gray hair brushed back and the lines in his face marked with the precisions of a Grecian statue."[40]

In the middle of the bank crisis, Tyler had to care for his badly ailing first wife. The frail Letitia had been sick for more than a year and was confined to her bed at the White House. She emerged just once, in late January 1842, for the wedding of her daughter in the East Room, a glittering affair. The president and doctors watched over her until her death in September 1842. Tyler's personal troubles increased as he was battling Congress and feuding with members of his cabinet.

His popularity with the public was at an all-time low. Many people disliked him. Hiram Cumming, who had apparently been shortchanged by Tyler in some way, denounced the president in scurrilous language. He wrote to Tyler, "You could not move without being offensive; something vile or deceptive would be exhibited with almost every word or deed. . . . When strangers saw or heard you, they would be struck with amazement. They at once perceived how weak, vain and pusillanimous you were. . . . They soon found you reckless, false and corrupt."[41]

While all this was transpiring, the president also found himself in the middle of a furious national debate over bondage. The northern anti-bondage crusaders assailed the slave-owner president as the puppet of states' rights Virginians and others in the South. Tyler insisted that he was the president of all the people, North and South, but few in the North believed him.

As he fended off attacks by antislavery northerners, he was assailed by pro-slavery southerners, who argued that as a Virginian, he needed to do more to protect forced labor. They suggested that he had come under the influence of Webster and that the two of them had formed a secret cabal with northern abolitionists. Webster was not only a famous antislavery champion but also a hot-headed champion. There had never been any question of his stand on the issue. "I regard domestic slavery as one of the greatest evils. . . . I would do nothing . . . to favor or encourage its further existence," he had roared. He was agreeable to some modifications on bondage, though, as evidenced by his support for Clay's Compromise of 1850.⁴²

Southerners warned Tyler about Webster. "The present condition of the country imperiously requires that a southern man and a slaveholder should represent us at their court," wrote an agitated Upshur to a Virginian friend. "Let this be as it may, if Tyler has any party at all, it is that party [Virginia's states' rights people] which he treats on all occasions with utter neglect."⁴³

Tyler was just one of a long line of presidents to be caught up in the slavery issue. It would grow and rage throughout America for another twenty years. It was such a divisive issue that in 1852 it divided the Whig Party, which collapsed a few years later, to be succeeded by the Republicans in 1855. In 1841 Tyler felt the full force of the bondage tsunami and, like all the other national leaders, did not know how to confront the issue.

While public figures throughout the land argued over forced labor, both the House and Senate passed the second, amended bank bill at the end of the legislative session in September 1841. Tyler promptly vetoed it as well, bringing on a storm of criticism from across the nation, where cities and villages were crippled by the financial crisis. Tyler was castigated by just about all the Democrats, and a large number of his own Whig Party members too. The Whigs were led by Clay, who told them never to give in to Tyler and that by doing so they would be turning their backs on their country. "It would be to give the legislative power into the hands of the President, and would expose you to the scorn, contempt and derision of the people and of our opponents. Do not apprehend that the people will desert you and take part with Mr. Tyler," he wrote Senator John Crittenden, a fellow Kentuckian.[44]

Webster immediately came to Tyler's defense. He said of the querulous Whigs spurred on by Tyler haters, "Those who deal only in coarse vituperation and satisfy their sense of candor and justice simply by the repetition of the charge of dereliction of duty, and infidelity to Whig principles, are not entitled to the respect of an answer from me. The burning propensity to censure and reproach by which such persons seem to be actuated, would probably be somewhat rebuked if they knew by whose advice, and with whose approbation, I received."[45]

While all this was going on, Clay hatched a major conspiracy to destroy the Tyler administration by wrecking the cabinet. Both the House and Senate had agreed to adjourn the legislative session the previous Thursday, unknown to everybody except the cabinet secretaries. The cabinet had assembled for dinner, by invitation, at the home of George Badger, secretary of the US Navy, on Lafayette Street. The entire enterprise was orchestrated by Clay, pulling the strings like a master puppeteer.

Clay believed the Tyler White House needed a big shake-up to right the national ship. While the department chiefs talked at the dinner table, Webster left and sat in the living room to separate himself from a cabal he knew was forming. Everybody knew how ambitious Clay was, and to counter that charge, he always pointed his finger at Webster, noting his "shocking" ambition.

At dinner, led by Clay, all the secretaries except Webster agreed to resign. To inflict the most possible damage on the White House, the resignations would all be handed in on Saturday, but some would resign at noon, some around 3:00 p.m., and some at precisely 5:00 p.m., giving the president little time to respond. He would have only Monday morning, before the congressmen went home at the end of the session at 2:00 p.m., to form a new cabinet, which seemed impossible.

Years later, Tyler's son John Jr. recounted the conspiracy as he outlined the resignation story. "It was deemed by the conspirators that the President would be utterly unable to form a new cabinet before the adjournment and, therefore, that he would be compelled to resign because of an impossibility to conduct his administration," wrote Tyler Jr. The cabinet secretaries reasoned that he had resigned political posts twice before, his anger getting the best of his judgment, and that he would, under such tremendous pressure, quit once more. "In fact [they believed] no other alternative would be left to him but resign through his inability to form a cabinet," added Tyler Jr.

Tyler Jr., who served as his father's personal secretary, was in the office with the president when the "nefarious" string of resignations started. Just after noon, Thomas Ewing arrived and handed in his resignation letter. Webster had preceded him by just a few minutes, though, and appears to have told Tyler of the scheme. Webster had tried all morning to get different cabinet secretaries to change their minds, with no success. Just after Ewing left the office, Webster turned to Tyler, with Tyler's son nearby, and said, "Where am I to go, Mr. President?"

"You must decide it for yourself, Mr. Webster," said the president.

Webster nodded positively. "If you leave it to me, Mr. President, I will stay where I am."

Tyler, with a broad smile on his face, rose from his chair behind his desk, walked over to Webster, and shook his hand and warmly. "Henry Clay is a doomed man from this hour," he said.[46]

Tyler maintained a calm demeanor during the cabinet resignations, but his friends and colleagues were very worried. Upshur was certain that Clay was plotting a mammoth scheme to destroy the country. "There is a deliberate purpose to make Henry Clay President of the United States, even at the hazard of revolution. The design is to embarrass the administration by withholding all needful facilities for carrying on the government, to distress the people by the severest pressure upon all their interests. . . . I should not be surprised to hear of populist outbreaks in all the large cities, and of desperate measures calculated to overthrow all law and order," he wrote.[47]

The resignation of nearly the entire cabinet stunned the nation. The men were applauded by most Whigs and Democrats but rebuked by Webster. "They had acted rashly," Webster told friends, and he blamed it all on Clay.

The cabinet debacle further damaged the relationship between the secretary of state and Clay, who had once been fast friends. Webster had thought so much of Clay that he told people privately that if he could not be president, the honor should fall to Clay. He saw Clay as a true patriot, intelligent, witty, hardworking, and a fine leader of the party. He was one of Clay's strongest supporters as early as the 1828 party convention. That friendship had now been eroded by politics.[48]

Ewing's reasons for leaving symbolized those of the other secretaries in the mass walkout. He told Tyler that "deeply as I was committed for your action upon it [the bank bill], you never consulted me on the subject of the veto message. You did not even refer to it in conversation, and the first notice I had of its content was derived from rumor."[49]

Each resigning member asserted that it would be impossible for Tyler to put together a new cabinet in just one and a half days, before the legislative session ended on Monday, and that this would mean the end of his administration.

Tyler, tipped off about the cabinet revolt by Webster, did not flinch in the face of the massive defection. He went to work right away, with the help of his son and Webster. By Monday morning he had chosen a new cabinet. "The almost entire work of reorganizing was thus to be accomplished by 'a president without a party' who, it had been confidently asserted, could not procure the aid of another cabinet in the administration of the government in the short period which remained," said Tyler about the job he had done. "I felt that a high and solemn duty had devolved upon me."[50]

The choice of new department heads was astute. They included important, highly respected people in the capital. The president's selections were lauded by the press. "The appointments are, on the whole, better than could be expected," said the *National Intelligencer*.[51]

The new secretaries were also all Whigs who were former Democrats, just like Tyler. It was part of a scheme, Tyler's enemies immediately fumed, to get the Democratic Party's support for Tyler in the 1844 election in an effort to defeat Clay, who seemed sure to run for president again as the Whig candidate. Clay had not announced, but his supporters were already holding rallies for him, and newspapers wrote of his 1844 campaign as a sure thing.[52]

Tyler scoffed at any discussions that he should resign. "My resignation would amount to a declaration to the world that our system of government had failed, from the fact that the provision made for the death of the President was so defective as to merge in the legislative branch of the government,"[53] he said.

The president was pleased with his new cabinet too. "We hope to sustain ourselves by no intrigue, but by a faithful discharge of our public duties . . . work faithfully to accomplish it," he wrote to a friend.[54]

He confided to Webster, "I would have each [new cabinet] member look upon each other in the light of a friend and brother. By encouraging such as spirit, I shall . . . advance the public good. Although we are to have a furious fire during the coming winter, yet we shall, I doubt not, speedily recover from its effects."

The one secretary who did not resign, Webster, was roundly denounced by his colleagues in the Whig Party. "If you identify yourself [with Tyler] and remain [in the cabinet] indefinitely, the public will condemn you," Clay said. Crittenden said that Webster was "ignoble" and needed to redeem himself by "the abandonment of Mr. Tyler." Another Whig said that Webster was "doomed."[55]

Crittenden and many others noticed a change in Webster's physical appearance after he decided to stay in the cabinet. Crittenden said he "looks like grim death." Poet Ralph Waldo Emerson, meeting him on a street, wrote that he looked "black as a thundercloud." (Webster, criticized from all sides in the remaining months of 1842 and the early winter of 1843, left office in May 1843.)[56]

Webster defended his decision to remain in the Tyler government in 1841 and never regretted it. Scorning his fellow cabinet members, saying they paid little attention to the national good and instead sought personal gain, he charged that "neither their candor or their sagacity deserves anything but contempt. I admit . . . that if a very strong desire to be instrumental and useful in accomplishing a settlement of our difficulties with England, which had then risen to an alarming height, then I confess myself to have been influenced by [that] personal motive. The charge . . . of seeking self-advantage I repel with utter scorn."[57]

By this time, it was not possible to patch up the differences between the president and Clay; their hatred for each other was too deep. Webster's decision to remain in the cabinet (he was involved in negotiations with Great Britain on several treaties) after everybody else left was an example of his support for Tyler and underscored the president's disdain for Clay.[58]

Shortly after the cabinet fled, in an unprecedented move, dozens of senators and congressmen from the Whig Party wrote a "manifesto" of complaints against Tyler, under the guise of an explanation for the failure of the bank bills, and went public with it at an outdoor meeting in Washington attended by more than seventy-five unhappy legislators. The president was charged with being a rogue chief executive, a schemer, and an enemy of his own Whig Party. He had lost his mind and could not "in any manner or degree . . . be held responsible for his actions." The manifesto said he had browbeaten legislators, lied to the public, abused his power, defrauded the courts, and practically destroyed democracy. It demanded just one term for Tyler as president, the right of Congress to appoint the treasury secretary, and a constitutional amendment that would limit the president's veto power so he could not meddle in congressional affairs. At the end of the incendiary document, in an unprecedented move, the legislators formally kicked the president out of his own party. The mass exodus of the cabinet and the manifesto demands would surely be the final two nails in Tyler's presidential coffin, his opponents believed.

Tyler dismissed the men with a wave of his hand. He said, as he had for years about politicians, that "party spirit [means] malice, ignorance and lies which I have seen so much of."[59]

Adding fuel to the political fire, John Botts, one of the authors of the manifesto, accused Tyler of treason to the party and the country and compared him to Benedict Arnold. "I conceived it impossible to serve my country and Mr. Tyler at the same time," Botts said, a view that had a considerable number of supporters among the Whigs. Underlying much of this concern was the party's fear that Tyler's shoddy work as president would result in the defeats of numerous Whig congressional and state legislative candidates in the next elections. (This came to pass. In 1840 the Whigs enjoyed a majority in the House of 133 seats to 102 for the Democrats, but in 1843 the Democrats gained the edge, 142 to 79).[60]

The manifesto touched off a string of bitter attacks on Tyler for vetoing both bank bills. The Whig press scorned him, and thousands of Tyler dummies were burned in effigy in front of large city administrative buildings and in village squares throughout the nation. A rowdy group of men marched on the White House, denouncing the president and shouting Clay's praises. Drunks stood beneath White House windows and scream epithets at the president.

At the same time, somebody—it is uncertain who—floated a wild rumor throughout Washington that the president was violently ill, suffering a severe brain fever that might kill him. When the rumor, which many believed, reached the White House, Tyler scoffed and said it was one more conspiracy and nothing else.

The arguments over a national bank at the center of the dispute extended back to 1832, when a bill was hotly debated and eventually vetoed by Andrew Jackson. There had been a bank during Washington's first administration, but its existence had been tentative since then. Now, ten years after the Jacksonian era debates, here was yet another debate and another veto. Millions of Americans were dismayed because they thought the bank bill, after compromises, was ready to pass—and Tyler killed it.

Life in Washington became ugly. More rumors said that Tyler was fatally ill. There were calls for his impeachment by numerous newspaper editors, North and South. Hundreds of threatening letters arrived at the White House. One newspaper reported that it feared the assassination of Tyler. It was not a false fear. In September 1841, a man wrote to Crittenden, "I received a letter this morning from a man in Russell County asking me if I thought it would be an unpardonable sin to go to the city and kill him [Tyler]. The fellow wrote as if he had a call to put him to death."[61]

TYLER WAS DESPONDENT at the Whigs for abandoning him. In the coming months, he fired 154 public officials, most of them Whigs, in retribution. Among the 154 were postmasters from towns and small cities who had no idea why they were being let go.[62]

The President did have some support from southern planters, but it was marginal. He had some friends among the northern Whigs, but it was limited, and those men were themselves threatened by leaders of the party. And behind all these inflammatory attacks on the president, arms folded across his chest in defiance, stood the titanic, larger-than-life Henry Clay. The Kentucky senator's hatred for Tyler was unmatched by that of any other congressman. It was not an anger of fury but anger that showed in the way he dismissed the president.[63]

Because of the political turmoil in Washington, the Kentucky senator clearly now had a chance to finally become president, even if he had to enter the White House through the back door.[64]

There was possibly another route to the presidency for Clay. Botts and others introduced a resolution calling for the House to appoint a special committee to investigate the possibility of removing the president from office, a measure that Clay took seriously. Tyler denounced them, writing a neighbor, Robert McCandlish, "Did you ever expect to see your old friend under trial for 'high crimes and misdemeanors'? The high crimes of sustaining the Constitution of the country I have committed and to this I plead guilty." He added that the critics were "using powers conferred by the Constitution from corrupt motives and for unwarrantable ends."[65]

Botts's efforts to impeach Tyler were joined by his yearlong string of denunciations of the President's kitchen cabinet, whose members Botts deplored. "[He has] looked only to the whisperings of ambitious and designing mischief makers who have gathered around him," Botts said, adding that "it will end badly for him. He will be the object of execration with both parties."[66]

Botts's efforts to get an impeachment appalled Tyler's colleague. Upshur said that Botts disgusted him and that Botts's impeachment effort was a case of "rudeness, wickedness and vulgarity. He has lost character to such an extent that an attack from him could not injure anyone."[67]

The proposed impeachment, and Botts's vituperative denunciations of the president, backfired. The people in his district, supporters of Tyler, turned on Botts. He was defeated in his reelection bid two years later by J. W. Jones and spent the remainder of the Tyler presidency on the sidelines, reduced to writing letters of complaint.[68]

Tyler was besieged by critics all his life. He was always annoyed by them and always described them in bitter language. In 1858, for example, he dismissed Missouri senator Thomas Hart Benton's book *Thirty Years in the Senate*, a work that was highly critical of Tyler. Tyler said the book would not make Benton an immortal statesman, as he had hoped. "[His views] will accompany him to the grave and be buried and forgotten with him. He was so prolix, and at the same time unreliable, from his excessive egotism and ill-regulated antipathies, that I would as soon undertake a journey through the Dismal Swamp as to wade through his ponderous folios," Tyler wrote.[69]

Tyler gained great solace from his friends and supporters, who loved him as fervently as his critics despised him. Upshur was one such friend. At the height of the *Creole* crisis, he wrote, "I can say with strict and literal truth that I have not heard from [Tyler] nor from any one member of his cabinet, any counsel, suggestion or opinion unbecoming an honest man and a true lover of his country. I do not believe that we have ever had an administration more truly devoted to the public good nor more free from every corrupt and improper design."[70]

Earlier, just before Christmas of 1841, Upshur had defended Tyler even further in a letter to Beverly Tucker. "We have all agreed, without a single exception, that our only course was to administer the government for the best interests of the country and to trust the moderates of all parties to sustain us. This is our firm purpose," he said.[71]

The *New York Herald*, one of the president's longtime supporters, stayed firmly in Tyler's camp. "Nothing can exceed the industry of the President. He rises early and retires late. Every hour of the day is devoted to his duties," the paper's editor said.[72]

Impeachment might have created a constitutional crisis. Under the Constitution at that time, the president had no power to appoint a vice president. According to rules on succession then, the next in line would be the president pro tempore of the US Senate, followed by the Speaker of the House. The next president would thus have been Senator Samuel Southard of New Jersey. If Southard did not immediately name a vice president, the wheels might have come off a few months later, since Southard died in May of 1842, and there was no Speaker of the House to replace him because of squabbles in Congress. There was no further succession specified in the Constitution, except a line that authorized Congress to elect whomever they wanted. That probably would have been Henry Clay. The Kentucky senator could have insisted that the election take place on the single day when there was no speaker or could have held up the election of Clay, and with his political clout, he would have prevailed.[73]

The impeachment idea was downplayed Crittenden. He told Clay there were not enough votes in the Senate to remove Tyler from office. Crittenden also told him that the move would probably engender unsympathetic views toward Clay among the public and would backfire politically. It might even cost Clay the 1844 election and give it to Tyler. The idea was tabled, for the time.[74]

Tyler breathed a sigh of relief. He certainly did not want to be impeached. He believed that his reputation had already been badly damaged by all the criticism. "The observation of my course for twenty-five years is not enough. I am placed upon trial and left to infer from the past that even after trial and a full vindication of my consistency, those of who all along had opposed me will still call out for further trials and thus leave me impotent and powerless," he wrote to John Rutherford, governor of Virginia.[75]

Upshur saw Congress itself as the opposition. "The great enemies of the country are in Congress," he said. "That body is, as one of the best of them frankly acknowledged to me, incompetent to legislate and, even if they were not so, they are so bound and fettered by party ties that they could not legislate to any advantage ; there lies the evil . . . the public faith and honor [are] left to take care of themselves."[76]

Another of Tyler's weaknesses throughout this period was his inability, through insensitivity, politics, and bad luck, to hold his cabinet together. In his four-year term he had a total of twenty-one secretaries for the six offices. He let some go, some resigned, and some died when a cannon on a US battleship blew up during a ceremony. The constantly changing cabinet wound up offering the president too much advice from too many people, the proverbial too many cooks in the kitchen.

Webster understood Tyler's problem and endlessly argued that the cabinet members did not help the country by resigning but hurt it. He wrote a friend, "You will have learned that Messrs. Ewing, Bell, Badger and Crittenden have resigned their respective offices. This occurrence can hardly cause you the same degree of regret which it has occasioned to me; as they are not only friends, but persons with whom I have had for some time a daily official intercourse. [But] I could not partake in this movement." He said of the conflict between the president, Congress, and the cabinet, "I regret these differences as deeply as any man, but I have not been able to see in what manner the resignation of the Cabinet was likely either to remove or mitigate the evils produced by them."[77]

Some members of the cabinet felt that the bank bill was the last straw. "I had not supposed, and do not suppose, that a difference merely between the President and his cabinet, either as to the constitutionality or expediency of the bank, necessarily interposes any obstacles to a full and cordial co-operation between them in the general conduct of the administration . . . but . . . the disapproval of the last bill made a case [for quitting]," said George Badger.[78]

Tyler also wasted valuable time and effort trying to smooth over differences with his old party, the Democrats, after he was jettisoned from his new one, the Whigs. He spent hundreds of hours currying the favor of key Democratic leaders to gain the Democratic nomination for president in 1844, since he knew he could not get the Whig nod. He went so far as to openly court Andrew Jackson, whom he had scorned since his swearing in as chief executive, writing numerous letters praising the general for various works of his administration. Failing to win the Democrats' love, the president, in his awkward political scrambling, won no one and lost everyone. The Whigs saw him as a traitor to party principles and, as usual, rallied around Henry Clay. The Democrats, who saw right through his scheme to jettison his Whig tag to gain their presidential nomination in 1844, loathed him. The president was undeterred. Tyler spent hundreds of additional hours working with politicians in both parties to cobble together a third party, with him as the head, to run against the Whig and Democratic nominees. Whigs were frustrated by his actions. "The traitor has destroyed the party," said Willie Mangum. At a dinner for a British diplomat, there was a toast for Queen Victoria. All the Whigs stood and cheered. Then there was a toast for Tyler. All the Whigs sat and none cheered.[79]

From early in Tyler's administration, the editor of the *Madisonian* and personal friends such as Upshur and Tucker urged him to abandon the Whigs, cease his efforts to go back to the Democrats, and form that third political party. They were backed in this effort by James Gordon Bennett, the fiery and influential editor of the *New York Herald*, who saw Tyler easily able to win the electoral votes in New York and Virginia and perhaps several northeastern states. Bennett, whose paper had one of the largest circulations in America, not only told readers that Tyler was a fine president under unfair assault from all quarters but made the rather startling claim that he was a descendant of George Washington.[80]

"Never did any administration—from the age of Washington to this day—occupy a more independent position—a more elevated platform," wrote Bennett.[81]

In addition to his other flaws, Tyler was also very sensitive to criticism. Negative remarks about him annoyed him, and he became paranoid and suspicious of everybody. The editor of the *Madisonian*, Tyler's unofficial organ, seemed to speak directly for Tyler on many issues. Of an attack by several newspapers on the chief executive, the editor wrote, "Was there ever impudence so unblushing? They advise him . . . as to what his honor requires who have zealously set themselves to work to strip him of all claims to honorable standing, who have sought to blacken his heretofore unsullied name . . . [and with the words] 'wretch,' 'traitor,' 'treason' and 'infamy.' . . . sought to destroy him."[82]

The entire US political system, torn by these upheavals, was stretched to the limit, and several key foreign diplomats saw disaster up ahead. Alexander Baring, Lord Ashburton, was in America and saw the circuslike political atmosphere firsthand. He later said he thought the entire American political network was going to collapse, "thinking it impossible that with so much disorganization and violence, the system could hold together."

Secretary of State Webster just shook his head at the animosity, confusion, and illicit schemes with which so many senators and congressmen were involved. "Leading friends of Mr. Clay have regarded nothing of so great importance as the promotion of his election. . . . I do not wonder that enlightened foreigners begin to doubt the permanency of our system," he said.[83]

In response to his critics, Tyler declared war on Clay and urged the defeat of practically any bill Clay proposed. He criticized Clay at every opportunity. Tyler went through his patronage lists carefully, making sure to cross out the names of any men remotely connected to the Kentucky senator. Clay's anger at Tyler's move could barely be contained. "The President is moreover jealous, envious, embittered towards me," he told friends.[84]

Politicians from all sides concurred, too, that Tyler, who had given numerous speeches condemning the overuse of executive power by Andrew Jackson, far exceeded Jackson in using the power of the White House. Tyler was, they said, two-faced.

Things simply could not get worse for the very tired, beleaguered president in the fall of 1841. But then, in early November, slaves aboard the *Creole* mutinied and sailed the seized ship to Nassau.

News of the capture of the ship, the freeing of the majority of its slaves, and the protection of the mutineers by the British government hit Washington, DC, like a bomb. Immediately, legislators, newspaper editors, and millions of Americans called upon Tyler to get the ship and its captives back, even if it meant a war with Great Britain. Louisiana senator Alexander Barrow bellowed that the United States should consider an invasion of the Bahamas. John C. Calhoun, author of the famous line "There is no honor in politics," thundered that the seizure of the slave ship was "the most atrocious outrage ever perpetrated on the American people."[85]

The American public was in an absolute fury and turned to the White House, looking for action. All of a sudden, Tyler, the most vilified man in America, had a chance to not only redeem himself but also to silence his critics, restore the Whigs' respect for him, gain the admiration of the Democrats, shred Henry Clay's political power, win the love of the press, and become America's hero.

※※※※※※

EVERYBODY HAD AN OPINION on the seizure of the *Creole*, everybody had their racial views, and everybody had their political views. But nobody, absolutely nobody, had any proof of anything. Who committed the murder? How exactly did it happen? Why? Who hurt the captain? How badly was he harmed? Were the doctors in the Bahamas taking good care of him? What about his wife, daughter, and niece?

How did the mutiny actually take place? Why did the mutineers sail to the Bahamas? Why not some other port? What were the mutineers like? Kind-hearted? Savage? Bloodthirsty?

Why didn't the crew stop them? Could the crew have stopped them? Why was such a small crew in charge of guarding 135 people?

Who did what and when?

Americans knew in brief why the slaves had seized the ship and where they had sailed to, but that was about it. The other side of the story would be forthcoming from the crew. America would hear that side shortly because the *Creole* was on its way to the port of New Orleans with its remaining crew and a few women who opted to stay on board. In that era, crewmen on a ship that had problems of any kind gave formal testimony, duly recorded, at a court in their next seaport stop. Officials in New Orleans would take down very lengthy testimony that described every incident on the ship. It would tell the crew's side of the story. The crew, of course, would build themselves up as brave men overwhelmed by the sheer numbers of their assailants. After their testimony, lawyers, government officials, and the American people would make up their minds about what the truth was, or what parts of the story were true.

Many interested people waited in New Orleans as the *Creole*, with its few remaining prisoners and skeleton crew, headed across the Gulf of Mexico, bound for the Crescent City.

CHAPTER FIVE

*Ashore in
New Orleans*

December 16, 1841

MADISON WASHINGTON KEPT CONTROL of his *Creole* crew in the hot, humid jail in Nassau. He was bigger than any of the prison's guards, who were impressed at his size. He used the same leadership skills in the prison as had on board the ship. He had worked on a plantation for years and had spent only one year as a free man in Canada. He was not a lawyer, but he knew not only American law also but British jurisprudence.

He reminded many of Denmark Vesey, hanged two decades earlier for leading his own slave rebellion. "He would never cringe to the whites, nor ought anyone who had the feelings of a man," wrote one Vesey biographer, who added that, as with the *Creole* and Washington, the strength of Vesey's revolt was "[due to] the extraordinary ability in the leader," who held the large number of rebels together as a unit.[1]

The same was said of Washington, who not only led the shipboard revolt but organized the men in the jail at Nassau, prepared their defense, and interceded for them with Bahamian authorities. He showed enormous skill, both at sea and on land. Washington had no knowledge of the dreadful things being said about him in a New Orleans court, where the newly arrived mates of the *Creole* gave their testimony about the mutiny and the sea voyage to Nassau. They accused

Washington and his fellow mutineers of murder, attempted murder, mutiny, and even piracy. The story they told, almost in unison with one another, was meant to not only condemn the mutineers but to exonerate all the shipmates. They needed to let the public and the owners of their ship know that they did all they could to salvage the vessel but were overcome by a very large gang of armed mutineers who nearly killed them, after murdering a passenger. They needed to paint the slaves as cutthroats who would do anything, even piracy, to obtain their illegal and immoral goals. At the same time, they had to showcase themselves as loyal and diligent crewmen who expertly sailed the *Creole* down the coast and had all good intentions of arriving in New Orleans but were overtaken in the shipboard revolt. They did their best physically and emotionally in the face of overwhelming odds. They did that and did it well.

The crew also painted a heroic picture of Captain Ensor, himself nearly killed by the so-called rabble in the fighting. No one pointed any finger of guilt at the captain or held him responsible for the ship's seizure. None of the crew reminded the courtroom audience that Ensor had failed to lock up the slaves in the hold or to lock the doors leading to and from the slave detainment center. All the captain's liberal policies, which helped bring about the takeover, were forgiven as the captain lay in a Nassau hospital, still recovering from the brutal mutiny. The testimony by the members of the ship's crew caused a fury.

Southerners who read the testimony in the newspapers were incensed that people who belonged to someone in the region had been given their freedom and that the nineteen ringleaders of the revolt had not been either hanged or turned over to US authorities. Emotions went deeper than that, though. Southerners smeared all African Americans and free blacks with the sins of the *Creole* mutineers. Clearly, southerners felt, forced laborers would revolt and escape at the slightest provocation, so they had to be watched. Security had to be tightened. The *Creole* incident showed what happened when discipline was lax. The testimony of the crew fired up all the hatred whites had harbored against blacks for more than two hundred years.[2]

In New Orleans and throughout the South, newspaper editors continued to fume that the snatching of the *Creole* violated a long agreed upon understanding between the United States and Great Britain that each country should return any ships, crews, or passengers taken in acts of piracy on the high seas. The slaves, in seizing the ship, had acted in the role of pirates, the editors howled. The situation was clear-cut.

Each virulent editorial in the South was met by one in a northern newspaper in favor of the slave ship takeover. The editor of the *Portsmouth Journal* of New Hampshire dismissed attacks on Washington by "Virginia abstractionists and slave breeders."[3]

"One cannot help being impressed with the capacity of the slaves for organization and leadership. . . . It required a good deal of native ability to perfect such organizations as some of them did, and at the same time keep their movements and activities absolutely secret [because] the slave system made originality and resourcefulness . . . impossible," observed one historian.[4]

As for the charge of piracy, advocates of the mutineers argued that in piracy, foreign abductors took a ship; here it was just slaves, who might be considered passengers since they were not legally captives that far out on the ocean.[5]

Supporters of the mutineers, hoping that Bahamian courts would free them, also believed that Washington's considerate handling of the whites after the takeover would count for a lot of goodwill. He had prevented angry slaves from killing several people, including the captain and his family. He had also spent a considerable amount of time tending to the wounded on the ship, white as well as black.

There had been a long history of takeovers or attempted takeovers on the high seas. The rebels on the *Creole* were not groundbreakers. They were just more slaves in a long line of people in bondage who had tried to gain their freedom.

The mutineers had to know, through word of mouth over generations, that dozens of gangs of captives had tried to seize their slave ships and that some had succeeded. Several countries had recognized them as free men. In 1825 captives had mutinied and captured the *Deux Soeurs* in Martinique. They killed eight crewmen. The ship was then sailed all the way to Sierra Leone, where courts freed the mutineers. Two years later, off the coast of France, captured men killed the entire crew of the *Augusta*, sailed it back to France, and also walked away free. The slaves who captured the *Decatur* in 1826 lost their mutiny, but when the ship docked in New York Harbor, most sneaked off and disappeared into the city. Wouldn't judges and juries in Nassau see the men of the *Creole* in that same light and release them?[6]

Washington knew that British policy had been to free men and women who wound up on British shores for just about any reason. The *Comet, Encomium,* and *Enterprise* had all been completely or partially wrecked in the Caribbean and their slaves had been freed upon their rescue by local fishermen and salvage wreckers under British law. A year after the *Creole* incident, the *Formosa,* traveling the same sea route and carrying thirty-eight slaves, was midway in its sail from Virginia to New Orleans when it was wrecked in the Bahamas. British officials there would free all on board that vessel.[7]

Washington may also have known, through the antislavery leaders he met, that the British went to extraordinary lengths to protect not only shiploads but also individuals who wound up on British shores. That was the case with Benjamin Parker, a black British subject living in Bermuda. He was apparently abducted by seamen from an American ship and taken to Antigua in 1839. About a year later, the master of a British ship, the *Eliza Kirkbride,* saw a man referred to as Parker and fitting his description in forced labor on a pilot boat in Charleston, South Carolina. The British government told US officials that he had been kidnapped. British consul William Ogilby started a search for him. "I have not been able to discover any traces of him," he said, following a search of every pilot boat in Charleston Harbor. Ogilby assumed that Parker had been sold to someone in the city or sent to a nearby plantation. Great Britain insisted that the US government find Parker and send him back to Bermuda. The Americans did nothing.[8] There was also the matter of justice for blacks in the revolt—justice that British officials had agreed years before was needed. Theodore Ward wrote in his play *Madison Washington,* "Is it any wonder others, deny our rights / As brothers / when they see us millions strong, / cowardly suffering such wrongs?"[9]

US abolitionist leaders stepped up their antislavery campaign as the mutineers waited for their trial in the Nassau jail, just block or so north of the two-story waterfront building complex that housed the offices of legislators and Governor Cockburn. The abolitionists saw the US government, not the British, as the villains. The editor of one antislavery newspaper criticized " the attempt made by the American Consul at Nassau to wrest the vessel from the British authorities, while in a British port by force of arms."[10]

While the mutineers stayed in jail, one day just as hot and tedious as the previous, Cockburn was very busy with the *Creole* case. The veteran administrator had decided to send the ship dispute all the way to London and let his superiors there make the final decision about what to do with the incarcerated Washington and his gang of rebels. Cockburn collected all the paperwork turned in by his attorney general, notes and requests from John Bacon, and all dispatches concerning the *Creole* that he had received. He wanted Lord Stanley, the colonial secretary, and Prime Minister Robert Peel to make a decision and tell him how to proceed. This took a considerable amount of time. It was fine administrative work and good politics. What Cockburn needed to do, and did, was administer justice while at the same time protecting himself. He could do so by laying out all the written information and opinions in front of his superiors back in London, offering no strong opinion of his own, and letting them bask in the glory, or choke on the blame. He was just a governor who carried out orders from the main office back home, nothing more and nothing less.

In his letters to his superiors, he emphasized that at no time did he or any of his aides or police in Nassau help the African Americans leave the ship. They left on their own and then drifted off into the town of Nassau. Cockburn and his aides did not alert the slaves to the departure of the ship to Jamaica, which most of them boarded, or assist them in any way to sail there. Any of those actions would have been considered illegal under the laws of the United States and Britain. The governor had been extremely cautious to handle the *Creole* issue as carefully as any administrator could. Back home in London, British officials were even more cautious, reaffirming their hands-off policy toward escaping people. In one note, Lord Aberdeen, the foreign secretary, wrote a British diplomat in the United States that Britain would "certainly do nothing to encourage mutiny either among slaves or freemen." [11]

One reason for this caution was that the Bahamas attorney general, G. C. Anderson, had become involved in a dispute following his visit to the *Creole* shortly after it had anchored in early November. Anderson told Cockburn and authorities in London that "[Zephaniah Gifford] stated that it was not his desire to detain on board his vessel any one of the persons who did not wish to remain, and that they had his free permission to quit her." But Gifford testified in his New Orleans deposition that Anderson had not said that. "The rest of you are free and at liberty to go on shore if they pleased," Gifford insisted the attorney general had said. It was a statement that might be construed to mean that he, a British official, was saying that the crown approved of whatever the escapees planned to do in the Bahamas and also approved of the takeover of the ship.[12]

Cockburn wanted to get rid of the slave ship anchored securely in the harbor because the longer it was in Bahamian waters, the stronger the argument of its Virginia owners, southern politicians, Secretary of State Webster, President Tyler, and the American press that he had illegally seized American property. He might also risk an attack by American warships on a mission to take back the *Creole*.

Cockburn authorized first mate Gifford, now the acting master of the ship, to sail it to New Orleans. Gifford had sufficient crew to take the ship to Louisiana. After loading up with supplies, he was on his way, the vessel's tobacco and flax still tied up in the middle of the hold. The ship carried 5 of the original 135 passengers—all women—who might have been afraid of living alone in the Bahamas and decided to move on to whatever lay ahead for them in slavery in Louisiana.

Captain Ensor, who had been put in a Nassau hospital upon his arrival to recuperate from his stab wounds, cuts, and bruises, was in no condition to sail the *Creole* across the Caribbean to the United States. He had numerous injuries that needed time to heal and required nursing care. He needed lengthy bed rest and daily attention from doctors. It was also cold back home in Richmond, and his battered body could use a month or two of sunny, eighty-degree days in Nassau. And a man in his condition would probably not survive an eleven- or twelve-day sail back to Richmond or the trip to New Orleans. Cockburn told Ensor that staying was no problem, that medical personnel in Nassau would take care of him at no charge, and that he could return home after he recuperated. His family stayed, too, living in a nearby house.

Cockburn said good-bye to Gifford and the crew of the *Creole* when they left Nassau Harbor on November 19, ten days after the ship arrived. The ship had a smooth sail to New Orleans, where its crew immediately became one of the biggest stories in the history of the Crescent City.

New Orleans was a unique city. By 1841 most of the South had stopped growing in population. Northern cities like New York and Boston were growing rapidly and turning into residential megalopolises and profitable commercial centers. But the people who ran the South were in no hurry for growth. Southerners were content to maintain their population size as long as the slave-driven economy was productive. To that end, more captives were brought in from plantations or were transported from one region to another.

Madison Washington and his fellow slaves had been transports. They did not know who would buy them in New Orleans. They might wind up in the fields of a sugarcane plantation or as warehouse workers in the Crescent City. The women might be field hands in meadows under a hot southern sun or work in easier jobs as domestics in the plantation house. New Orleans was special because it was a seaport for travel from the United States to the Caribbean, Mexico, and Central and South America. Its streets teemed with Anglo-Americans, Creoles, French, Haitians, freed blacks, and forced laborers. Pirates roamed through its swamps. The port, with its sugarcane exporters, was prosperous. New Orleans had some of the best restaurants and bars in America, and music resonated through the night. It was the Emerald City of America in 1841.

All that remained for Governor Cockburn in Nassau now was the disposition of the nineteen mutineers. He had been told they needed to remain incarcerated until legal authorities in the Bahamas and London decided what to do with them. The problem was that the mutineers had killed someone and nearly killed the captain and some crew members. They had committed numerous criminal acts, any one of which would have resulted in execution or a prison term if it had been committed on land. Cockburn told his aides at Government House at the side of the water that the situation was a mess. But he added with some assurance that it might be remedied quickly if the Bahamian and British courts simply took the attitude that the acts had taken place in international waters and therefore were not Great Britain's problem.

Proslavery southerners turned his argument upside down and charged that even if a ship were sailing in international waters, the captives remained people in servitude. Even if the ship was taken to a port governed by a country that had outlawed slavery, those men and women were still slaves. The location of the slaves did not matter—just their bondage. "Now there is nothing more clear that, according to the laws of nations, a vessel on the ocean is regarded as a part of the state to which she belongs . . . and that if forced into a foreign port by an unavoidable necessity, she loses none of the rights that belong on the ocean," charged Senator John C. Calhoun, who also argued long and hard that all new US territories and states had to allow slavery to protect the slave-driven cotton business. To outlaw bondage would be "contrary to that equality and advantages which the Constitution was intended to secure,"[13] he said.

Would the British see the issue that way? If they did not, the result would be an international uproar and might prompt President Tyler to declare war on Great Britain and attack Nassau. Cockburn did not want that.

The Talented Governor Cockburn

Cockburn was probably the very best person England could have in the governor's office in the Bahamas. He knew the American official and unofficial mind-set from his years as a British official in Canada. His jobs there had also taught him how to work with people of all kinds to resolve differences, and resolve them in the government's favor. He had extensive governmental skills but also knew how to work within the community. The skills he had learned in the very cold north of Canada enabled him to work well in the very hot Caribbean and the Bahamas. He knew, the morning the slave ship anchored in his harbor, that he had a delicate international situation on his hands. He had to think through every step he took. He had to keep in touch with British leaders in London and John Bacon in the Bahamas. He could not take any rash steps toward the Americans because the issue had become political right away. Cockburn knew, without reading any American newspapers, receiving any letters, or talking to anyone, exactly what would happen: southern planters would howl; newspapers in the South would demand the mutineers for trial and newspapers in the North would scream that the Americans were once more bending to the will of England; Tyler would bellow for the return of the ship and its passengers; all Americans except ardent abolitionists would criticize him and his superiors in London for letting the *Creole* dock there and butting in on American business practices; and the eyes of all leaders of Caribbean nations, regardless of their policy toward runaway slaves, would be on him. The governor would be setting precedent for the entire area.

There was another factor, and that was the wide rift over England's outlawing of slavery on its shores or the shores of its possessions in 1833. The decision came right when the cotton industry was booming in America. It was expanding rapidly because of forced labor, and in fact even more slaves were needed for the production of cotton. So while bondage was becoming more and more important to half of America, the South, it had ceased to be important to England. Consequently, anything that England did in the world of slavery was seen as a political affront to the South and to America in general. Everything became political. The governor was aware of that and tried not to anger the United States or its minister in a dispute that could quickly become volatile.

The *Creole* incident hit British and American politics like a cannonball. In both nations, some leaders believed that other disputes might already lead to a war between them. The two countries were involved in a severe dispute over the location of the boundary between Maine and Canada. They were in hot arguments over the US–Canadian border north of Oregon Territory.

What the British did not realize was that throughout the boundary negotiations, led by Webster for the Americans and Lord Ashburton for the British, was that Webster had worked with the editors of both Whig and Democratic newspapers in Maine to get more favorable coverage of his talks. Those newspapers had for years sided with Maine political figures about the border with Canada. Webster convinced the editors to soften their stand and embrace various compromises. This would not only make the talks with Lord Ashburton easier but would help build a stronger bridge between the United States, Great Britain, and Canada. The editors succumbed to Webster's political charms.

The United States still fumed over the 1837 burning of the steamship *Caroline* by a British citizen. And now the British were boarding US ships in search of African Americans. Prior to 1812, the British had boarded American merchant ships in search of sailors they claimed had deserted from the Royal Navy. They grabbed American sailors who had in fact never been in the Royal Navy and forced them into service. This frequent practice enraged Americans and led to the War of 1812. Now, in 1841, the British were proud of their boarding actions in search of slaves. British ships did not just chase and seize US slave ships but chased any ship they found on the Atlantic and suspected of being involved in bondage. Many blamed British guilt for having been involved in the slave trade for so many years prior to 1833. They were going to rid the whole world of slavery, all by themselves, to make up for their earlier transgressions, numerous critics in the United States and Europe said.

Another issue that irked the British was extradition. Many criminals had fled Canada, crossed the border, and settled in the United States. Britain and Canada wanted better extradition procedures in the Webster–Lord Ashburton treaty so they could get those lawbreakers back.

The mutineers in their jail cells in the Bahamas were anxious. If they were returned to the United States, the very least punishment they would get, even as only runaways according to tradition, was a year in jail—if they were not hanged. Cockburn was even more anxious at his office as the waves of the Caribbean Sea rolled up gently on the nearby beaches and sea breezes bent the palm trees outside his window. What would happen now?[14]

Across town, John Bacon, steeled in his cause by Gifford, Ensor, and others, was determined to get the nineteen imprisoned slaves sent back to the United States to stand trial. He wrote Webster a lengthy letter about the *Creole* incident and, like Cockburn, added every single piece of paper he could find connected to the case, including copies of testimony by mates and other crew about the mutiny, the murder of Hewell, and the savage attack on Ensor.[15]

In a strange way, Bacon was glad the incident had happened. He had been on the job in the Bahamas for only a year and wanted to stay. A post in the Caribbean was a sought-after assignment in the diplomatic corps because of the sunny weather, warm climate, and chance to work with other English-speaking people. He was happy to have something to do, something serious to do, and wanted to perform well to impress Webster, himself in office just eight months.

Lord Stanley wrote Cockburn back shortly after he received his letters and bundles of paperwork on January 7 and reassured him that everything he had done in the slave ship matter was legal and in line with department guidelines and that he had provided the crown with much information and evidence to permit officials to make a decision in the case. They were happy to have him. Lord Stanley turned the matter over to crown lawyers in the office of the Doctors' Commons. The lawyers wanted to put the *Creole* issue to rest as quickly as Cockburn did and reached a series of decisions within just three weeks, extremely fast service for that office.

The Crown's Secret and Unknown Verdict

In a determination reached by three lawyers, the Doctors' Commons ruled that the seizure of the ship was not a crime of piracy or plunder, just an effort of slaves to secure their freedom, and therefore the nineteen mutineers could not be tried in a British court in London or in Nassau. Since the murder had been committed on an American ship in international waters, not on a British ship or on a Bahamian island, there was no cause for charges in Nassau. If anyone was to try the mutineers for murder, it had to be the United States. Since the United Kingdom did not have an extradition treaty with the United States, the mutineers would not be sent back to America. The lawyers also noted that under Britain's treaty with the United States, although criminals could be transported from the Bahamas to the United States for trial, that decision was voluntary—as a friendly judicial gesture outside the extradition treaty. The lawyers told Lord Stanley and Cockburn that the crown had decided not to do that. They agreed with everything Cockburn had done and added that Bacon's charge that the British had liberated the slaves was false; the mutineers had liberated themselves and had legally walked off the *Creole* under their own power, with no assistance from any British officials in the Bahamas.

To emphasize the crown's stand, Lord Stanley added a letter to the legal findings. In it, he reemphasized that Cockburn had not tried to liberate the slaves from the ship and did nothing to encourage the mutineers to go to Jamaica to work after they left the *Creole*. Since the slave ship case was "within the limits of British territory, within which limits the condition of slavery is not recognized by law & being charged with no crime they voluntarily quitted the vessel on board of which there was no legal power to detain them."

In short, Lord Stanley told Cockburn that everything he had done was right, and he backed up every legal theory Cockburn had used. The governor had the complete support of the crown. Lord Stanley's letter and the verdict documents were tossed into a diplomatic pouch and taken to a ship that would deliver them to the Bahamas. The trip would take a month, maybe longer. While Cockburn waited for that verdict from London, all hell broke loose in New Orleans.

Tyler, Webster, Lord Ashburton, and a Resolution?

Southern newspaper editors condemned the ship's takeover shortly after it arrived in New Orleans and its newly returned mates and crew gave their formal protest in court. The editor of the *New Orleans Courier* asked for "punishing the hypocrites [British] whose end and aim is the destruction of southern property—American liberty and independence." The editor of the *New Orleans Bulletin* wrote that the city had been "thrown into flames" by the accusations of the crew in their depositions and demanded that the United States finally stand up to the British.[16]

Other southern editors said that a slave ship was a slave ship no matter where it was, that a ship sailed into a port by mutineers "loses none of its attributes of nationality," and that the same laws applied to blacks on the ship in Nassau "as [to those] manacled in a Virginia jail."[17]

The mutineers, they wailed, had to be brought back to the United States, marched into a courtroom in chains, and found guilty of hijacking, attempted murder, and murder. The nineteen mutineers had to be hanged, and right away, as a message to all unruly blacks.

In Washington, DC, President Tyler stroked his chin as he listened to his aides and friends argue about the *Creole* in his second-floor office at the White House. Could there be a way to win the slave ship fight and, at the same time, win favor with both the North and South. He knew that he was not a crafty statesman and negotiator like Henry Clay and did not have the diplomatic experience of John Quincy Adams. He was despised by just about all the influential people in the nation's capital. In fact, his interference to the crisis might make him an even bigger loser and not the winner he wanted to be and believed he should be. He was the president, after all, accidental or not.

Everywhere he looked, his world seemed dim. The press criticized him on a regular basis. He was ridiculed in the diplomatic corps. Tyler's public approval was running at record lows. He was being badgered by senators and congressmen every day on one issue or another. He was once again called a traitor to the Whigs, this time by Representative Edward Stanley of North Carolina. The congressional criticism never ended. South Carolina senator James Hammond lambasted the White House, writing that the country needed to gather its arms for war against England. The United States was "ready for it," Hammond wrote. He added with rancor that "with Tyler at the head of affairs and such an unprincipled and cowardly secretary of state as Webster," the nation was in deep trouble.[18]

John Tyler immediately understood the importance of the *Creole* case and what it could do for him. He spoke out against the seizure of the ship, sided with all in favor of getting it back along with its captives, and swore vengeance upon

England and the Bahamas. In a very bold public move, he asked Congress for a substantial increase in the military appropriations budget—$2.2 million—to build warships and to train men in case military conflict with Great Britain began. That was a nearly 10 percent overall increase and a 30 percent increase in naval spending. It would be the highest military spending until after the Mexican War five years later.[19]

To seal the deal with the British to get back the mutineers, he needed a veteran politician, a slippery negotiator, and a sneaky political manipulator. Tyler had all three in Webster. He called his secretary of state to the White House for a chat about strategy to handle the *Creole* crisis. The seasoned Webster would think of some scheme. It was Webster, after all, who had just won a political tussle by getting the editor of Washington's most powerful newspaper, the *National Intelligencer*, to let him write three unsigned editorials. All in the nation's capital believed that the newspaper editor had written them and not a politician. No one suspected Webster had penned them, and the secretary certainly did not let on that he had. Other important newspapers reprinted the editorials, giving Webster even more clout yet never suspecting the editorials were from his hand. Tyler was aware that the veteran senator and now his secretary of state knew everybody in Washington. He could get things done at summer parties and winter dinners—and in many newspaper offices—that even the president could not accomplish.

But what Tyler did not understand about the secretary of state was that Webster was saddled with a mountain of work and had a very small staff, fewer than a half dozen men. And one those men, his chief clerk, was his son Fletcher, whose presence on staff caused a lot of grumbling about nepotism. Webster was hopelessly understaffed and toiled as hard as he could to run the department. Then, suddenly, he had the *Creole* case on his desk and a skeleton crew to assist him. Webster and his staff were completely overwhelmed by the case and its international complexities.

Tyler told Webster to push hard to get the US minister to England, Edward Everett, to lean on the British prime minister, Robert Peel, to send an emissary to the United States. Then Tyler could persuade the emissary to come down hard on the mutineers in far-off Nassau. He told Webster that he needed to win this diplomatic engagement so that the nation could rest assured that the US government would never again let a foreign power seize its ships and slaves.

Having said that, the president then let everyone within earshot know that he and Webster would get the job done—and soon.[20]

The narrowly directed, harsh letter that Webster sent to Peel through Everett was a shining example of tough diplomacy, because Webster, Tyler, and the US Congress really had no legal leg to stand on. Webster told the British leader that the *Creole* was an American ship owned by an American shipping company carrying American men and women in forced labor down the coast of Florida, an American state. It was taken violently by its passengers, acting as illegal mutineers, and sailed to Nassau. There, he lamented, the Bahamian government, with the cooperation of the British, had let the ship dock and welcomed all its passengers to the island. They should have been rounded up and sent packing to America in chains, he insinuated. In private, he noted that international law prohibited any nation to interfere with vessels from another country that had sailed into its port by "stress of weather or otherwise." This, Webster and Tyler emphasized, was exactly what had happened with the *Creole*. Under the "otherwise" heading, the mutineers had taken the ship and sailed to the Bahamas. They had to be returned to America.[21]

There was a large diplomatic problem. As everybody knew, there was no slavery in the Bahamas. Upon landing, the 135 American captives were free. Worse for Webster, the United States and England had no extradition agreement. The American government could not force the British to give up the slaves.

But Webster got around that problem quite neatly. He argued that he was not talking about British law but about "comity and usages of nations." Simply put, he said that the British needed to help the Americans in this crisis of domesticity in an unofficial and friendly way just as, always, the Americans would help the British in a similar crisis involving British citizens who sought asylum in the United States. If the British did not cooperate, Webster warned in a careful phrase, "the peace of the two countries. . . . would always be in danger."[22]

Webster's memo to Everett and the British was so highly praised when it was published in the *Congressional Globe* that Clay ordered Congress to print an extraordinary one thousand extra copies to be distributed to various American and British officials. Most of the US Congress was now behind Webster, and Tyler, in the crusade.

In the hoopla over Tyler and Webster's demands to have the *Creole* returned, all seemed to overlook Britain's strident policy on slaves who landed on the shores of their colonies by any means at all. And no matter how much British diplomats, such as Lord Aberdeen, the foreign secretary, reiterated that policy, few in America paid any attention. After a whole winter and spring of American flag-waving, Lord Aberdeen made the same argument he had made in November. He wrote to the US ambassador at the end of April 1842, nearly half a year after the mutiny on the brig, that all African Americans were free on British soil but that criminals had to be dealt with.

THE REMAINDER [except the mutineers] were informed that there was no charge against them and as far as the authorities of the island were concerned, they were released from all further restraint. They accordingly availed themselves of this freedom. All landed from boats which had assembled for the purpose of conveying them to the shore. . . . The demands of Mr. Everett are utterly at variance with the laws of England. Upon the arrival of the *Creole* in the port of Nassau, the negroes on it at once became free and Her Majesty's government possessed no legal power or authority to restore them to a state of slavery.

LORD ABERDEEN ALSO ADDRESSED the issue of the mutineers and said "they could not be tried in the [Bahamas'] courts for an offense committed out of British jurisdiction and if not recognizable by these courts, it was equally impossible to transfer the accused persons to the courts of any other nation," adding that such a possibility was granted by extradition treaty but that there was no real treaty between the two countries. Lord Aberdeen added, too, that the British considered charges of piracy against the mutineers but had found none. He told the American that leaders of the House of Lords, many of them lawyers, concurred unanimously with the decision of the judgment tribunal. He insisted that no British official had aided the *Creole* in its arrival in Nassau and certainly no British official had suggested to any of the mutineers that they would find freedom on the Bahamas.

Lord Aberdeen glossed over the charge that in the past, England had returned cargo from wrecked ships. "Any supposed analogy between human beings and the objects of merchandise must necessarily be imperfect and defective," he said.

He also explored American laws that pertained to the *Creole* case, stating that many freed black British citizens traveling to southern states on business for northern companies, even shipping companies, had been jailed, sometimes beaten, and later released. England did not ask for them to be released because it could not interfere with the laws of American states, just as America could not interfere with the laws of British colonies. It was a perfect comparison; all Americans dismissed it.[23]

In his letter to the American ambassador, Lord Aberdeen went further. He quoted the Declaration of Independence, saying that all Americans were entitled to "Life, Liberty and the pursuit of happiness" and then said that the declaration apparently had been discarded so that each individual state, and not the nation, could decide who had liberty and could pursue happiness and who could not. He added, too, that Canada had returned an American criminal to Arkansas but there had never been any return of British criminals who fled to the United States for the protection then knew they would receive. "There are persons enjoying entire impunity who are stained with crimes of the deepest dye, and whose surrender has been demanded by the British authorities, but demanded in vain," he said.[24]

It was a solid, ironclad defense of a clearly written British law on slavery. The British were satisfied with it and the Americans were not.[25]

The issue was a natural one for the bombastic Henry Clay to embrace. He was publicly a champion of forced labor, although privately he told friends that he was opposed to the institution on moral grounds. On political and economic grounds, it made sense to him, and in slave-driven Kentucky, he needed to defend it to get reelected year after year. But the issue was more than that for him. It gave him a chance to also defend the nation against its former foe, Great Britain, and to strengthen his national image for the upcoming 1844 presidential election. He could be a champion of the South and the North at the same time. "The liberty of the descendants of Africa is incompatible with the liberty and safety of the European descendants. . . . Their liberty, if it were possible, could only be established by violating the incontestable powers of the states and subverting the Union and beneath the ruins of the Union would be buried , sooner or later, the liberty of both races," he said.

He continued, "What would be the conditions of those two races in the slave states upon the supposition of the immediate emancipation? Does any man suppose that they would become blended into one homogenous mass? No human law could enforce a union between the two races."[26]

In the bleak winter of 1842, national politics had turned into mayhem. "All is confusion, chaos and disorder here," said a frustrated Clay of Washington. "No system! No concert of action! No prospects of union and harmony."[27] But the *Creole* incident offered an opportunity to bring some unity to Washington. With the assistance of Clay and the national media, the president and his secretary of state were becoming national heroes.

Support was not solid everywhere, though, and that worried Webster. To strengthen his hand, the secretary explained the situation to him US Supreme Court justice Joseph Story, hoping that he would side with Webster and Tyler. No one in the world knew more about slavery, mutinies, and international law than Story. A respected author of works on international disputes, he had handed down the decision that had freed the mutineers on the slave ship *Amistad*. Surely, Webster believed, Story would see the distinct differences between the *Amistad* case and that of the *Creole*. Story did not. He stunned Webster by telling him bluntly that the two cases were the same. Story said that the British did not have to return the *Creole* slaves under any circumstances. Lacking any legal backing from Story and the Supreme Court, Webster had to convince the British that future friendliness between the two countries was more important that a public relations victory over this tiny incident in the slave world, and he had to do it fast, faster than the rising tide of anger in Congress, the media, and the public.

The diplomatic game of talks and threats became heated, and heated quickly, on both sides of the Atlantic. Many in America feared that the *Creole* incident would lead to war. Some hoped that a war *would* break out. One member of Congress even stood up on the floor of the House and called for an armed attack on Nassau. "The British," William Channing argued, were "an angry menace."[28]

Webster assured the president that Everett would have no difficulty in getting the ambassador to persuade British government officials to dispatch a negotiator to America to diplomatically resolve the *Creole* problem—right away.

Webster was happy to do the president's bidding because he saw the *Creole* affair as a marvelous opportunity and yet another way to strength his bid to become president in the next election. The 1840s was an era in which American newspapers ran thousands of stories about British–US relations. Even small newspapers in upstate New York and far-off Maine kept up with news from

England. The press attention he would get in the *Creole* battle would give Webster a glossy veneer as a presidential candidate in 1844. Neither he nor anyone else believed that Tyler would run for president on his own in three years. Tyler was strictly a seat warmer for the next nominee, and Webster felt confident that he would be that nominee. An impressive diplomatic victory in the *Creole* difficulty would give him an aura of foreign policy expertise and make more formidable than any other candidate, even Clay. Tyler might claim victory in the dispute, if there was one, but the newspapers would let the voting public know that Webster had been the man in the ring, the man landing the blows for America in the *Creole* scuffle.[29]

As Americans fumed, British officials raced to develop a plan to solve the slave ship problem, because they certainly did not want a third war with America. The first thing they needed to do was name an emissary, demanded by the Americans, and that was Alexander Baring, Lord Ashburton, former head of the banking firm of Baring Brothers. Lord Ashburton was the perfect choice. He was as American as any Brit could get. He owned a million acres of land in Maine, had visited the United States several times, and had married the daughter of William Bingham, a Philadelphia banker and former US senator.[30] He had worked in his father's business, Hope and Company, for many years and later renamed it with his brothers. The company had tentacles of influence throughout Europe, and few made business moves without consulting Lord Ashburton and his brothers. The Duc de Richelieu once said, half seriously, "There are six major powers in Europe—Britain, France, Austria, Hungary Russia, Prussia and Baring Brothers."

Lord Ashburton, professionally and personally, was a strong supporter of British–American relationships and always had been. His political credentials were impeccable. He had served in Parliament from 1806 to 1835, making many friends in that chamber. He also had extensive professional credentials and had served as Britain's minister of trade seven years earlier, starting that job just after his parliamentary terms ended. That job established his friendships with several prime ministers and cabinet secretaries.[31]

Fixing the *Creole* problem was just part of Ashburton's mission, though. He was also in America to solve a dozen or so other problems in trade and land boundaries, troubles that had escalated tensions between the two counties. If they could be resolved, tensions could be eased.

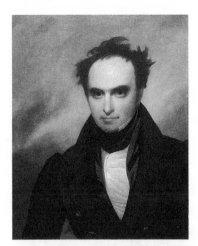

FIGURE 1
Daniel Webster, Tyler's
secretary of state, was put
in charge of negotiations
to win the *Creole* dispute.
(Painting by Francis
Alexander, National
Portrait Gallery.)

FIGURE 2
President John Tyler,
the "accidental president,"
who became chief
executive on the death
of William Henry
Harrison. (Painting by
George Peter Alexander
Healy, National Portrait
Gallery.)

FIGURE 3
US representative
John Quincy Adams of
Massachusetts, a former
president and staunch
abolitionist. He and other
congressmen led debates
on the *Creole* and its slaves.
(Painting by George Caleb
Bingham, National Portrait
Gallery.)

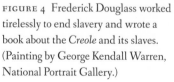

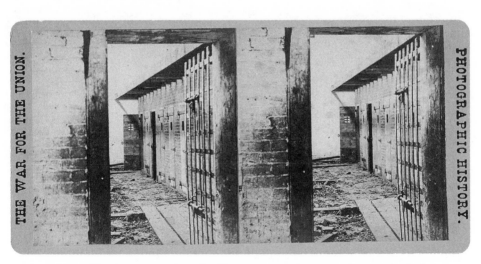

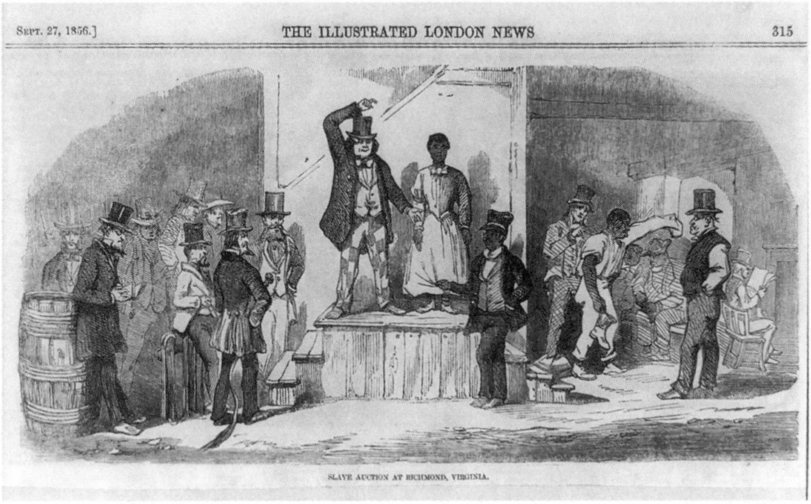
SEPT. 27, 1856.]
THE ILLUSTRATED LONDON NEWS
315
SLAVE AUCTION AT RICHMOND, VIRGINIA.

FIGURE 6 This slave auction in Virginia was similar to one the slaves on the *Creole* were headed for in New Orleans before they seized their vessel on the high seas off the coast of Florida (Library of Congress).

THE WAR FOR THE UNION.
PHOTOGRAPHIC HISTORY.

FIGURE 7 This slave pen in Alexandria, Virginia, was similar to one where mutiny leader Madison Washington was held before he was put on board the *Creole* for its trip to New Orleans in 1841 (Library of Congress).

FIGURE 8 This drawing of Nassau shows the town itself and boats in the harbor. The
drawing was given to Governor Alexander Cockburn in 1841, just a few months prior to
the arrival of the *Creole* and its slaves (Bahamas Archives).

FIGURE 9 This 1864 photo shows Nassau in the era when its residents did business with the Confederate States of America. Southerners used Nassau as a port because the Union navy could not attack them in British territory (Bahamas Archives).

FIGURE 10 Bay Street, the main avenue in Nassau. The street was crowded with boardinghouses, small hotels, shops, a tavern, and an icehouse (Bahamas Archives).

FIGURE 11 Henry Clay, a Speaker of the House, was appalled at the seizure of the *Creole*. He predicted it would open the door to other slave ship mutinies and ruin maritime trade on the Atlantic coast. (Painting by John Sartain, National Portrait Gallery.)

FIGURE 12 Henry Wise, a crafty Virginia politician and states' rights champion, was one of President Tyler's early supporters. He fought Tyler's enemies in Congress and back home in Virginia.

FIGURE 13 Judge Joseph Story was the key Supreme Court justice in the *Amistad* rebellion case in 1839 (National Gallery).

FIGURE 14 Hearings for the *Creole*'s slaves and meetings
between the US ambassador and Governor Cockburn were held
here, at Government House (Bahamas Archives).

FIGURE 15 Antislavery champion
Representative Joshua Giddings
of Ohio (Library of Congress).

FIGURE 16 John Minor Botts was
a longtime Virginia politician from
Richmond and a close friend and
political ally of President Tyler. He
served in Congress during the *Creole*
crisis (Library of Congress).

FIGURE 17 Louisa Adams was the wife of congressman and former president John Quincy Adams, a strident abolitionist. She served as her husband's hostess and attended numerous meetings of the abolitionist cabal that lobbied furiously to free the slaves on the *Creole*. She was also one of Washington's most prominent social leaders and a patron of the city's theaters (Library of Congress).

FIGURE 18. Beverley Tucker, from a wealthy Virginia family, was a Virginia judge and a friend of President Tyler. He lived in Williamsburg, where he was Tyler's neighbor and a professor at the College of William and Mary. Tucker was a fiery states' rights champion (National Gallery).

FIGURE 19 John C. Calhoun became secretary of state in 1844 and, with Tyler, pushed for the annexation of Texas. Calhoun joined Tyler in threatening a war with Mexico if it invaded Texas. Earlier, he called British support of the *Creole* mutineers an insult to the United States. (Painting by George Peter Alexander Healy, National Portrait Gallery.)

FIGURE 20 President James K. Polk won all the credit for the annexation of Texas as a slave state, but President Tyler did most of the early work. Tyler wanted to annex Texas to make up for the political loss he suffered in the *Creole* incident. (Painting by Charles Fenderich, National Portrait Gallery.)

He was eager to go. He started packing numerous trunks as soon as Peel asked him to sail to the United States. He was in such as hurry to cross the ocean that the final memorandum from Peel concerning the goals of his talks had not even been written when his ship slipped out of its British port. The paper work caught up to him later. The weather was cold and rainy, the Atlantic windy, and the waves high. Friends in England told Lord Ashburton that hardly anyone traveled to America at that time of year and that the trip would be miserable. He did not care. The new emissary could not wait for the captain to hoist his anchor and head for the United States.

Why was he so eager to sail? It was not just the chance to serve as an emissary and prevent a war. It was a chance to see one of the oldest friends he had in America, Daniel Webster. The two men had met on Lord Ashburton's prior trips to the United States and liked each other immediately. Everyone said that they bore a striking physical resemblance to each other, both with large heads, receding hairlines, dark eyes, and dark, thick eyebrows. Lord Ashburton was a bit more bald than Webster, something Webster always kidded him about. They laughed easily at each other's jokes, enjoyed reading the same authors, listened to the same music, saw the same plays, shared the same American friends, and were fans of the same sports. Webster was one of the best dressed men in America, sporting expensive, well-fitted suits in his numerous appearances at Congress and at the White House. Lord Ashburton was also a well-known fashion plate. He was said to be one of the best dressed men in the world, spending hundreds of dollars on suits at the best stores in London.

Their wives were even closer friends than they were. The Websters had lived with the Barings at Lord Ashburton's palatial estate, the Grange, on an 1839 visit to England, a trip partially funded by the Barings. In addition, Webster had worked as the paid legal counsel and representative in America for the House of Baring. This reunion of the two old friends was, of course, carefully planned. Lord Aberdeen, England's foreign secretary and a close friend of Peel's, told Lord Ashburton that his "known friendly relations" with Webster "were among the chief inducements to selecting him."[32]

Lord Aberdeen told Everett much the same thing. "[I] had been mainly influenced by a desire to select a person who would be peculiarly acceptable to the United States as well as eminently qualified by the trust," he wrote him.[33]

Webster told Tyler that the selection of Lord Ashburton, his friend, was a clear signal that Britain wanted to resolve the *Creole* issues, and others, as quickly and amiably as possible. This was a good sign. Lord Ashburton, too, saw hope in his deployment to America.

He had plenty of time to think about his reunion with Webster, because the terrible storms on the Atlantic that his friends had predicted did occur. The ship's captain could make little headway against the strong winds, and his vessel was blown hundreds of miles off course. The ship arrived in America more than a week after it was scheduled to drop anchor.

A very weather-beaten and seasick Lord Ashburton walked down the gangway in New York on April 2, 1842, very happy to stride onto solid land. He was full of bluster, though, despite the treacherous voyage. He did not take his ill wife on the journey but arrived as the head of a large party of Britons eager to solve the political problems of the two nations. With Lord Ashburton were three secretaries, five servants, three horses, and a dozen large trunks. That was not all. He and his eight companions had to wait for hours on the crowded dock until laborers unloaded his large, elegant carriage, which he would use to travel about in America.[34]

Lord Ashburton told everyone he met that he could not wait to begin diplomatic talks with Webster and that he was hopeful of resolutions acceptable to all. He told everybody, too, that Peel had given him the authority to approve all treaty decisions and a resolution in the *Creole* matter right there in the United States. No one back home would reverse his decisions. There would be no waiting. Back in London, Lord Aberdeen backed up Lord Ashburton's statement about sole authority and added that the prime minister and other cabinet officials were certain that Lord Ashburton and Webster could reach conciliatory agreements in a short period of time. Lord Ashburton told New Yorkers that he expected all the issues, especially the *Creole*, to be resolved soon and that negotiations would take no more than six months, a rather speedy conclusion for talks that involved a number of contentious issues.

Lord Ashburton and his entourage moved to Washington and stayed at a house at Sixteenth and H, a few blocks from Webster's home, and soon began to enjoy the Washington social scene. He and his aides attended numerous parties and receptions, plus official government functions. The burly, well-dressed Lord Ashburton was frequently seen strolling through the city. He stopped and engaged in conversations with hundreds of Americans and quickly made himself a popular diplomat.[35]

Both Webster and Lord Ashburton saw trade between the two nations as critical. They did not want quarrelsome battles over geographic boundaries to create animosity between the countries and certainly did not want the sticky *Creole* issue to wreck commerce that had been highly profitable for both sides. It had been thirty years since the War of 1812, and England and the United States were both hoping to enter an era of good feelings about each other. The *Creole* could ruin that, and both men worked hard to avoid that outcome.

Webster and Lord Ashburton were all smiles in public, but in private both fretted over the outcome of their talks because of the ever-growing national furor over the *Creole*. Many in Congress and just about all newspapers howled that the friendly, cozy relationship that old buddies Webster and Lord Ashburton shared was corrupt and that the outcome would not benefit either country but only the two men. Both diplomats denied that, but most people distrusted them from the first day Lord Ashburton walked down the gangplank of his ship and stepped foot on to American soil. The pair, many Americans argued, would reach a cozy agreement on many issues but the *Creole* and its slaves would be ignored. Immediately, enemies of Tyler and Webster said there could be no compromise on the *Creole*—the nineteen mutineers had to be returned home.

Another problem was that Lord Ashburton had completely misjudged American unhappiness over the *Creole*. He saw the incident as just another bondage dispute and did not realize the size of it. He did not understand the American sense of honor and that the South saw the *Creole* case as the supreme test of it. Southerners paid no attention to the laws on slavery in the United States, the Bahamas, or England. All they knew was that American honor had been offended and that England, the villain, had to release the mutineers to make up for the slight. Lord Ashburton did not completely understand this and in fact did not even put the incendiary issue of the slave ship at the top of his list when he sat down with Webster that spring.

He wanted to resolve the boundary issues in Canada and any maritime issues but did not want to confront Webster, Tyler, or the American people on the specific story of the *Creole*. He told Webster that it was too volatile and that he did not want it to explode in their faces. Webster quickly agreed.

He remembered what a hot issue the *Amistad* mutiny had been, and that had involved Africans from far way who did not speak any English, not American slaves from across the river in northern Richmond who spoke perfect English. They agreed that if they did not talk about it, the *Creole* issue might go away. Webster carefully backed off on charging the British with any serious crimes and called their actions in the *Creole* incident just "officious interference," a term he made up and that no one completely understood. Besides, they told everybody, they were working on paths to eliminate bondage wherever they found it and that somewhere within that campaign, the *Creole* issue would be resolved. Webster added that he was "not intending to surrender any point of national interest or national honor in the talks about slavery in general but did not want to talk about the details of the explosive *Creole* case."[36]

Besides, Webster and Tyler were getting no legal support in the *Creole* case anywhere. After Justice Story turned down Webster's appeal for legal help he turned to Hugh Legare, the US attorney general, a Democrat. Legare turned him down too. He told Webster that if a man murdered someone in America and fled to a foreign country, he could be turned over to US authorities. However, if a foreign country refused to do that, as countries nearly always did in the cases of runaways, the United States could legally do nothing about that. The freedom of even a murderer was protected by the laws of that country.[37]

In all his notes to Lord Ashburton, Webster carefully avoided any confrontations. Lord Ashburton had made it clear that the *Creole* case was off the table. He hadn't had much time to study the issue, so he really could not discuss it with Webster. He pushed the controversy as far away from his hands, and the hands of the British government, as he could. But Webster talked and wrote about the *Creole* debate constantly. At one point he wrote, "Your lordship's . . . large experience in commercial affairs cannot fail to suggest to you how important it is to merchants and navigators . . . that they should feel secure against all but the ordinary causes of maritime loss," cleverly avoiding mention of the *Creole*. At the end of the note, in even more verbal wizardry, Webster wrote that "instructions shall be given to local authorities in the islands which shall lead them to regulate their conduct in conformity with the rights of [US citizens] and the just expectations of their government."[38]

Lord Ashburton, a cagey negotiator, told Webster that, in the end, all slave return cases would be treated individually and that local laws, meaning British crown laws, would prevail in each situation. But he seemed to leave open the chance that in some cases the crown might make an exception. In reality, the crown would not.

There was something else on Webster's mind. The *Creole* case was causing feuds in Washington and at the center of them was John Quincy Adams. It was Adams, he remembered vividly, who had won an acquittal for the Africans on the *Amistad* just two years earlier. He had done so by presenting the personal stories of the slaves—tales of their wives, parents, children, and jobs back home. He made the courts see them as people and not just captives. What if Adams, buoyed by the *Amistad* victory, somehow jumped into the *Creole* case as a defense lawyer for the nineteen men sitting in jail in Nassau? What if he sailed down to the Bahamas and represented them in front of either British or American judicial panels? He had turned the *Amistad* foreigners into beloved heroes. Webster could imagine what he would do with the *Creole* slaves. How would he describe their leader, Washington, enslaved because he had tried to rescue his wife, still toiling in slavery? Would he elaborate on men on board who had lost wives and children to slave traders? Tell stories of whippings in the shadow of the halls of Congress? Talk of the starvation of American bondsmen and bondswomen? Describe the rat hole slave pens in Virginia? The dreadful auctions in New Orleans? Buyers callously holding open the jaws of men, women, and children to check their teeth before purchase? Webster closed his eyes whenever he thought of the spellbinding Adams in front of judges and juries with those stories.

And Webster knew that Adams despised him. Adams hated the entire Webster family. There was no better proof of that than two notes in Adams's diary from the summer of 1843. Adams was in a rage over Webster's son and head of staff, Fletcher Webster. Adams accused him of sending him a letter that was "impertinent" and that showed him to be "bloated with self-sufficiency as an executive officer." He charged in a second diary note that a second letter from Fletcher was "as impertinent, as ignorant and as insolent as the former. Into what hands has . . . the department of state fallen?" In the same entry, he sneered that Daniel Webster had gone to Marshfield to shoot snipes, to fish for trout and to patch up on some shameful rents."[39]

Webster and Tyler had their hands full with Lord Ashburton because his view of the *Creole* story was very different than theirs and included some mistakes. Not only did Lord Ashburton misunderstand American honor, but he did not understand the details of the case either. From the start, he thought Webster and the Tyler government saw the mutineers in Nassau as fugitives and were seeking to reclaim them. This misunderstanding slowed down the talks. The British minister spent an extraordinary amount of time trying to explain to Webster that England would not permit the United States to charge the mutineers with piracy. Under piracy laws, American lawyers could try the mutineers as pirates in Bahamian courts. But the Americans had turned down each offer of a piracy trial since the *Creole* had dropped anchor in Nassau. The British publicly said they did not know why the Americans did not try the mutineers as pirates, but privately they all knew, as Webster knew, that there was no evidence that the mutineers had acted as pirates.[40]

At the same time, those in the antislavery crusade in America, and there were many, insisted that while the ship had to be returned, and in fact it had been and was in New Orleans, its passengers had to be given their freedom, since the boat had been anchored in foreign waters. They badgered Lord Ashburton about Britain's stance that the ship was more important than the slaves. Lord Ashburton also had problems with his friend Webster, who was irritable throughout the summer of negotiations. Lord Ashburton said that Webster was prone "to have unreasonable, ungracious and difficult moods."[41]

What kind of an agreement could Lord Ashburton and Webster reach? And would anybody on either side of the Atlantic pay any attention to it?

Added to all that stress was another factor. The summer of 1842 was one of the hottest in US history, and nowhere was the temperature hotter, or the humidity more oppressive, than in Washington, DC. The heat threatened to render Lord Ashburton incapable doing any work. "I must throw myself on your compassion," he wrote Webster. "I contrive to crawl about in this heat by day and to live my nights in a sleepless fever. . . . I shall positively not outlive this affair if this is to be more prolonged."[42]

Lord Ashburton's arrival in America should have been hailed by all, but it was not. By the time that he had disembarked, the British in the Bahamas had released all the captives except the nineteen mutineers. Southern slave owners demanded prosecution of the mutineers. At the same time, antislavery leaders in America hailed the release of the 116 men and women and urged Bahamian officials to let the mutineers go too. All America was in an uproar and either for or against the people on board the *Creole* and for or against Great Britain too. Or were they? England was an enemy for taking an American ship, but it was, for many abolitionists, a hero for releasing the slaves.

To stem the tide of criticism, President Tyler released all official correspondence about the ship to the newspapers, which printed it. Tyler believed that the dissemination of information would quell the public uproar, but it merely inflamed it. Even the *Madisonian*, the president's primary supporter, was lukewarm in its defense of Tyler, chortling that he was upholding the Constitution and should have more followers than he did.

Tyler resented that too gentle pat on the back and really resented several southern state legislatures that demanded that he get the mutineers back and put them on trial somewhere—anywhere. At the same time, Tyler felt very confused. As the president, he felt he had to get all of the *Creole* captives back. As a politician, he knew he had to get them back to placate the South and gain its votes when he ran for office in 1844. Tyler, though, had been against slavery all his life, as his father had been before him. As a senator, he had offered a bill to eliminate the slave trade in Washington, DC, which was defeated. The bill appalled his southern colleagues in the government, especially those in his native state of Virginia.[43]

If Tyler was confused over the issue, Lord Ashburton was *really* perplexed. He could not understand why Tyler was so agitated. He wanted the mutineers back and yet was opposed to slavery. He wanted the slaves back to please the South but did not want them back, because that would displease the North. The president did not want a war but threatened a war. Tyler agreed with Congress but at the same time disagreed with Congress. Lord Ashburton saw Tyler not only as a bad president but also as a very poor politician. He was "weak and conceited" Ashburton wrote friends. He added that he was a scared leader who wielded no power in America because of his position as an "accidental president."

The British ambassador was adamant that Tyler was not a qualified leader for the American people and that the longer he stayed in office, the more difficult relations with the United States would be. Tyler had "strong opinions about the *Creole* case and is not a little disposed to be obstinate on the subject," Lord Ashburton wrote home. He added in another letter that the president "is very sore and testy about the *Creole*."[44]

At one point Lord Ashburton, overheated and worn down by diplomacy, was ready to leave the negotiations and sail home to England, leaving the contentious *Creole* issue unresolved. He was not throwing in the towel over the *Creole* but over the Maine–Canada boundary dispute. Local politicians from the two states constantly meddled in the talks between the British ambassador and the secretary of state. Finally, in the early summer of 1842, Lord Ashburton signaled to Webster that he had had it with the talks and was going to flee the United States as quickly as he could. Webster sent this message to Tyler, who called Lord Ashburton to the White House to smooth over the talks and at any cost to keep him in the United States.

That winter and spring, Tyler seemed agitated about everything, not just the *Creole*. He was being battered by the press, jeered at in Congress, and ignored by the people. Americans noticed it and so did other foreign visitors to the White House. British novelist Charles Dickens, then on a literary tour of America that brought him much fame, was disappointed after first meeting with President Tyler. He said that the president "looked somewhat worn and anxious and well he might, being at war with everybody."

Tyler grumbled to all that he worked too hard, was saddled with too many responsibilities, and spent all day and all night on work that brought him little gain. In a letter to a friend from Virginia, dated just a few months after the *Creole* crisis, Tyler lamented about his job as president.

MY COURSE OF LIFE is to rise with the sun and to work from that time until three o'clock. The order of the patching business is pretty much, first, all diplomatic matters; second, matters connected with the action of Congress; third, matters of general concern falling under the executive control; then the reception of visitors and the dispatch of private petitions. I dine at three and a half o'clock and in the evening my employments are miscellaneous—directions to secretaries and endorsements of numerous papers . . . again, after candlelight, part from all business, until ten at night, when I retire to bed. . . . What say you? Would you exchange the peace and quiet of your homestead for such an office?[45]

TYLER GOT INTO EVEN MORE TROUBLE. With Webster's assistance, he named a politician from Maine as an illegal secret agent, with a handsome bank account provided by Tyler's office. This man was to conduct a propaganda campaign throughout Maine to make Lord Ashburton think that all Maine was behind the proposed US boundary line offer. His efforts were discovered pretty quickly and wound up in numerous newspapers just as Lord Ashburton and Webster sat down to talk about the *Creole*.[46]

Over the previous thirty years, since the War of 1812, England had grown tremendously as a world power. Its navy was the largest and most notorious in the world, and in 1815 the British army had defeated Napoleon at Waterloo. Since then, the British army had won several other conflicts and was feared throughout the world. Lord Ashburton told Lord Aberdeen and Prime Minister Peel, though, that America was much stronger than they suspected and that Great Britain would lose a war with America, its third straight. That loss would erode England's military prowess in Europe.

That was probably not true, so why did Lord Ashburton say that? He never fully explained his stand, but perhaps he simply wanted England to agree to end the *Creole* standoff. He pressured his superiors very hard to do so, even though they had told him, and the Americans, that he had all the power to make decisions.

Tyler and Webster saw Lord Ashburton's vacillating as a sign that he was not a good negotiator and could be bulldozed into agreeing to do what America wanted. This made the upcoming talks between Webster and Lord Ashburton not only difficult but dangerous.

Tyler was keenly aware of the importance of Lord Ashburton's trip to America and did all he could to make him feel at home during his stay, starting with a glittering White House dinner in honor of Lord Ashburton and his entourage in June 1842. More than one hundred of the most influential people in the nation's capital attended the event, where Webster introduced Lord Ashburton to the president, who personally and on behalf of the government welcomed him warmly.

Tyler needed a peace accord with Lord Ashburton, but he was not about to capitulate on anything. "The idea of my conceding to Great Britain anything? Fudge!" the president roared.[47]

The formal talks between Webster and Lord Ashburton began in early April 1842. The first of three issues they wanted to settle was the attack on the *Caroline* several years earlier, led by a British citizen. The second was the boundary line between Maine and Canada, and the third the suppression of the American slave trade on the Atlantic and Pacific Oceans. The *Creole*, it turned out, was fourth and last issue, but no one paid much attention to it until later, a huge mistake by both Lord Ashburton and Webster.[48]

The British emissary knew that the public was in a frenzy to get the ship back, but he underestimated the ugly mood in Congress toward Great Britain. Many congressmen were still smarting over anti-American British tactics prior to the War of 1812. Lewis Cass, the minister to France, who would later become an influential congressman and run for president, bellowed that Britain's stopping of merchant vessels to search for slaves was the exact same tactic (that time involving American seamen) that had started the War of 1812. It was as disgraceful in 1842 as it was prior to that war, he said.[49]

Chasing Slave Ships on the High Seas

British officials countered that the United States was belligerent in its relations with the crown over the suppression of the slave trade on the high seas. In 1807 Congress had passed a law eliminating the arrival of Africans in the southern states. The law did little to stop this trade though. As part of its 1833 laws eliminating slavery anywhere in its empire, the British had authorized stopping and searching ships suspected of carrying Africans. If any were found, they were taken aboard British ships, sailed to British colonies or England itself, and then released. The United States refused to permit the boarding of its ships, and England had to honor that ruling. Subsequently, dozens of slave vessels, when spotted by the British on the oceans, ran up the US flag, keeping boarding parties off their decks and protecting their human cargoes.[50]

In many cases, though, British captains with "reason to believe" that a ship was carrying Africans boarded and inspected it with armed soldiers. An example was the American ship *Douglass*, boarded by a party of soldiers from HMS *Termagant* off the coast of Africa. In the ship's log of October 21, 1839, the *Termagant*'s captain wrote:

> 11 a.m. Hove to and boarded the American brig *Douglass*. Light airs and cloudy, with rain. Sent an officer and party to examine brig; found her with slave cargo.
>
> 2 p.m. Sent an officer and party of men to take charge of the brig being engaged in the slave trade

5 p.m. Made sail.

8 p.m. Calm and fair. Brig in custody.[51]

Shortly afterward, a Lieutenant Seagram, an officer on the *Termagant*, reported to his boss, Admiral George Elliott, that interviews with several men on the *Douglass* showed not only how the slave trade worked but also the duplicity of the American slave owners and the American consul in Havana, from where the brig had departed on its journey to buy Africans. The *Douglass* was an American ship but traveled from Cuba. It was run by seven Spaniards, not Americans, and was bound for the Brass and Bonny Rivers in Canada to put its captives on another ship. That ship, built in Baltimore, carried no slaving equipment in order to deceive British naval captains.

The lieutenant's interviews with the Spaniards, through an interpreter, also revealed that the American consul in Cuba, N. P. Trist, had authorized the *Douglass* to carry two cannons and if necessary to fire on any British ship trying to overtake it. "A debate took place previous to the boarding whether they should fire, or not, into the boats of her majesty's brigantine *Termagant*, and they also had ready bags containing musket balls for the aforesaid purpose," wrote Seagram, who said the *Douglass* did not fire because the crew feared an all-out bombardment by the *Termagant*. "Our attempts point out very clearly the spirit of opposition to our attempts to suppress the slave trade by an American authority while covering a slave cargo with the American flag," Seagram added.[52]

The British boarding of suspected slave ships had strong international support. In 1841 the British proposed the Quintuple Treaty, which authorized the boarding of ships and was signed by Austria, Great Britain, France, Russia, and Prussia. The British asked the Americans to sign it but were met with vociferous opposition in Congress. The idea was dropped.[53]

While Webster and his old friend Lord Ashburton squabbled over land boundaries and while congressmen from both major parties parried with each other in the halls of Congress, the mutineers of the *Creole* slumbered in their hot Nassau jail, waiting for word on what Governor Cockburn, the Bahamian court, and courts in England would do next.

There was much talk about Madison Washington, the leader of the mutiny, He was hailed as a hero by most Bahamians for saving the life of the captain, guarding the captain's family, caring for the wounded, and bringing the ship into Nassau in a peaceful manner. Some shook their heads at him, though, because in being so kind, he had tied himself up legally. A Captain Fitzgerald, a British commander in Nassau, told friends "how foolish the [mutineers] were, that they had not, when they rose, killed all the whites on board, and run the vessel ashore and then they would have all been free and there would have been no more trouble about it."[54]

Many others agreed. Previous shiploads of blacks had been freed when their vessels had crashed on reefs and underwater rocks. They merely separated themselves from the captain and crew and sought out the bands of Bahamians who arrived quickly at the wreck site. Washington, perhaps unwittingly, did not do that, and his kindness toward the captain and crew set up him and the others for homicide charges.

Washington insisted to his jailers and the other mutineers that they all were free because they were in the Bahamas and that courts there would back them up on that assertion. Nothing they did on the ship mattered, he kept insisting. He reminded his fellow mutineers that black freedom newspapers all asserted that the British were lenient with runaways. "The chains of bondage fall from their limbs once their feet have pressed English soil," wrote an editor of the *Liberator*. Washington had complete confidence in his case, despite the worry of many others.[55]

Many in the Bahamas and the United States were perplexed at Washington's skills as a leader and mutineer. He had exhibited none of them when he was a forced laborer in Virginia. He had not planned any insurrection while he was free in Canada, and certainly not a shipboard takeover. It was because he had not been targeted as an insurrectionist, though, that he was so successful at that job. Nobody feared him. Ever since the Nat Turner rebellion a decade earlier, southerners had been on the lookout for rebellious insurrectionists. "It was the suspicion eternally attached to the slave himself, suspicion that a Nat Turner might be in every family, that the same bloody deeds might be enacted over at any time and at any place," James McDowell said in the Virginia State Legislature in 1832, a year after the Turner rebellion.[56]

Washington escaped the net, too, because the exclusionary laws of Virginia at that time covered only slaves who had actually been involved in an insurrection or lived in counties where an insurrection had taken place. Virginia's leaders were certain that this policy would save them from insurrections such as Washington's. "Conspiracies of slaves have been plotted in several states of the Union and excited the serious attention of most of the states in the South," said the governor of Louisiana, who added that barring rebellious blacks was the answer. "The total prohibition of slaves into the state is the only safe method of avoiding the danger which threatens us."[57]

Southern leaders were enraged that Washington had slipped through the net and become the ringleader of the *Creole* rebellion. "If any person should by word or deed excite freed Negroes or persons of color to conspire or rebel, such persons shall be deemed guilty of felony," stated a law in North Carolina. Under it, rebel leaders such as Washington would be given thirty-nine lashes and imprisoned for one year.[58]

No one in the Bahamas or the United States could understand how Washington, a cook, had become so knowledgeable about the views of both Canada and England about slavery, their intense opposition to it, and all the tiny loopholes involved in their laws against it. How had he become so smart so fast, and how had he conveyed the feelings of these foreign powers to his mostly uneducated fellow mutineers? Washington told his men that he had learned all this through newspapers, pamphlets, and meetings with abolitionists on his way south to free his wife. He told the Bahamian officials nothing about his knowledge though. He just shrugged, but they knew he had a deep understanding of British law. That had led him to Nassau and might lead him to freedom too.[59]

After the takeover of the *Creole*, as Washington sat in jail in Nassau, southern leaders once again howled that to free Washington would encourage other rebels like him. Hundreds of ships carrying captives followed the same general route from the Virginia area down to New Orleans. If Washington were not punished, they said, slaves on those ships might lead a similar mutiny, causing more death and destruction. Madison was quickly becoming an example of what a slave leader looked like. Southerners desperately wanted him to be an example of a man swinging on a rope from a wooden crossbeam atop a gallows.

They also raged that the future would not just be populated by mutinies on the high seas but revolts on land too, in all the southern states. "If we may not safely sail on our own coast, with our slave property on board, because Great Britain may choose to deny our right to hold property in slaves, may she not, with equal propriety, extend the same rule to our cotton and other staples," roared John C. Calhoun.[60]

Many agreed with him. "The revolts which occurred and plots which were discovered were sufficiently serious to produce a very palpable disquiet . . . undertone of uneasiness," wrote a historian later. By 1841, for more than one hundred years, dozens of slave owners and overseers had been murdered by concoctions of plants and roots, mixed together to become poisons secretly administered by slaves. According to southerners, this rebelliousness had to stop.[61]

Those undertones were everywhere. Captive plantation workers led miserable lives and for generations had yearned to be free—by any means necessary. What slave populations did not need, planters agreed, were hostile men and women continually riling up the workers toward a plantation mutiny of some kind. The *Creole* was a vivid reminder of that daily fear.[62]

The fear was not new. It had existed since 1772, when British courts handed down the Somerset decision, which stated that any slave brought to England from somewhere else was immediately free. Almost all American newspapers had written about the court ruling, and American planters trembled when they read the stories. The only way to prevent revolts, the southerners maintained, was to keep their captive workers in line and troublemakers far away.[63]

Plantation owners in the northern part of Virginia, where Madison Washington was from, were particularly nervous because political leaders in that area often spoke and wrote against slavery. Thomas Jefferson, although ambivalent about bondage all his life, wrote that African Americans "were deprived, were forever deprived, of all the comfort of life, and to be made most wretched of the human kind." A fellow Virginian, Patrick Henry, had written that "we find men, professing a religion the most humane, mild, meek, gentle and generous, adopting a principle as repugnant to humanity as it is inconsistent with the Bible and destructive to liberty."[64]

The infamous Nat Turner revolt was not what scared southern planters. What terrified them were all the others, not so widely reported, and the revolts that might yet come. In the introduction to his book *American Negro Slave Revolts*, historian Herbert Aptheker wrote of that fear: "[Nat Turner] was not an isolated, unique phenomenon, but the culmination of a series of slave conspiracies and revolts." The last thing southerners wanted was publicity about the *Creole*. That could be read by both whites and blacks. Blacks, southerners agreed, had to be kept "in their ignorance" of revolts. That kind of publicity would lead to many more *Creoles*. Such press coverage had worried planters for more than half a century.

In 1800 the editor of the *Virginia Gazette* had written, "The public mind has much been involved in dangerous apprehensions concerning an insurrection of the Negroes.[65] By then the nature of slavery had changed. Thousands of slaves from plantations had been either moved or sold to new owners in cities, particularly seaports or river towns, where they worked in warehouses, stores, and factories. In the cities, they had far more freedom than they had had on plantations. They lived in apartments or boardinghouses. They went to bars, congregated in dark alleys, and held parties. In Richmond, African Americans even danced with white women in taverns, gambled alongside white men in casinos, and drank in white-owned saloons. They had enormous freedom and wanted all of it.

Also in 1800, led by Gabriel Prosser, Virginia slaves plotted a massive uprising. Part of the plan was to kidnap the governor, James Monroe (who would later become president), and murder dozens of merchants. The plot was uncovered and the leaders were hanged, but it was a frightening reminder of how dangerous life could be within a world of angry black men and women. People throughout the South were frightened also by the rising tide of antislavery forces. These people, loud and fierce in their views, could be found all over the nation by 1841, when Madison Washington and his men seized the *Creole*.

<hr />

IT IS DIFFICULT TO PINPOINT the exact start of the American antislavery movement—the effort to abolish it, totally and immediately. The Quakers, a nonviolent religious group in Pennsylvania, issued an antislavery statement in 1688. An antislavery law was passed in Rhode Island in 1652, but it was often violated. The first formal abolition society, in Pennsylvania, was founded in 1775; Benjamin Franklin later became its president. By the 1780s, numerous antislavery letters appeared in American newspapers. Vermont forbid bondage in 1777, and all northern states had outlawed it in some form by 1804. Northern courts, starting with Massachusetts in 1783, uniformly ruled against bondage. There were sporadic and small black freedom groups in southern states. In the

1830s, the *Liberator* and other abolition newspapers began publication in the North, although few lasted very long. Thomas Jefferson, George Washington, and other national leaders spoke out against slavery. Religions were against it, claiming it was un-Christian. American abolitionists pointed proudly to England, which had eliminated the institution in a series of laws through 1833.

The problem with the anti-slavers, though, was that their numbers were small, preventing them from winning many elections and subsequently, having much power. They also lost the big battles in Congress, such as the 1820 Missouri Compromise. Then came the *Creole*. The emotionally battered leaders of the abolitionist movement suddenly had new life.

✣✣✣✣✣

CHAPTER SIX

In the Creole's Wake, the Abolitionists Storm Washington, DC

✣✣✣✣✣

Summer 1841

AT THE BEGINNING OF THE 1840s, the antislavery movement was losing its strength. A national backlash against antislavery supporters had followed Nat Turner's bloody revolt. America's antislavery societies had feuded with each other at the end of the 1830s and at the start of the 1840s. They had stumbled into, and allied themselves with, James G. Birney's grand scheme to form a third national political party, the Liberty Party, to halt forced labor. Many people paid attention to Birney. He was not an amateur politician trying to win an election to bring attention to the antislavery cause. He had worked in politics for years and was an astute political organizer. He started his career in government by working on Henry Clay's congressional campaign. A few years later he was elected to the Kentucky State Legislature as a member of the Democratic-Republican Party. Two years after that he moved to Madison County, Alabama, to run a large cotton plantation with several slaves he had purchased. Soon afterward, he won election to the Alabama State Legislature. Birney did not make much money on the plantation and lost a considerable amount of money gambling on horse races. He later sold the plantation and became a highly successful attorney in Alabama. He became fervently opposed to bondage after he left his plantation and became a member of the American Colonization Society. In 1835 he moved to Cincinnati and started the *Philanthropist* newspaper. He joined the antislavery society there but left after a dispute. His political wandering ended with the formation of the Liberty Party in 1840. He ran for president on its ticket that year.

The Liberty Party did not do well in any election. Its candidates, led by Birney for president, were crushed in the 1840 presidential and 1841 local elections. Birney had made one of the strongest appeals to wipe out slavery up to that time. He said that "slavery was impoverishing our country, breaking up our schools, effeminating our men, converting female amiableness into ungovernable fury, and bringing the judgment of God upon our churches, whose members and whose ministers live, and are supported in their ministry, by the fruits of unrighteous exaction."[1]

New York antislavery crusaders battled the antislavery champions in Massachusetts, who took on the crusaders in Pennsylvania. The factions could not even agree on a city in which to hold a national convention, so they postponed it. The editors of the different black freedom newspapers feuded with each other and called each other names. "The pseudo Abolition Society [of Massachusetts] must go down to the vile dust from whence it sprang," wrote one editor about another's party, "unwept, unhonored and unsung."[2]

Their fund-raising drives had gone dry. It was only the money of the wealthy Tappan brothers, Arthur and Lewis, from New York, and money the abolitionists secured on trips to England to visit antislavery friends there, that kept the movement afloat. The Tappan brothers had first started a dry goods business in Boston and then moved the New York City to start a silk importing business, which made them rich. They published the *New York Journal of Commerce*, a mainstream newspaper that featured strong antislavery editorials. The Panic of 1837 crushed their silk importing venture and nearly put their newspaper out of business. The wily businessmen, seeing huge financial growth in New York City, then founded the Mercantile Agency, a credit rating service that grew into a very successful enterprise (it was the predecessor of Dun and Bradstreet). By the early 1840s, the Tappans were back on their feet financially and devoted all their time and money to the antislavery cause, despite its problems. They were famous for their devotion to the cause and willingness to fund it, aiding groups, publications, and administrative agencies to stamp out bondage. They helped nearly everyone in the cause in some manner.

The plight of the abolitionists was so dire in the early 1840s that when one, Edward Southwick, asked John Quincy Adams what he should do when he reached a southern state to discuss captivity, Adams said abruptly, "Turn around and go home."[3]

The antislavery leaders had no luck in the courts either. Federal and state judges refused to make any affirmative rulings abolishing slavery and limited themselves to tiny sections of the issue. In the case of *Prigg v. Pennsylvania*, handed down in 1842, the US Supreme Court overturned Pennsylvania's efforts to protect runaways from slave catchers. It was yet another sign that the US government would always protect slavery.

In the fall of 1840, a group of reformers met at the Chardon Street Convention in Philadelphia for three days. Their plan was to rally the antislavery devotees, present a new liberation platform, attract press attention, and raise money. They failed at everything and were seen as a joke by the movement's leadership. "Madmen, mad women, men without beards, Dunkers, Muggletonians, Come-outers, Groaners, Agrarians, Seventh Day Baptists, Quakers, Abolitionists, Calvinists, Unitarians and Philosophers—all came successfully to the top, and seized their moment, if not their hour, wherein to chide, or pray, or preach or protests," charged *Liberator* editor William Lloyd Garrison.[4]

The battles within the antislavery crusade had made Garrison the head of the movement, but after the Chardon Street Convention failed, more than half of the members fled. A new and different part of the antislavery crusade's attack failed too. That was the well-rounded but not very strong argument that if slavery was not halted, it would divide the nation and cause a dreadful civil war.[5]

Finally, a number of abolitionists were not just fiery but downright mean-spirited. They showed no intentions of ever compromising with anyone on any aspect of the issue. Some of them, such as David Walker, excoriated not just politicians but all white people. "The whites have always been an unjust, jealous, unmerciful, avaricious, and blood thirsty set of beings, always seeking after power and authority . . . in fact, take them as a body and they are ten times more cruel, avaricious and unmerciful than [heathens] ever were . . . it is positively a fact that that they [take] vessel loads of men, women and children and in cold blood and through devilishness, throw them into the sea and murder them in all kinds of ways," he said in 1829, criticizing slave ships carrying blacks from Africa as well as transports taking the likes of Madison Washington by sea from Virginia to New Orleans.[6]

The movement had lost most of its power and its future looked bleak.[7]

But then, all of a sudden, antislavery societies found a new home, new leadership, and a new voice. All this originated from a very unlikely source, journalist Joshua Leavitt, who had arrived in Washington, DC, as a correspondent for a black freedom paper, the *Emancipator*, in the very hot summer of 1841. Leavitt, a former Congregationalist minister, was full of ideas and ambition. His vision was limitless and his dreams unbounded. He not only argued that bondage was immoral but that it was bad for the country. In the pamphlet "The Financial Power of Slavery," he argued that the South's reliance on forced labor was ruining the US economy.

He was in Washington not just to write stories against slavery but to work to bring about the institution's end. He had a two-level attack plan. The first part of his scheme was to convince numerous congressmen from the Whig Party, the more reform-minded of the two parties, to change their views. For years the Whigs had argued that slavery was an economic issue and was therefore needed to help southern planters maintain their businesses. Leavitt and others convinced many of them, in an intense lobbying campaign over that summer, that forced labor was not an economic issue but a moral one. "I regard it as the dictate of sound wisdom to make opposition to slavery the leading object of public policy. I feel so sure I am right that I cannot be satisfied without doing all in my power to bring the people to my view," Leavitt said. His friend Theodore Weld put the issue into rhapsodic language that could still be understood by all. "The business of abolitionists is with the heart of the nation rather than with its purse strings," he said in 1836. Weld also molded a powerful argument to refute planters' long-held contention that the Bible authorized slavery. Quoting scripture, Weld told his followers that the Bible holds "man stealing" as illegal everywhere and punishable by death. He said the authors of the Bible did not mean that "man stealing" meant kidnapping. It mean enslaving a man, which steals a man's spirit. Therefore, Weld said, the Bible actually stood firmly against slavery.[8]

Weld could write beautifully or he could be biting and cryptic. His rage showed in his words, including these: "Try [a slave], clank the chains in his ears and tell him they are for *him*. Give him an hour to prepare his wife and children for a life in slavery. Bid him make haste and get ready their necks for the yoke, and their wrists for the coffee chains. Then look at his pale lips and trembling knees and you have a nation's testimony against slavery."[9] Many leaders of the movement had come to agree with Weld by 1841.[10]

Leavitt and his acolytes convinced the Whigs, too, that many northern farms with paid workers earned higher profits than similarly sized southern slave plantations. One reason, he said, was that laborers in the South, in the misery of bondage, did as little work as possible for their owners. In framing slavery as a moral issue, Leavitt told the Whigs, they could appeal to everybody, not just businessmen. Leavitt told them too that under the antislavery umbrella, the Whig Party could fight for a hundred different causes. That way, he told party leaders, the Whigs could attract not only their regular supporters but hundreds of thousands of people opposed to bondage. It was the same argument Abraham Lincoln would make to the leaders of the brand-new Republican Party when he joined it in 1856, fifteen long years after Leavitt's exhortations to the Whigs in Washington, DC. Leavitt was reasonably successful. By the fall of 1841, dozens of Whig congressmen had joined his cause. "[The Congressmen are] determined to carry the war in upon the enemy—to shift the plan of campaign and attack slavery at every point," wrote one anti-bondage leader.[11]

Leavitt was just one of many antislavery leaders, and independents, who argued that paid workers produced far more than those working as forced laborers. They had been saying that since the 1770s, but their pleas fell on thousands of deaf ears.[12]

The second part of Leavitt's strategy was to establish a select committee of antislavery congressmen and to give them, and the movement, a physical presence—a national office—in Washington. There were plenty of lobbies in town, so why not one more?

As soon as he arrived in Washington, Leavitt had identified a loosely put-together group of House members who hated forced labor and wanted to end it. Some of the congressmen, such as William Slade and John Mattocks of Vermont, Seth Gates of New York, Sherlock Andrews of Ohio, Nathaniel Bordon of Massachusetts, and Francis James of Pennsylvania, had little power or influence. Weld told friends that Gates, who contributed a lot of money to the cause, was "as timid about speaking in public as [poet] John Greenleaf Whittier."

Mattocks led Leavitt to think that he would lead the group and dazzle all with his rhetoric. He said he was the biggest liberal in the country. But when pressed about his availability as a speaker, Mattocks backed away from Leavitt. He said, "Speeches? Never made one in my life."[13]

But there were two men who showed tremendous promise in Leavitt's eyes. They were Joshua Giddings, a young antislavery firebrand from Ohio, and former president John Quincy Adams. Physically, Adams was an aging shadow of his former self. "He is about five foot, eight inches in height very bald, with low forehead, and nothing about the shape of his head that indicates unusual talent, yet his physiognomy has something of an intellectual appearance. He is truly regarded as a venerable personage," said Giddings. The anti-bondage champions had not liked Adams during his single term as president but had warmed to him considerably when he so ably defended the mutineers of the *Amistad* and won an acquittal for them. Now, in 1841, he was a hero of the antislavery movement. Leavitt also saw, stacked in the halls and offices of Congress, huge canvas bags filled with "end bondage" petitions, containing more than four hundred thousand signatures and sent from all over America. They were lined up along the walls and piled up on top of one another.[14]

The petition campaign, coordinated by young Weld, had been a huge success. Weld's philosophy was that if someone signed a petition, they would see themselves as attached to the movement and remain a member forever. "Neglect no one. Follow the farmer to his field, the wood chopper to the forest," he told the petition distributors. "Hail the shop keeper behind his counter. . . . Let no frown deter, no repulses baffle. Explain, discuss, argue, persuade."[15]

Leavitt reasoned that if he could put together a committee of antislavery congressmen and support them in the press, he might find some success and strengthen the movement. Adams, he thought, would be the leader. The former president, who would go on to serve nearly eighteen years as a Massachusetts congressmen, was famous as a former chief executive, had lots of political friends, and wielded enormous influence. He had no trouble attracting press attention. He was also recognized as the man who best understood the forced labor situation. Giddings was a hardworking representative and willing to do the research, and cajoling, that Adams did not have time to do. Adams was in wobbly health, though. He was seventy-four, and age had started to slow him down. "[I am] with a shaking hand, a darkening eye, a drowsy brain, and with all my facilities dropping me one by one as the teeth are dropping from my head," he lamented. What could he do in his state for the crusade, he wondered. The answer was clear: "My conscience but presses me on; let me but die upon the breach."[16]

The rest, Leavitt assumed, would fall in line behind the leaders. That small handful of men would then attract more congressmen to their cause. In time the rest would swing over.

A group of congressmen was not enough, though. The movement needed a physical office, a central point where people could visit the abolitionist leaders, send their petitions, and mail money. The group found it in Ann Sprigg's boarding house at First Street and Pennsylvania Avenue, just a few blocks from the White House. She operated the boardinghouse to earn money after the death of her husband. When residents of the house walked out the front door, they looked directly at the massive Capitol and the sight energized them.

The group used rooms in the house as an office. Several congressmen even moved there. It was common for congressmen to live in boardinghouses during their stays in the capital, since there were no apartment houses then and few hotels. The antislavery crowd liked the arrangement, and as the days and weeks went by, the men brought in more and more luggage, clothing, and personal belongings. They set up bookshelves in their rooms and hung small paintings on the walls. The boardinghouse became a home away from home. Soon, more antislavery congressmen moved in, completely filling the house, with several of them doubled up in bedrooms.

Sprigg was at first terrified to have so many crusaders under her roof. She was afraid that other prospective boarders would shun her and that her business would suffer. Just the opposite happened. "This house is the only boarding house in Washington which has all of its rooms and beds occupied," said Weld.[17] The other boarders did not mind being surrounded by black freedom champions. "They treat brother Leavitt and myself exactly as though we were not fanatics," Weld laughed. "And we talk over with them at the table and elsewhere abolition just as we should at home."

To protect herself from potential trouble, Sprigg removed slaves her late husband had owned from the premises and replaced them with eight free black men. She could not bear the idea of abolitionists preaching to her slaves. She had friends who worked for the Underground Railroad transport them to northern states over the next few days. It was rumored, but never proven, that Sprigg was herself an agent in the Underground Railroad.

The boarders all had dinner together at a long table, presided over by Sprigg at the head of it. The men there, especially members of the select committee, often discussed the plans and programs of different organizations in the crusade. (A few years later, Congressman Abraham Lincoln from Illinois became a boarder.)

Weld, from upstate New York and one of the early tenants, was one of the premier antislavery rabble-rousers in the nation. The group housed at Sprigg's eagerly solicited Weld to be their chief lobbyist because of his fame in the crusade, his contacts, his skill as a writer and researcher, and his never-ending, till-the-last-breath hatred of bondage.

Weld was an easy man to notice. He was tall and thin, walked with a slouching gait, wore old shoes, and never brushed his coats. He let his hair grow too long and scraggly at times and rarely combed it. He had a high forehead, thin nose, sensitive mouth, and thick, bushy eyebrows. He possessed a rich, full voice. The abolitionist was usually seen as a strident and difficult person. "I hope that young man never gets married," one woman said of him when he was a bachelor. "He will break her heart."

Weld had other shortcomings. He was critical of himself and his friends. He had a short temper and often burst into tirades. He was absent-minded, impatient, and antisocial. Weld also felt guilty that he had a limited education and frequently fought with his wife, women's rights advocate Angelina Grimke.[18]

As a speaker, though, whether behind a lectern in an old fine hall in a city or on a wooden platform in some small, rural village meadow, illuminated by bright torches, he was powerful. He managed, in just a few moments, to capture the audience and take them with him on his antislavery ride. Before she met him, his Grimke said of his public appearances, "As soon as his countenance became animated by speaking, I found that it was one which portrayed the noblest qualities heart and head beaming with intelligence benevolence and frankness." Despite their marital disputes later, she always maintained her admiration for his speaking prowess.[19]

The abolitionists liked him, and that permitted him to achieve great things in the black freedom movement. Weld, the grandson of a minister, did not get his professional start in the anti-bondage drive though; he got it as a champion of labor. He studied with the great reformer Charles Finney at Hamilton College in New York. Shortly afterward, he became a nationally recognized advocate for manual labor and went on two- and three-week cross-country excursions, lecturing on the virtues of manual labor. He was then hired by Arthur and Lewis Tappan to be the spokesman for their Society for Promoting Manual Labor in Literary Institutions. He traveled more than ten thousand miles and gave 236 public addresses on labor. One of his stops was in Cincinnati, where he suddenly left his job and became a student at Lane Theological Seminary in 1833. Ohio was an antislavery hotbed in the 1830s, and Weld was converted to the cause. Along with other Lane students, he went to dozens of meetings and helped organize numerous rallies and protests. The students held heated public debates on forced labor over an eighteen-day period and pledged to free all the slaves in the area. The debates gained Weld an early standing as an abolitionist leader and earned him national publicity.[20]

The college, its board members furious, shut down the antislavery group. Eighty percent of them quit school. Weld left the educational institution too and became an agent of the American Anti-Slavery Society in New York. There he teamed up with James Birney and the Tappans, who were then becoming leaders against forced labor. He began to write essays against bondage in 1834, in addition to organizing rallies. One of his great early successes was to poke holes in the slave owners' longtime insistence that the Bible authorized slavery. "The advocates of slavery are always at their wit's end when they try to press the Bible into their service," he wrote.[21]

Weld also paid little attention to the planters' frequently repeated claim that since they were good to their slaves, no one should complain. "The slaves in the U.S. are treated with barbarous inhumanity. Over-worked, underfed, wretchedly clad and lodged. . . . insufficient sleep. . . . [Many have] front teeth broken off," he said in a book that was highly praised for its graphic and often brutal descriptions of bondage.[22]

He scorned southerners for their claims that slaves were property and not people and made his point in excruciatingly researched essays. He added that southerners could have forced laborers only because their narrow-minded state courts approved of the practice.[23]

Weld wrote fiery essays that read like stump speeches, and people enjoyed reading them. In 1835 he wrote Liberty Party leader Birney, "May God purify us, gird us for the conflict, give us faith and then we shall stand unscathed by the flames which burn around us."[24]

He was also good at defining the antislavery movement as a crusade that was looking for ardent true believers, not just tepid joiners. He wrote in 1836, "If your heart aches and bleeds, we want you. You will help us. But if you merely adopt our principals as dry theories, do leave us alone. We have millstones enough swinging at our necks already."[25]

He became editor of the *Emancipator*, married Grimke, and moved to New Jersey. There, Weld, Grimke, and her sister Sarah wrote *American Slavery as It Is: Testimony of a Thousand Witnesses*. This book and his work at the *Emancipator* brought him national fame as an anti-bondage leader and led Leavitt to hire him as the chief lobbyist for the Washington group.

Weld's reception at Sprigg's was similar to the reception he received in Congress and elsewhere in town. People were courteous to him. Even proslavery congressmen were gracious. Weld was pleased. After all, in New York, he had been seen as a rabble-rouser and feared for his safety. Here there was calm. He wrote to his wife, "I do not feel that I am in any special peril. I have been, you know, for months together in hourly danger of assassination. When I ran the danger, I felt it, but my duty not to heed it was plain and I never lost a moment's sleep on account of it. . . . We are not the agents God has chosen for the deliverance of the slave if fear of anything swerves us from duty."[26]

Weld's happiness in Washington was further enhanced when Giddings took him to the White House for the annual New Year's Day reception, where Weld met President Tyler and other Washington dignitaries. Giddings then escorted him to the home of John Quincy Adams, whom Weld had never met. On this visit, Weld learned that rumors that Adams and his wife fought with each other all the time were untrue. Weld also learned that Grimke was a second cousin to Adams through some complicated genealogy.

Weld had several key tasks as the chief antislavery lobbyist. One, not written down anywhere, was to try to preserve peace between the congressmen and others in the movement, who were always arguing over goals, methods, and leadership. Tempers were often frayed, and personal animosities got in the way of progress. "All hope of fusing into one the various divisions of the anti-slavery host seemed to me utterly vain. Deep, irreconcilable, personal animosities and repulsions . . . make such a cooperation impossible," Weld wrote.[27]

He himself was guilty of this. After his marriage to Grimke, he saw all those who criticized his wife as his enemy and the enemy of the movement. Such feuds lasted for years and slowed down the antislavery crusade. Weld was certainly not alone. Once the campaign started to gain publicity, in the late 1830s, southerners began to criticize it, and its leaders bristled at the attacks. Their thin skin and constant debates with critics hurt their cause.[28]

Weld possessed a sharp tongue, too, and no one was spared. His own sister-in-law fell victim to it in 1837. After one of her lectures, he said that she lacked "an interesting and happy manner of speaking; that your manner is monotonous and heavy and instead of increasing the power of truth uttered, weakens it." She did not agree.[29]

The next step was political organization. Giddings came up with a name for the group of congressmen: the Select Committee on Slavery. The congressmen acted as a well-oiled machine. One congressman would introduce a bill and serve as sponsor of the legislation while the others would back him and lobby for it. Another bill would be sponsored by another man. This way the work was divided up evenly. The lobbying group also showed the rest of Congress that the committee had not only had numbers but also organization and power—power that would grow over the years.[30]

The new committee had its problems, though, and each member realized it. The congressmen had their hands full with national matters and troubles in their home districts. They spent about half the year in Washington and half the year back home. The issues they wanted to attack—fugitive slave laws, laws on slave catchers, the annexation of Texas, the admission of Florida as a state, and the interstate forced labor trade—needed research. So they brought a dozen or so antislavery experts to Washington for months at a time to study the issues and work as lobbyists. They made a grand appeal to similarly minded societies for money and men.

Weld was pleased with the work Leavitt had done, admired the dedication of the congressmen, and more than anyone else saw the need for the Washington office. He was also impressed with the determination of Leavitt and the representatives to make antislavery a permanent plank on the Whig election platform. Weld was tired of the crusaders' unending desire to attach the antislavery fight to a third party, because third parties went nowhere in general elections. It was the classic political Don Quixote idea of charging the castle, knowing that no matter what you do, you will lose. "These men are in a position to do for the anti-slavery cause in a single speech more than our best lecturers can do in a year," Weld said of the men in the group. "The fact that men NOT sent to Congress by a third party [the Liberty Party] are ready to take such ground, will more than all things else open the eyes of abolitionists, who far and wide are getting so intoxicated with third parties and relaxing their grasp on the conscience of the South, and North."[31]

Weld was not alone. A half dozen influential leaders of the movement agreed with him, each telling friends that a third party based solely on the antislavery movement could not succeed. *Liberator* editor Garrison, who despised third parties and parties in general, told friends that America was better off with a smooth-running government than with third parties, which he said bred anarchy.[32]

Weld told friends and his new congressional colleagues that they faced an uphill struggle. "That slavery has begun its fall is plain . . . but its fall will be resisted by those who cling to it. . . . The end will be slow. Woe to the abolitionists, if they dream that their work is well-nigh done," he told all.[33]

In fact, Weld, hired as a buoyant champion for the movement, secretly and prophetically began to believe that only a war of some kind would end bondage. "Nothing short of miracles, constant miracles, and such as the world has never seen, can keep at bay the two great antagonistic forces. . . . They must drive against each other till one of them goes to the bottom. . . . It cannot be arrested. The end must come."[34]

The group needed money to pay Weld's salary, expenses, and rent for rooms in the boardinghouse, which people in the nation's capital soon started to call Abolition House. Without outside help, they simply decided to pay all the costs out of their own pockets, a considerable expense. They did not mind doing so.[35]

They all realized that the Select Committee on Slavery, as an ad hoc cabal, had no influence. Not only did it have no power, but it, and all the abolitionists, had become a punching bag for the entrenched southern political leaders. Southern congressmen and senators routinely referred to Adams as "mad." Senator William Preston of South Carolina said that the crusaders exercised "domineering influence" and were "calumniators" and charged that they had "impugned the honor of the South." He added that the leaders had "declared war on women and children, a war that spares no sex, respects no age, pities no suffering that consigns our hearts and altars to flames and blood." Senator Alfred Cuthbert of Georgia accused the abolitionists of trying to start a national race war.[36]

Local people shunned the crusaders too. When abolitionist James Thome tried to give a speech in Granville, Ohio, residents set fire to the schoolhouse where he was scheduled to speak. Amos Dresser was physically forced off the lecture platform in Marblehead, Massachusetts. At a Presbyterian church in Circleville, Ohio, where Weld was giving a speech, a gang of anti-abolitionists hurled dozens of rocks through church windows. One hit Weld in the head, cut open his forehead, and forced him to sit down. Shortly afterward, in Berlin, Ohio, Marius Robinson was dragged out of his house in the middle of the night, stripped, tarred and feathered, and chased into a nearby woods. John Alvord was pelted by dozens of eggs during one of his talks. Frederick Douglass was another victim of egg tossing at a talk in Harrisburg, Pennsylvania. "They came equipped with rotten eggs and brickbats, firecrackers and other missiles, and made use of them somewhat freely, breaking panes of glass and soiling the clothes of some who were struck by the eggs," said William Lloyd Garrison, who was on the speakers' platform with Douglass.[37] Meetings of numerous antislavery societies were broken up. Homes of leaders, including Lewis Tappan, were sacked. Some black churches were burned.[38]

In Washington, the select committee was just a happy handful of strident antislavery legislators to whom few people paid attention. They had no real power, even with Adams in their midst. The total number of people openly opposed to forced labor in the country was about two hundred thousand, and that was a padded number. They made up a small percentage of the 17 million American citizens—a rather powerless fighting force.[39] And, they moaned, that number had stalled, just like the movement. They had a lot of fire and steam, and smoke too, with the irascible, hardworking Giddings, often noted for his thatch of wild curly hair, among them. There was no attention being paid to them in Congress, in the mainstream press, or in the public. In the cold winter of 1841, for the crusaders, all seemed bleak. Yet they plunged on.

And then, with no warning whatsoever, the *Creole* was taken by Madison Washington and his fellow rebels as it sailed in the Atlantic. Abolition House suddenly had an enormous amount of ammunition for its cause. The *Creole* dispute gave the Select Committee on Slavery a significant boost in esteem and enormous publicity at a time when it desperately needed it. The mutiny electrified the population and gave new life to the bondage issue. Capital residents devoured it. Southerners wanted the ship and its slaves back. Northerners wanted the ship back, and many of them wanted the nineteen mutineers returned too. Others did not want the mutineers back on American soil but wanted them to be free to live in the Bahamas or wherever else they wished to reside. Feelings were mixed, and differences of opinion fueled long and loud debates. *Creole* talk dominated conversations in stores, homes, and taverns. The press had not published much on the antislavery movement since the *Amistad* trials. Then, without warning, there was a huge, headline-grabbing story. And unlike the *Amistad* litigation, it involved not foreigners but Americans from Richmond, just ninety miles south of the nation's capital. The slave ship takeover was the best thing that could possibly have happened to the Select Committee on Slavery and to the cause itself. Weld, torn away from his cubicle at the Library of Congress to hear the news, was euphoric, as were the other members of the committee, especially Adams and newcomer Giddings, who saw eternal promise in the *Creole* case.

Black leaders jumped to the defense of the *Creole* mutineers, and none was more forceful than Frederick Douglass, who saw the men as genuine heroes. They were not African heroes, he told his large crowds, but American heroes. "There are many Madison Washingtons and Nat Turners," he said later, "who would rise if northerners [would take] your feet from their necks and your sympathy and aid from their oppressors."[40]

Shortly after the *Creole* seizure news reached the nation's capital, the Select Committee on Slavery met to adopt a strategy to widen discussions of the mutiny in Congress itself. The major obstacle was that a gag rule forbade Congress from discussing the bondage issue. The select committee hated that rule, but it had been in place since 1836, at the constant insistence of southerners who did not want the heated issue debated by anyone. "For such a purpose, so wicked, so inexplicably mean, the Southern slaveholder calls [men] to lie down like whipped and trembling spaniels at their feet . . . our Republican spirits cannot subject to such condition. God did not make us, Jesus did not redeem us, for such vile and sinful uses," said abolitionist Gerrit Smith of the rule in 1838. He was one of its many northern critics.[41]

Its chief critic in 1842 was former president John Quincy Adams, who had frequently jousted with its defenders on the House floor. Adams had opposed the gag rule since the moment it was introduced in 1836. That morning Adams stood in the well of the House chamber and angrily said, "I hold the resolution to be a direct violation of the Constitution of the United States, of the rules of this House and the rights of my constituents."

He was booed by the southerners as he was nearly always booed. "I said it amid a perfect war whoop of 'Order!'" he joked as he recounted the incident in 1837.[42]

Adams had been concerned about the damage forced labor was doing to America for decades, but he ignored the issue for many years. As late as 1807, the Massachusetts politician did everything he could to avoid talking about slavery. That winter there was a heated debate on the floor of the Senate, where he sat in a large brown leather chair as one of the two senators from Massachusetts. Every leading speaker in the Senate, except Adams, took part in the debate. Determined to avoid the issue, he merely sat and listened. "I took, and intend to take, no part in the debates on this subject," he wrote with great finality in his diary that night.[43]

Twelve years later, in 1819, Adams sat at a meeting with President James Monroe. According to Adams, Monroe "said the feeling against slavery was so strong that shortly after the close of our revolution many persons had emancipated their slaves, but this had introduced a class of very dangerous people, the free blacks, who lived by pilfering and corrupted the slaves and produced such pernicious consequences that the [Virginia] legislature was obliged to prohibit further emancipation by law. The important thing now was to remove these free blacks."

In his diary, Adams did not object to anything Monroe had said at the meeting.[44]

Also in his diary, Adams criticized the Colonization Society, which was devoted to moving thousands of black people from America to Africa. "Their project of expurgating the United States from the free people of color at the public expense, by colonizing them in Africa is, so far as it is sincere and honest, upon a par with [the project] of going to the North Pole and traveling within the nutshell of the earth."[45]

A month later he sat in the office of Virginia judge George Hay and listened to him denounce the antislavery movement. "Hay said he had a great avidity for all papers concerning the project for abolishing the slave trade, a project which he believed would ultimately fail, which had already produced incomparably more mischief than good. And which he had no doubt would continue to be pernicious."

Adams voiced no objections to Hay's view.[46]

By 1819 Adams understood that the southern senators were playing a game, and he disliked it. "The slave-drivers, as usual, whenever this topic [slavery] is brought up, bluster and bully, talk of the white slaves of the eastern states, and the dissolution of the Union, and oceans of blood, and the Northern men, as usual, pocket all this hectoring, sit down in quiet and submit to the slave-scourging republicanism of the planters," he groaned.[47]

He had to admit, though, that the senators and congressmen from the pro-bondage states were splendid orators and good backroom arm-twisters; that is why they nearly always got their way. "The slaveholders are much more ably represented than the simple freemen. With the exception of Rufus King, there is not either in the House or Congress from the free states a member able to cope in powers of the mind with William Pinkney or James Barbour," he said, adding that no antislavery men in the House could argue with forced labor representatives such as John Randolph or Henry Clay.[48]

Adams had wished for an antislavery knight in shining armor in Congress for more than twenty years. Back in 1820, after listening to a long discussion about a Rufus King speech in the House, he noted,

THE SLAVEHOLDERS CANNOT HEAR [bondage speeches] without being seized with cramps. They call them seditious and inflammatory when their greatest real defect is their timidity. Never since human sentiments and human conduct were influenced by human speech was there a theme for eloquence like the free side of this question now before Congress. . . . If but one man could arise with a genius of comprehending, a heart capable of supporting and an utterance capable of communicating those eternal truths that belong to this question, to lay bare in all its nakedness that outrage upon the goodness of God, human slavery, now is the time and this is the occasion upon which such a man would perform the duties of an angel upon earth![49]

THE YEAR THAT HE APPLAUDED KING was the year the Missouri Compromised was passed to prevent hostilities over the forced labor question. Adams just shook his head about its adoption. "A law for perpetuating slavery in Missouri, and perhaps in North America has been smuggled through both houses of Congress," he wrote glumly in his diary. He hoped that a series of large organizations would be formed to end bondage, but he doubted they would. "The cement of common interest produced by slavery is stronger and more solid than that of unmingled freedom. The slave states have clung together in one unbroken phalanx," he said.[50]

That same winter he began a campaign to forbid statehood for any territories that sanctioned bondage, and he took yet another slap at those states in which slavery had been legalized or might be. "A state which should undertake to establish it would put herself out of the pale of the Union, and forfeit all the rights and privileges of the connection," he wrote.[51]

The crusade gained some newspaper coverage and was discussed throughout the Union. In the summer of 1835, Adams wrote in his diary, "There is a great fermentation about the subject of slavery at this time in all parts of the union. . . . Public opinion running everywhere stronger and stronger into democracy and popular supremacy contribute all to shake the fetters of servitude. The theory of the rights of man has taken deep root in the soil of civil society. It has allied itself with the feelings of humanity and the precepts of Christian benevolence. It has aligned itself with religious doctrines and religious fervor." He told friends that antislavery societies were organizing all over the country and getting themselves funded.[52]

He taunted southerners over their gag rule, which they thought would preserve bondage forever. Each and every year, he read a petition involving slavery to challenge the rule and anger southerners. One time he introduced a petition signed by twenty-two bondsmen and innocently asked if that was all right under the gag rule. Southerners opposed his motion with great fury, in a discussion and denunciation of Adams that lasted three full days. The Massachusetts congressman was vilified. He was threatened with censure and being kicked out of the House. One southern congressman even suggested that the House sergeant at arms arrest Adams and have him thrown into a nearby prison.

He warned all that the issue was dangerous. "We are in a state of profound peace and over pampered with prosperity, yet the elements of exterminating war seem to be in vehement formation, and one can scarcely see to where it will lead," he said on August 11, 1835. He had been complaining about slavery for years, but his discomfort with the institution started to heat up that summer. Slaves had been lynched in Mississippi, and there had been riots by abolitionists in Baltimore. In Charleston, anti-bondage pamphlets were taken out of the US mail to make certain that no one in South Carolina read them.[53]

A year later, in 1836, Adams warned Congress that slavery could lead to a war between its supporters and enemies. In early March 1842, he told Giddings that the question might lead to bloodshed. "In the case of a servile war, involving the free states of the Union, the question of emancipation would necessarily be the issue of the conflict. All war must end in peace, and peace must be concluded by treaty. Of such a treaty, partial or universal emancipation would probably form an essential, and the power of the President and Senate of the United States over it would be coextensive with the war," he said.[54]

He stated further, "From the instant that your slave holding states become the instrument of war, civil, servile or foreign, from that moment the war powers of the Constitution extend to interference with slavery."[55]

In 1837 antislavery representative William Slade offered a petition that he knew would be turned down because of the gag rule, but James K. Polk, future president and at the time Speaker of the House, made an error in parliamentary procedure that allowed Slade to speak about his petition. Adams was delighted. "The whole herd were in combustion," he chuckled at the slavers. "Polk tried to stop him half a dozen times, but was forced to let Slade go on. The slavers were at their wit's end," Adams wrote in his diary.[56]

His delight in mocking the forced labor empire was often tempered by his sadness over the troubles brought to the nation by the issue. In November 1837, he was saddened by an attack on the printing presses of abolitionist publisher Elijah Lovejoy of Alton, Illinois. He called the attack "the most atrocious case of rioting which ever disgraced this country" and lamented to friends that the slavers had destroyed Lovejoy's presses during three previous attacks on his office. This time the assault was fatal. "The mob assembled in the night, sur-rounded the warehouse and demanded that the press should be delivered up to them. It was refused. They assailed the house with musketry, forced their way into it, set a fire on the roof of the building, shot Lovejoy dead, wounded several others till the press was delivered up to them, which they broke into pieces and threw into the river."[57]

By 1842 his most recent engagement on the gag rule had been during the previous spring's legislative session. He had defended the antislavery move-ment in a two-week-long heated debate over the gag rule. As always, he lost, but this time the discussion was vicious. Adams insisted that the root of the debate was not pro- or antislavery feelings but southerners' hatred for north-erners. Representative Kenneth Rayner of North Carolina went into a loving description of Sir Walter Scott's novels and said that the wealthy cavaliers who ran the vast plantations of the South would team up with tens of thousands of non-slaveholding "mountain men" to battle the northerners. He became angrier and angrier as he spoke. At the end of his short speech, he threatened that northerners would one day find themselves swimming in "a sea of graves" if they continued in their campaign to end bondage.

A *National Intelligencer* reporter was fed up with the viciousness of the gag debate and wrote that the House had become a "bear garden." Other reporters said that the House was sick of Adams. One wrote that he "causes more mischief than ten men."

Adams had become the punching bag for the antislavery movement. He was roundly criticized no matter what he did. In 1842 Representative Thomas Marshall of Kentucky hurled a volley of epithets at him. They were "a flaming preamble charging me in substance with subordination of perjury and high treason and resolutions that the House might well expel me," said Adams.

At the end of the speech, Marshall invited Adams to visit a southern state.

"To be lynched," said Adams.

"Very likely," answered a scowling Marshall."[58]

Tyler allies discounted any talk against forced labor and told those in favor of getting rid of the gag rule that the president not only supported the gag rule but also envisioned a plantation-style United States that was constantly expanding as an agrarian nation.[59]

Nobody had ever broken the gag rule, but the *Creole* troubles inspired Weld, Giddings, and Adams to try it in the early winter of 1842. They agreed to in-troduce a set of resolutions concerning the *Creole* and slavery. The uproar the resolutions would cause would open the door in both houses of Congress for loud and earnest debates on both the slave ship and the slavery issue in general.

The resolutions were written primarily by Weld, with help from Giddings, but Adams, the old leonine wizard from Massachusetts, jumped the gun on everybody.

He had dinner with the members of the select committee the night before a January session of Congress and worked himself into a frenzy debating slavery and politics with them. His fists were clenched and his jaw set in anger as he railed about the issue and his Senate colleagues. "The old patriarch talked with as much energy and zeal as a Methodist at a camp meeting. Remarkable man!" wrote Weld. Later Weld told his wife that "the old nestor . . . has smitten the whole host with . . . discomfiture."[60]

Adams would start his new campaign the very next day, he told the committee, because a member had asked the House to remove him from his seat on the Foreign Relations Committee because of his feelings on slavery. It was a door-opener. He could refute the suggestion and at the same time, since it involved the subject of bondage, launch into the first-ever denunciation of it in Congress. It was the perfect opportunity, and he was the perfect man to seize it.

Overnight, Adams changed his mind. He looked up at the House gallery the next morning and saw Weld and his friends sitting there. He noted their smiling faces as he rifled through the large stack of papers, documents, letters, and notes piled up on his wide wooden desk. Adams was five feet seven, 175 pounds, with a shining, nearly completely bald head. He looked like a lion perched behind a thick jungle bush waiting for his prey. "As he sat in the middle of the House, with his immense petition rolled around a kind of windlass to sustain it, his excitement was manifested in the flaming redness of his bald head which acted as a chronometer of his audience," said Julie Gardiner, who sat in the packed gallery that day. (She would marry John Tyler in 1844, two years after his first wife died.)[61]

Adams did not want to talk about being dismissed from the Foreign Relations Committee, though. He had a scheme, and this plan brought a little smile to his lips as he unveiled it. The congressman casually pulled a small slip of paper from the middle of a large stack of documents on his desk and peered at it intensely.

He had in his hands a petition from forty-six people in the farm community of tiny Haverhill, Massachusetts, who demanded the dissolution of the United States over the bondage issue. Next he produced a petition from the residents of a small town in Pennsylvania. They complained that Congress, in protecting slavery in the Creole mutiny, was going to take the United States into a third war with Great Britain. Adams asked Congress to consider both petitions, just as it had considered hundreds of petitions from citizens across the land for years.

Adams rose from his seat, raised his hand, looked about the House chamber, and with great haste said he was against the destruction of the country suggested by the good citizens of Haverhill. He had always told citizens angry about the issue that the greater good was always the whole, united America, He did not want it cut in half or, as many suggested, three or four different countries. He was against that, but he demanded that the issue be debated, despite its reference to slavery. As he knew he would, Adams created a firestorm, a "snarling debate," he wrote in his diary, on the floor of the House. He was constantly interrupted by congressmen, northern as well as southern, Democrats as well as Whigs, who demanded that he sit down and be quiet. "It was a hot debate," he wrote at home that night. "The gag rule! The gag rule!" He blithely ignored them all. "If before I get through every slaveholder, slave trader and slave breeder on this floor does not get materials for bitter reflection it shall be no fault of mine!" he snapped at them, and he kept on talking.[62]

Looking down at him from the packed gallery, watching him intently, was a very confused Weld. He and his fellow black freedom advocates, sitting among hundreds of spectators, were thrilled, however, when the former president began bellowing. "He lifted up his voice like a trumpet, and howled under his dissecting knife . . . a perfect uproar like Babel would burst forth every two or three minutes," said Weld, noting his enemies' displeasure as they squirmed in their seats.

Whig leaders hated Adams for his diabolic speech about the Haverhill petition and for breaking the gag rule. The Whigs, unfortunately for them, were equally divided among the pro- and antislavery states, by regions North and South. They had to hold their two selves together, a feeling similar to Abraham Lincoln's statement of seventeen years later that "a house divided against itself cannot stand." The southerners needed the northerners, and the northerners needed the southerners. Nobody needed the irascible old John Quincy Adams.

He was in the fight of his life. "I am in the midst of that fiery ordeal and day and night are absorbed in the struggle to avert my ruin,"[63] he said.

So the southerners decided to get rid of the very difficult Adams once and for all.

They were going to ignore what he had to say about bondage and the red-hot *Creole* case, which he had been talking about since the November takeover of the vessel, because that was not an argument they could use to harm him legislatively in the winter of 1841—it was too public and too incendiary. No, a squabble on house rules and the gag rule would suffice. In just a few days, they could rid themselves of the blustery old windbag from New England forever.[64]

Representative George Washington Hopkins of Virginia leaped to his feet and asked the speaker if the members could simply hold Adams's resolutions up in the air and set fire to them. He was turned down. Also incensed at Adams's petitions, Thomas Gilmer of Virginia offered a resolution to censure Adams and kick him out of the House of Representatives.

"Gilmer consumed nearly two hours in his long meditated and bitterly rancorous speech against me," wrote a heated-up Adams in his diary that night.[65]

Dozens of others roared their approval that afternoon. In short order, caucuses were held, and a vote to put Adams on trial in the House carried easily, 118–75. Amid all the debates, Thomas Marshall said Adams was guilty of "perjury and treason." One of the resolutions passed by Congress not only called for his ouster but reminded him that he should be grateful that this was the only punishment his foes sought. Virginia's Henry Wise, who hated Adams, called the Massachusetts congressman "a white-haired hypocrite" and compared him to Benedict Arnold and Aaron Burr. The fanatical Wise accused him of trampling on history and wailed that he "preyed upon the dead like the vampire."[66]

Just a few months earlier, in June 1841, Wise had delivered a blistering six-hour attack on the black freedom leaders and Adams in the House. He had started each sentence with a loud clatter or words and then lowered his body and head farther and farther until, bent at the waist, he was prone and lying his desk. As his body dropped lower and lower, for dramatic effect, he dropped the tone of his voice down to a loud whisper. In that whisper he continually chanted, "abolition . . . abolition . . . abolition . . ."

"He represented me as a fiend, the inspirer and leader of all abolition," said a startled Adams in self-defense.[67]

The cabal of politicians allied against Adams in the winter of 1842, the year of the *Creole*, was led by Marshall. Adams was nervous as he stared at the list of congressmen at home and counted up the votes prior to his trial. He added up one hundred congressmen who owned slaves and would definitely vote against him. There were forty who represented the free states, but "they were in the league of slavery and mock democracy," according to the Massachusetts congressman, "and would break me on the wheel if their votes could turn it round." So what did he have left? About 120 free state supporters, but he knew that many of them simply did not like him and would take this opportunity avenge some slight of his over the years. The vote to boot him would be close.[68]

Marshall, whom the old man despised, was chosen because he was a Whig, like Adams, and because he was the nephew of legendary US Supreme Court chief justice John Marshall, whose genius would surely rub off on young Tom, who had just turned forty. The Whigs were so mad at Adams that they did not offer him any support at all. He had to rely on his new, young, trusted friends in the antislavery movement, the men of Abolition House. They met with him at his Washington home the night before the first day of the House censure and expulsion trial. They arrived one by one, shivering a bit in the winter air, even though most had large overcoats and scarves wrapped around their necks and top hats tugged down on their foreheads to retain heat on the chilly night. Adams's wife, Louisa, welcomed each of them as they trudged through the door into the center hall. Adams had not expected them, so he busied himself getting chairs into the living room and straightening it up. Louisa rushed to the rear of the house to make tea and coffee. Hastily prepared cakes were brought out on a tray. As soon as they sat down and stretched their legs, the men were all business. They began talking about the House trial, with references to bondage and the *Creole* problem. They talked and talked. They were there for two reasons. First, they wanted to help Adams plot his strategy and offer some talking points. Second, they wanted him to know that although everybody seemed against him, they were in his corner and would cheer him on every day of the trial and be there for emotional and moral support as long as he needed them. Then Adams rose. "The aged statesman listened attentively, but for a time was unable to reply, laboring under great apparent feeling. At length he stated that the voice of [our] friendship was so unusual that he could not express his gratitude," wrote Giddings.[69]

Weld, who was keeping track of the news about the imprisoned mutineers of the *Creole*, offered to do all the research and writing of briefs that Adams would require for his defense in the next few days. A smiling Adams was happy to have the assistance, especially from Weld, a man he was growing to like. This latest forced labor flap, over the *Creole*, had done much to cement their friendship, and he was glad to have him at his side as he played Daniel walking into a congressional lion's den of slaveholders.

In his opening statement, Marshall, a House rookie who sported a beard, stood behind his desk. Surveying the gallery with his eyes, he vilified Adams, telling his fellow congressmen that the old man was guilty of "high crimes" and "treason" and that with the residents of tiny Haverhill he was trying to destroy the government of the United States and wreck the Constitution. Congressmen cheered him on, and Adams's few abolitionist supporters were "depressed," according to Giddings.

The venerable old representative from Massachusetts then rose and looked about the room. From where he sat, he had a good view of the speaker's chair, high up over the assemblage in front of a far wall, surrounded by flags. He could see the Democrats, all sharp-eyed and angry, many with their arms folded. He could see his fellow Whigs, most of them angry too. His eyes peered up at the gallery and saw that it was jammed with spectators, practically shoulder to shoulder. Some in the front row leaned forward, resting their arms on the rail. He noticed a good hundred people standing against the wall behind the back row of the gallery to watch the duel of words about to unfold. The dark brown colors of the desks and chairs struck him as making the chamber quite formal. It had been a place where history had been made often and, he surmised, would be made again that day. After a moment or two, he pointed to the clerk and asked him to read the Declaration of Independence. The stunned clerk had to get a copy and then stretched it out on his desk. He began to read it. "When in the course of human events . . ." he started and then stopped.

"Proceed! Proceed!" Adams said, and the clerk went on. No one in the House understood where Adams was going.

He looked around the House chamber. The Democrats seemed surprised by the reading of the declaration, which had been signed by Adams's father and written by his father's good friend Thomas Jefferson. The Whigs were puzzled too, because the turn to history was not what they expected. They expected the weather-beaten old man to hurl fire and brimstone at his attackers. This was a bit of a shock.

The clerk continued. "Whenever any form of government becomes destructive of these ends, it is the right of the people to alter or abolish it."

"Go on," said Adams.

"It is their right, it is their duty, to throw off such government."

"Stop!" said Adams.

He looked around the enormous hall and paused for a long moment to give everybody there a chance to remember who he was. He was John Quincy Adams, the former president of the United States, and, just as importantly, a man whose father had not only been president himself but had taken part in the writing of the Declaration of Independence and had participated in the Revolution. There, in front of them, in this balding old man in his seventies and the ghost of his father, was a connection to the war, the founding of the republic, the writing of the Constitution, and everything that Americans held sacred. He was not only the center of Congress that moment but the center of the universe.

Then Adams began to speak, telling the crowd that the issue was not the devout group of residents in Haverhill and their concerns about bondage. No, he said, it was not four dozen men and women in Haverhill who were tearing apart the government. It was the slaveholders who were wrecking America. "There is a concerted system and purpose to destroy all the principles of civil liberty in the free states," he said. He warned that if petitions were disallowed, then habeas corpus would be next, and then trial by jury, freedom of the post office, freedom of speech, and freedom of the press. He said he did not want the dissolution of the Union but begged for a better Union.

He cut into every aspect of life in the southern states, charging that the North was superior to the South in all respects. He said South Carolinians had wantonly kidnapped freed blacks in the North and enslaved them on southern plantations. He argued that northern schools were better than those in the South and that northern industry, commerce, and shipping were far better than those industries in southern states. He blasted the "miserable highways, deserted plantations, dilapidated dwellings and general poverty" of Virginia and once again accused slaveholders of trying to start a war with England over the *Creole*.[70]

He spoke as a statesman, not an angry congressman, very unlike the opposition's Marshall. There was "a calm fearlessness and majesty that furnished the highest illustration of the moral sublime that I ever witnessed in a popular secular assembly," said Weld with great pride. Giddings added, "His manner was calm and self-possessed; his voice clear and firm; his words measured, his venerable form erect under the weight of more than seventy years. There he stood, confronting a power which for more than half a century had controlled the councils of the nation."

The first of the slave horde to attack Adams was Wise of Virginia. His assault was all bluster and chaos, and he did not even mention the Haverhill petitions. He accused Adams of a long string of political attacks on others, of stirring up the northerners against the southerners, and said that his involvement in the *Creole* affair showed that he really did want the United States to become involved in a war with Great Britain. Wise, getting more and more overheated, even accused Adams of being a British agent. He made little sense and drew little applause when he finished his speech.

The House took a weekend break from the trial, and Adams spent it preparing what would be a withering attack on both Wise and Marshall on Monday. The weekend also gave the congressmen hell-bent on crucifying Adams time to reflect on their stands, and they did. The great planter wall began to crack. It cracked only slightly, but it cracked.

The trial resumed on Monday. All the seats on the House floor were filled, and the gallery was packed. Hundreds of spectators and reporters crammed the spaces along the back wall of the chamber and the gallery. Hundreds more were jammed into the hallways leading to the gallery doors. More than a dozen senators left their offices and went to the House to listen to Adams speak, forcing their way through the thick crowds to do so.

At first Adams relied on soaring rhetoric, appealing to those in the crowd and especially those in the press, whom he hoped would carry his message to the country. "For half an hour he breasted the torrent of excitement with a calm fearlessness and majesty that furnished the highest illustration of the moral sublime that I ever witnessed in a popular secular assembly," wrote Weld with glee.[71]

After that preamble, Adams dropped his dignified air and lit into both Wise and Marshall with the passion of a knight, lance in hand, rushing down the list in a medieval joust. He said the House had to be reminded that just a short time earlier, Wise had come into it "with his hands and face dripping with the blood of murder, the blotches of which were yet hanging upon him," referencing the dreadful duel in which Wise had foolishly agreed to participate as the second to Representative William Graves of Kentucky, who had shot and killed Representative Jonathan Cilley of Maine. Neither man had a genuine grudge against the other but wound up in the duel over a supposed insult to a third man. They found themselves on a familiar dueling field in Bladensburg,

Maryland, with percussion rifles in their hands. It was an awful morning. The two men raised their rifles and fired. They both missed. The pair insisted on another confrontation and both missed again. Then there was the third, and fatal, shooting. Graves aimed carefully and hit Cilley in the chest. The Maine congressman lurched forward, one hand holding his chest and the other hand on his knee for support, and then toppled over dead. Wise had then intemperately published an account of the duel. (He had engaged in a duel himself in 1832.) The capital and the nation were in an uproar over the duel. How could two congressmen who did not even share a dispute fire at each other, with one killed, in that ugly ancient battle of honor. People immediately compared it to the murder of Alexander Hamilton by Aaron Burr in 1804.

Giddings was sitting close to Wise at the time of the Adams speech and watched him during the duel accusation. He looked "tortured," wrote Giddings.[72]

Adams then tore into Thomas Marshall, working hard to keep the intellectually rather dull Marshall quite separate from his brilliant uncle. "The Constitution of the United States says what treason is and it is not for him or his puny mind, to define what high treason is and to confound it with what I have done." He added disdainfully that Marshall needed to go to "some law school" to find out what the law was. "My last missile upon Marshall was an exquisite blast upon bondage by Marshall himself in his letters to the *Commonwealth* newspaper. He writhes under it in agony. . . . Marshall was sprawling in his own compost," said Adams in his diary.[73]

Marshall stood thirty feet from Giddings during Adams's accusations, his arms folded across his chest, tightening as the old man attacked him. "His cheeks were pale with emotion, and the whole contour of his face gave an expression of deep mortification," wrote Giddings. Marshall was humiliated

A few days later, Marshall walked into the House chamber as Adams was attacking another victim, this one a congressman from Pennsylvania. Marshall shrugged and said to a friend, "Well, if he has fallen into Adams' hands, all I can say is, may God have mercy on his soul."[74]

That night Adams was visited by Weld. Adams was gleeful, certain that he was now winning the debate and confident that the opposition would soon give in. "He was fresh and elastic," said Weld, "like a boy." Adams was boasting. "I am ready for another heat!" He then talked for an hour about the attack he planned for the following day. He did so, said Weld, "in a voice loud enough to be heard by a large audience. Wonderful man!"

In addition to his hatred of slaveholders, Adams was beside himself with anger over the coverage of his trial in the newspapers of the nation's capital. "I charge the newspapers of this city with injustice to me, the *Globe* being daily filled with abuses and invective to me while I am here on my trial, and the reporters of the *Intelligencer* suppressing the most essential part of my defense," he wrote later.[75]

He was too quick to criticize the press, though, because the majority of the newspapers made him look good in his duels with the slaveholders in the House chamber. Weld brought him copies of all the newspaper in town the next day. "Mr. Weld was here this morning with a cheering report with the impression of my defense on Thursday, Friday and Saturday upon the current of popular opinion," he said, a big smile on his face.[76]

The tide had turned. Representative Joseph Underwood of Kentucky said that if Adams was guilty of treason, he should be hanged, and he sneered that was not about to happen. John Botts of Virginia, who hated all antislavery supporters, admitted on the floor that Adams was really not a true abolitionist. Thomas Arnold of Tennessee thought it was pointless to even debate the gag rule because the rule had seen its day. "[You] might as well attempt to dam up the waters of the Niagara as attempt to stay the right of petition," he said. A dozen or so other slaveholders were mild in their criticism of the former president as he talked on through the afternoon. The drama of the debate seemed over, and many of the representatives stared off into space as Adams discussed the case against him.[77]

The next day, following discussion with numerous congressmen about the gag rule and the *Creole*, Wise and Marshall returned to the House chamber humbled men, a little wary of backlash from constituents now sympathetic to the old man. Marshall said that he had never intended to charge Adams with treason and knew him as a patriot. He accused Wise of trying to get the "patriot" booted out of Congress. Adams rose and told all that the debate had just begun and that he intended to keep it going for three weeks or more because he needed time to gather hundreds of documents for his defense. The debate went on for one more very long week. In the middle of it, Adams rose and waved a letter he had received. It contained an assassination threat, including a song called "Stop the Music of John Quincy Adams." The death threat and the sympathy he then received solidified his support not just from the Whigs but from Democrats and even many southerners. On February 2, an exhausted Thomas Gilmer, who had written the resolution calling for censure, agreed to withdraw it if Adams agreed to withdraw the Haverhill petition. Adams did and the great House trial was over. The Massachusetts congressman was the clear winner.

The thoroughly defeated Wise said that Adams was "the acutest, the astutest, the archest enemy of southern slavery that ever existed." After that session of Congress, the battered Marshall, who had also feuded with Henry Clay, retired from public life.[78]

The crusaders were effusive in their praise of Adams. Giddings wrote,

HE HAS MADE THE ENTIRE SOUTH TREMBLE before him. I have with my own eyes seen the slaveholders shake and tremble through every nerve and joint while he arrayed before them their political and moral sins. The power of his eloquence has exceeded any conception which I have heretofore had of the force of words of logic. He has, in my opinion, opened a new era in political history I entertain not the least doubt that a moral revolution in this nation will take its date from this session of Congress. I am confident that the charm of the slave power is now broken.

THE SOUTHERNERS WERE CRESTFALLEN. Four southerners on the Foreign Relations Committee, which Adams chaired, quit their posts the day after he was exonerated.

After the trial, Adams, Giddings, Weld, and the other abolitionist leaders increased their talk on the *Creole* and the need for England to free the muti-neers. Giddings and Adams shared the same view of the African Americans on the *Creole*—that they were protected by natural laws. Adams had argued in the *Amistad* case, and other antislavery champions had argued in other cases, that while states control the law within their borders and the federal government between the states, nobody controlled the law on the high seas, in international waters. There, Giddings said, and Adams had always said, African Americans were free men and women.

Many in the government agreed with them, as they had agreed about the *Amistad*. "They became free men when taken by voluntary action of the owners beyond the jurisdiction of the slave states," Charles Sumner, later a senator from Massachusetts, said emphatically. In fact, the court ruling had added that since the men on the ship were free, they had the legal right to kill the crew members trying to put or keep them in bondage, a strong point in the decision to free the men. Adams, after his trial, asked the same question about the *Creole* and reminded his critics that the *Amistad* was all about Africans from halfway around the world who had been kidnapped and the *Creole* was about Americans in slavery from right across the Potomac River who had mutinied to defend their rights. The *Creole* case, he told all, was legally far stronger.[79]

Ironically, just twelve days after the *Creole* was seized, Adams received a Bible signed by the three leaders of the thirty-five mutineers on the *Amistad*. A good omen or dumb luck?[80]

One factor in the *Amistad* case was justice. "What is justice and was this justice?" Adams had asked the Supreme Court in 1839. Now, in the winter of 1842, he sought justice for the men and women on the *Creole*.[81]

The arguments of Adams, Giddings, Weld and other antislavery leaders won over many northerners but failed to impress southerners. The southerners were adamant in their belief that the 2.5 million people in bondage in the United States at the time of the *Creole* mutiny had to be kept in bondage. Senator James Hammond of South Carolina wailed that they were "the greatest of all the great blessings which a kind Providence has bestowed upon our glorious region."[82] Millions of southerners agreed with him.

The Strained Start of the Webster–Ashburton Talks

Lord Ashburton and his friend Daniel Webster had problems when they sat down to start their negotiations over the *Creole* and the Canada–Maine boundary line. First, the British did not want to enrage the US government by freeing all the slaves from the *Creole* and ignoring noble gestures on the part of Tyler and Webster to get the slaves back to, as they contended, their rightful owners. Tyler insisted that the issue was not just escaped slaves but murder and attempted murder, which surely, he told Lord Ashburton, were separate, criminal charges and put Washington and his colleagues into a special category.[83]

At the same time, the British did not want to anger the South through the freeing of the 116 non-mutineers and a court ruling on the nineteen mutineers.

England had extensive and important trade with the southern states. They provided not only cotton but numerous other commodities that Great Britain did not want cut off; it could not survive without them. So the English walked a fine line, constantly beating their chests over their antislavery stance while at the same time looking terribly concerned over how to handle the *Creole* affair without offending the South and its millions of residents.

Part of the British diplomatic attack was its time-honored policy of deference. British diplomats treated all with great respect, always acknowledging their claims in any argument. This philosophical approach worked in Europe, but since the Revolution and the War of 1812, their negotiators found it difficult to use in America. Frederick Douglass mocked them for their haughty attitude toward Americans. Speaking of the US position on the *Creole* years later, he said, "The British government treated it with the utmost deference—for they are a very deferential people. They talked about honorable and right honorable, lords, dukes and going through all of their Parliamentary titles, and sent Lord Ashburton over to this country to tell us, of course, that that very deferential people could not send back 'the niggers.' So, Uncle Sam could not get them and he has not got them yet."[84]

While Lord Ashburton and his superiors back home worried about that, the southern leaders discussed similar concerns. The southern states were agrarian, with few factories, and needed all the manufacturing imports they could get from England. They did receive a number of implements from northern states but had a heavy and quite busy trade with British companies and British ships. They could not let the *Creole* issue blow up their long-standing, necessary, and profitable trading relations. All had to be careful. They were dancing on glass.

Northern abolitionists faced a similar problem. They howled bitterly that Washington and his mutineers had to be let go and given their freedom in the Bahamas, and that any and all refugees in the Bahamas or any other foreign country had to be awarded freedom. At the same time they argued that England had no right to interfere with American shipping and was overplaying its hand in maritime negotiations. They were against England for stepping into an American problem but proud of England for doing so. It was a delicate and, at the start of the Webster–Ashburton talks, a seemingly unsolvable problem.

❦❦❦❦❦❦

The Crucifixion of Joshua Giddings, the Abolitionists, and Anybody Who Supported the Mutineers aboard the Creole

❦❦❦❦❦❦

Winter 1842

FIRST-YEAR CONGRESSMAN JOSHUA GIDDINGS, an antislavery champion from Ohio—a fashionable dresser whose head was topped by wild curly hair that always caught people's attention—began his first term in a lustrous manner when he boarded a train to Washington City to take his place in the House of Representatives. He found, to his delight, that he was seated across from Davy Crockett Jr., the teenage son of the famous former congressman, Indian fighter, and the hero of the Alamo, where he died in 1836 in a battle for Texas's independence from Mexico. The younger Crockett was very friendly and amiable toward Giddings and the others seated nearby. Everybody liked him. He did not resemble his dashing, already legendary father at all. "The son appears to possess few of the leading traits of his father. He seemed to be a modest, unassuming man," wrote a disappointed Giddings in his diary a few days later.

The train, carrying several other midwestern congressmen and merchants, rumbled through Maryland, making a clackety-clack sound as it chugged along, rolling slightly. The passengers could look out the windows at meadows, forests, rivers, lakes, ponds, farms, mountains, waterfalls, lone residences in the middle of low-slung hills, silos, herds of cattle, wild rabbits, and farmers walking behind animals over hard, frozen ground in a December land often chilled by snowfalls. There were villages of a few small buildings stuck at intersections of dirt highways, their roofs jutting upward into a clear sky. There were tiny towns and large cities, such as bustling Baltimore. The train cut through land by day and by night, with lamps and torches illuminating a blackened world. Giddings and the others slept at night as the train clattered through the countryside. They woke in early morning as the sun slowly rose over the forests outside the train windows.

The train pulled into the Washington station just after 7:00 p.m. The train station was a busy, hurly-burly world full of clamor, loud noises, and people dressed in all kinds of clothing rushing this way and that, all of which Giddings noted with disgust in his diary: "The moment we stopped we were surrounded on every side with runners, porters, hackmen and servants—one calling to know if you would go to Gadsby's [hotel], another if you would go to Brown's, another if you would take a hack, etc. They are a source of great annoyance which the police ought to prevent."

His annoyance with Washington was compounded a few days later, December 3, 1838, the day he was sworn in as a congressman, when he saw colleagues he had idolized when reading about them in newspapers back in Ohio. "I confess I was disappointed in their appearance. There was not that dignity of carriage about them which I expected," he wrote.[1]

At first, President Martin Van Buren did not impress him either. "He is small of stature, has a low forehead, is very bald with eyes sunk far back in his head. His general appearance is not prepossessing. Indeed, to a casual observer he would present the appearance of a man of ordinary character; nor do you see any evidence of extraordinary intellect," Giddings said. Then he reassessed the president: "[When] you look him square in the face [though] you are at once impressed with his shrewdness and intelligence. He converses fluidly and rapidly."

A few weeks later, following the president's annual New Year's Day reception, Giddings went to the home of former president John Quincy Adams, who was also hosting a holiday reception. Giddings could not control himself in his admiration of Adams, who was apparently one of his lifelong idols. "His name will hereafter fill the brightest page of American history," he wrote in his diary. "His countenance glowed with benevolence and kindness . . . a specimen of greatness."[2]

Just a few days later, on December 11, the House of Representatives passed yet another gag resolution, forbidding any discussion of bondage on the House floor. It carried, 126–73, so quickly that Giddings did not get a chance to understand what it meant. Giddings did notice the bravura character of John Quincy Adams that day. The former president rose to object to something, and the speaker asked him to stop talking because he was out of order and knew he was out of order. He kept talking anyway, moving his head from side to side and waving his arms, peering up at the ceiling and the heavens at the same time, speaking louder as the speaker asked him to sit down in ever louder terms. "The uproar increased and the Speaker, rising from his chair in great agitation and excitement, with stentorian voice, called on the House to assist him in enforcing the rules," wrote Giddings with great delight, like a spectator at a raucous boxing match.

Suddenly, Adams closed his mouth, pulled the sides of his jacket to his waist, and plopped down in his leather chair with a loud thud, to be heard no more. Giddings, and all in the House chambers, were amused.[3]

There were times when Giddings was perplexed by Adams, though, such as the day in early January 1839 when Adams refused to vote for a resolution to abolish slavery in the District of Columbia. "He said that he was prepared to abolish the slave trade between the states and to recognize the independence of Haiti. He assigned no reason for any of his opinions [and] he seemed to convince the South that he was not so great an enemy to them as they had supposed, and some of the northern members seemed to think he was not so strongly opposed to slavery as they thought him to be," wrote Giddings, a bit confused by Adams's actions.[4]

Giddings did not laugh about the differences between southern and northern delegates, who seemed to be from two entirely different countries, each one fully prepared to go to war against the other on just about any issue one could name.

"During this week every member present must have witnessed the high and important bearing of southern men—their confident and bold assertions, their self-important airs, their overbearing manner; while the northern men, even on the subject of slavery, are different, taciturn and forbearing. Our northern friends are, in fact, afraid of these southern bullies. We have no northern man who dares boldly and fearlessly declare his abhorrence of slavery and the slave trade," said Giddings, who was stunned by the control southerners had over the House.[5]

Northerners even feared discussing forced labor, and that bothered the hot-headed activist from Ohio. "At the South, the general impression is that [abolition] is designed to create a general rebellion among the slaves and have them cut their master's throats. At the North, they have no definite idea of the meaning of abolition and northern men appear afraid to come out and declare their sentiments . . . they keep a distance from the subject," he wrote in his diary.[6]

The cowardice of northerners to openly discuss bondage in Congress appalled him. He told friends that he, for one, would do so as frequently as possible, even if people warned him not to do so because it would upset the southerners in the House and violate the sacred gag rule.

Giddings decided to speak out about servitude as often as he could, at first introducing a bill to eliminate the slave trade in the District of Columbia, which was killed in committee, and then talking to dozens of northern representatives about bondage. His mostly unwanted conversations about slavery would, three years later, get him into enormous trouble.

Giddings, who did not see himself as a gifted orator, admired those who were, especially Sargent S. Prentiss, a proslavery congressman from Mississippi and a member of a group that Giddings disdained. He gushed over the thirty-five-year old congressman's verbal skills that first chilly December in Washington. The remarkable thing about Prentiss, who walked with a limp, was that he rarely used notes and could speak effectively for hours. When he first arrived in Congress, he came as the winner of a disputed election and had to defend himself. He did so in a nine-hour speech over the course of three days, given almost entirely without notes, that mesmerized the packed chamber. Giddings wrote in his diary that the House gallery was jammed with people—women and girls, blacks and whites, masters, mistresses, wives, and servants. "Prentiss either chained the audience in breathless silence, or convulsed them with laughter. His irony was of the most bitter kind, his invective solemn and impressive, and his eloquence lofty and commanding. For three hours the partisans of the administration sat in torture and withered beneath his castigation," Giddings wrote delightfully, adding that all the boardinghouses and hotels in Washington held up their dinner service until Prentiss finished his remarks.[7]

People had enormous hopes for young Prentiss, but he had to leave Congress after one term to straighten out tangled land dealings and a string of gambling debts back home. He left Mississippi to avoid trouble, moved to New Orleans, and died there of a combination of alcoholism and cholera at the age of forty-one.

Giddings was determined to become as good a speaker as Prentiss and several days later thought he had his chance. George Jones had represented Wisconsin in the last Congress and was defeated in his reelection bid. He came to Congress anyway and insisted on being paid until the end of the year, money he charged Congress owed him. He was not paid. His insistence at collecting his congressional salary caused a huge stir, and Giddings, angry, planned to introduce a resolution to deny Jones his pay. He was told that Jones was a well-known duelist and that if he disagreed with Giddings's resolution, which of course he would, he might challenge him to a duel, take him outside the Capitol, and shoot him. Giddings certainly did not want to be shot dead at work. He wrote Jones a diplomatic letter, saying that if he had objections to Giddings's resolution, he should tell him before he introduced it. There was a miscommunication, though, and Jones never answered the letter. The next day, just as Giddings was about to speak, the letter was forwarded from Jones to the chairman, who read it out loud to the chamber.

Giddings's friends were astonished that he would actually stand to denounce the hot-headed and dangerous Jones. Giddings held his ground and tried to speak, but just as he was about to do so, someone jumped up, got the attention of the chair, and began to talk. Then someone else did the same, and then another and another while Giddings sat. Finally, seeing an opportunity, Giddings jumped to his feet and was recognized by the chair. He read his resolution and then made the House members laugh with a funny story. (George Jones did nothing.) The ice was broken for the rookie from Ohio. Encouraged by his maiden speech, he told himself that he was not a poor speaker after all. "I have now fairly made my debut and today I fancied, on entering the hall, greeted more warmly than heretofore. Members who had previously barely paid the passing salutation now came to my seat, with great politeness inquired about my health and many of them congratulated me upon the favorable reception to my speech," he said proudly.[8]

Giddings tried, on several occasions, to introduce anti-servitude legislation, which was forbidden, but each time he made members see that he was sincere in his efforts and that he would, if were reelected, become a leader of the antislavery cause.

Then, in February, he was stunned by the sight of a group of men and women in bondage, chained, moving through Washington. He wrote bitterly,

THIS DAY A COFFLE OF ABOUT SIXTY SLAVES, male and female, passed through the streets of Washington, chained together on their way South. They were accompanied by a large wagon, in which were placed the more feeble females and children as of such tender years as to be unable to walk. A "being" in the shape of a man was on horseback, with a large whip in his hand, with which he occasionally chastised those who, through fatigue or indolence, were tardy in their movements. This was done in the daytime, in public view of all who happened to be so situated as to see the barbarous spectacle.[9]

ON FEBRUARY 7, Giddings sat back in shock when he heard that over in the Senate, Henry Clay had denounced the antislavery coalition. "That is property [slaves] that which the law declares to be property," Clay said, setting himself up as a proslavery champion. Clay had also said that Giddings's district in Ohio was full of antislavery supporters, and he criticized them all. Giddings was as stunned as everyone else. "He had attacked them without mercy," said Giddings.

Giddings dismissed Clay's speech as just rhetoric because Clay was getting ready to run for president again and needed the votes of southerners, but the speech turned many northerners against Clay. It hurt him in the North as much as it helped him in the South.[10]

The Ohioan sat down at his desk and wrote a note to Clay, asking if he now believed that Congress had no right to abolish servitude in the District of Columbia. The next day, Clay stopped at Giddings's desk to discuss the issue, but Giddings was not there. Later, the two finally met and discussed the issue, but there was no resolution. "The conversation became dull and with a cold invitation by Clay to call and see him, he left," the congressman said of Clay.[11]

Angry at Clay's new and strident views on slavery, Giddings decided to break the gag rule. He waited until an innocuous bill about building a bridge across the Potomac River was introduced to ask for recognition. He got it and, with hardly anyone paying attention, leaped to his feet and reminded people that forced labor was still legal in the nation's capital, where the bridge was going to be constructed. "It is known, sir, that the slave trade in its worst and most abhorrent forms is being carried on here to an alarming extent," he began, but he was called to order and told to stop talking by the speaker. Giddings ignored him.

He continue, "We are told by some honorable gentleman that the subject of its continuance cannot be discussed in the House; that a dissolution of the Union would follow as the inevitable consequence of any interference with the traffic on the part of Congress. On the other hand, I have come to the conclusion that northern men, who have from their infancy been bred to the love of liberty, where every precept impressed upon their youthful minds, every principle."

Now dozens of representatives began to shout at Giddings, imploring not to break the gag rule and discuss servitude. He went right on, talking louder as the noise from others increased and remaining calm as anger seethed in the faces of dozens of congressmen who sat near him. "Every principle of their matured years has habituated them to think of the slave trade with disgust and abhorrence, to contemplate it as only among barbarians and uncivilized nations, to look upon it upon it with horror," he said. Here, Giddings looked at the chair, but the chairman said nothing. He went on as more southerners jeered him. "It is my opinion that such men can never consent to continue the seat of government in the midst of a magnificent slave market. I say it distinctly to the committee, to the nation, to the world, that northern men will not consent to the continuance of our national counsels where our ears are assailed while coming to the capital by the voice of the auctioneer publicly proclaiming the sale of human, of intelligent, beings."

Giddings again looked at the chairman, who saw his dangerous speech, so far, as still legitimately tied to the bridge funding bill.

Giddings then sailed into an attack on the gag rule, telling his colleagues, getting louder and louder in their distaste for his remarks, that thousands of northerners had sent congressmen petitions on forced labor that had never been heard in the House. He charged that Congress was holding America in a "legislative straitjacket" and that all of their lips had been "hermetically sealed."

He then switched back to the bill. He said that northerners could not vote for a bill that improved the life of a city that sanctioned slaves living in its houses and working for masters on its streets. He continued on that bill-connected theme for several more minutes, adding that it would be immoral for him, representing an Ohio district whose citizens objected to servitude, to vote for a bill to build a bridge in a slave city. "It is wrong, sir. It is palpably wrong," he said. Giddings looked down at his notes and talked a bit more about the bill. Then he announced that he was going to ignore the gag order and speak freely about servitude as long as he was a congressmen.

There was an uproar in the House. Giddings ignored it and passionately went on, although the noise was deafening. "On the beautiful avenue in front of the Capitol members of Congress, while on their way to the capitol, during this session, have heard the harsh voice of the inhuman auctioneer publicly selling human beings They have also been compelled to turn aside from their path to permit a coffle of slaves, male and females, chained to each other by their necks, to pass on their way to his national slave market."

The roar of objections rose to a crescendo level. The chairman cut Giddings off immediately and he was forced to sit down.[12]

Later, at home, the Ohio congressman was bitter about being cut off. He wrote about the decision, "Much excitement prevailed and the House became a scene of perfect confusion and uproar. Some seemed to enjoy this much; among those the venerable ex-President [Adams] laughed heartily and coming to my seat advised me to insist upon my rights, not to be intimidated by the course taken by the Southern men. This confusion lasted for about one hour and I suppose, for the purpose of restoring order, the chairman . . . decided that I was out of order."[13]

The speech, or attempt at a speech, had failed but at the same time succeeded because it marked the unknown, rookie congressman as a major player in the anti-bondage movement in Congress. His mail, mostly antislavery, increased dramatically, and other members of Congress befriended him.

Of course, there was a downside to his emergence as an antislavery champion. Southerners hated him. On the day of his speech and in subsequent House meetings, he was insulted by them and often ridiculed or ignored. Giddings was heavily criticized in southern newspapers and seen as the new Antichrist.

This position was not new; he was used to that. Shortly before he made the speech, he had delivered another in which he accused the federal government of aiding slave catchers who sought runaways harbored by Indian tribes in Florida. The speech infuriated southerners, who saw him using one issue, the Indian tribes, to talk about the banned issue of slavery. One Congressman, Representative Edward Black of Georgia, picked up a Bible on his desk, marched across the House chamber, and stood right in front of Giddings, waving it in his face. Pointing his finger at him, Black said that Ohioans in Giddings's own district were unfair to free blacks who lived there. "Thou hypocrite. First cast the beam out of they own eye," he shouted. Then, trembling, unable to control himself, Black howled at Giddings that if he ever visited the state of Georgia, he would be hanged. Several more congressmen formed a line behind Black and took turns insulting and threatening Giddings.

The Ohio congressman knew what they were doing. They were trying to push him into a duel. He did not take the bait and later wrote that he would never fight a duel with anybody for any reason.[14]

The Ohio congressman did not see the *Creole* incident as just another that had to be somehow swept under the rug, as did so many southerners. He likened it to the *Amistad* case, to which he attached both solemnity and dignity. "[It] struck at the very existence of slavery. Were these degraded, ignorant, superstitious heathens entitled to life and liberty?" he said of the *Amistad* mutineers. "Had the Creator endowed them with these prerogatives? The court, clad in judicial robes, the Attorney General and numerous members of the bar, Governor Baldwin, acting as prisoners' counsel for the Africans, associated with Mr. Adams, who had long since left the Presidential chair, with the honors and blessing of a nation; the vast audience, the solemn bearing and dignity of the court and officers—all conspired to render the proceeding one of high moral sublimity."

The *Amistad* defense, argued so brilliantly before the US Supreme Court by John Adams, was a national landmark in American jurisprudence, and Giddings was convinced that the *Creole* case would be too and that generations of Americans in the future would refer to it in any conversation about slavery.[15]

IN THE MONTH AFTER JOHN QUINCY ADAMS'S VICTORY in his House expulsion trial, the crisis over the *Creole* heated up considerably. Congressmen, senators, and newspaper editors discussed it daily. Some large organizations argued for the release of the nineteen mutineers still in jail, and other large groups argued against it. Diplomats around the world bitterly debated the case. In Washington, the men who lived at Abolition House met almost on a daily basis and talked about it. They needed to get the British high court to free the mutineers, but they also saw that they could use the *Creole* for a higher purpose.

The House gag rule against any discussion about bondage in America, voted in to placate southern slave owners, had been in effect for years. Different Whig congressmen, including Adams, had offered resolutions to overturn it, but they had all been defeated. Adams's supporters in Congress saw the *Creole* as their biggest opportunity to defeat the gag rule. The mutiny on the slave ship had drawn enormous press coverage and generated a thousand bar conversations. The abolitionists wanted to use the *Creole* publicity to get the gag rule removed. Then, with freedom to discuss forced labor in Congress, the representatives could talk about the *Creole* and work, with new public power, to force Britain to release the nineteen mutineers. That would begin a new era of discussions that the crusaders were sure would bring about the destruction of bondage in the United States in just a few years.

There were two problems, however. The first was that it was an uphill fight. Whoever offered the resolution and led the charge would be vilified by the slave owners and many non-slaveholders too. Second, the man who had the best chance to destroy the gag rule, Adams, who had led the fight against it for years, was too weak from his House trial to do so.

He told his friends at Abolition House that he could offer support and ideas for resolutions to remove the gag rule, but he was just physically worn out and could not do it himself.

He was also mentally fatigued. "My mind is in the condition of a ship at sea in a hurricane, suspended by an instantaneous calm. The brain heaves ... the body totters, and I live in a perpetual waltz. The presentient to the sudden termination to my life is rather cheering to me than painful," he wrote a few months later.[16]

His new acolyte, Joshua Giddings of Ohio, stepped forward to carry the torch. He and Adams came up with a clever plan. They would offer a group of resolutions about the *Creole* and bondage, not a resolution to overturn the gag rule. The House talk on the resolutions, if allowed, would in effect bring down the gag rule simply by its occurrence. Giddings's nine resolutions stated that:

Congress, as a federal agency, had the power to abolish slavery in each of the states.

Each of the states still had the power to authorize servitude within its boundaries.

The federal government had jurisdiction over all laws pertaining to sea traffic and any subject connected to shipping or cargo. The states had ceded these rights when the Constitution was passed.

Slavery, being an abridgment of the natural rights of humans, could exist only by force of municipal law and therefore was confined to the land jurisdiction of the power creating that law (not the ocean).

People on board a ship on the high seas, outside the jurisdiction of any state, were not subject to the laws of a state but subject to the laws of the United States.

When the *Creole* sailed out of the jurisdiction of Virginia, the people on the ship ceased to be under Virginia laws and became amenable only to US law.

The men and women on the *Creole* violated no US law and therefore could not be punished.

Any efforts to re-enslave the *Creole* passengers were in violation of US law and incompatible with national honor.

Attempts to exert national influence in favor of the coastwise slave trade or to maintain a commerce in human beings were subversive to the rights and injurious to the feelings and interests of the people of the free states and unauthorized by the Constitution.

Giddings turned them in to the House clerk on the morning of March 21, 1842, so they could be studied by members of Congress. He naively thought the study would be done quickly and that the resolutions would be approved for House discussion and printed in Washington newspapers so that members of the public could read them too. Then, he naively believed, the resolutions, or most of them, would be passed and the gag rule would be defeated, or a special vote on the gag rule would be scheduled and then it would be defeated. He had no idea of the utter firestorm he would create, a firestorm that nearly burned down the House of Representatives and that literally shook the government of the United States to its foundation.

The resolutions were read aloud by the clerk. Someone then asked for a second reading. The clerk read them again, slowly and clearly.

The reaction from southerners was swift. They were outraged. Congressman Isaac Holmes, from South Carolina, trembling as he spoke in very angry tones, said that "there are certain topics, like certain places, of which it might be said, 'fools rush in where angels fear to tread.'"

Giddings might have expected that from a southerner, but the next member to speak, Horace Everett, was from Vermont. He spit his disdain out. "I want to express my utter abhorrence of the firebrand course of the gentleman from Ohio." William Fessenden, a first-term congressman from Maine, and John G. Floyd of New York insisted that there be no immediate vote and that the resolution be tied up by the chair for some time. Caleb Cushing, a longtime activist, stunned the chamber when he stood to speak. "They appear to be a British argument on a great question between the British and American governments," he said of the resolutions, "and constitute an approximation to treason on which I intend to vote 'no.'"

Others suggested that to avoid a no vote, Giddings withdraw the resolutions and present them at a future date, when they could be debated calmly. Giddings, seeing that he was in for a rough fight and might lose, agreed. He thought that was the safest way out at that moment, and so did many others. Then, unexpectedly, John Minor Botts of Virginia got recognition from the chair and rose amid all the clamor.

An agitated Botts said that he had just scrawled a resolution on a piece of paper. The resolution said that what Giddings was trying to do, clearly to Botts, was drag the United States into a war with Great Britain over the *Creole*. He said that to do so "mutiny and murder" on the *Creole* were to be justified. Then he said that "the conduct of [Giddings] is altogether unwarranted and unwarrantable, and deserving the severest condemnation of the people of this country, and of this body in particular."[17]

Noise and arguments raged from one side of the House chamber to the other. Adams had been bad enough, but now this rookie from Ohio had the gall to try to not only wipe out the gag rule but also get the House to approve the mutiny on the ship, including the murder. The noise level rose by the minute until the speaker gained quiet and, banging down his mallet, adjourned for the day.

Botts's charges brought about a 128–68 vote for a censure debate. Giddings, fearful that the debate would result in a vote in favor of censure, spent the early part of the night working on his defense. At the end of the evening, he walked over to Adams's house. Adams was glum. He told Giddings that he would probably be censured. Giddings said he could easily defend himself, but Adams cut him short and said that by the rules and the manipulation of the "slavery party," as he called the Democrats, the censure vote would be taken without him having a chance to explain his resolutions. Young Giddings was stunned.

"You are not as familiar with the slaveholders' character as I am," said Adams. "Slaveholders act from impulse, not from reflection; they act together from interest, and have dreaded of the displeasure of their constituents when they act for slavery."

He added that, in the end, the Democrats usually won. "They have threatened and entreated, bullied and wheedled, until their more simple adversaries have been half coaxed, half frightened into a surrender of their principles for a bauble of insignificant promises," he had written back in 1821. He felt the same way now.[18]

He also told Giddings that the slaveholders, and officials of the southern states, would do anything to retain the slave power that controlled the South— lie, cheat, and steal. Just one year later he was proven correct when it was reported that officials in various southern states had falsified the 1840 census to dramatically increase the number of blacks who were deemed mentally incapacitated in an effort to show that most blacks were mentally diminished and should never be freed and allowed to roam among "normal" people.[19]

Giddings was certain that under the rules, he would be allowed to discuss both his resolutions and his right to remain in the House as a representative from Ohio. He paid no attention to Adams's warning about the slavery party and its power to get its way. He insisted on speaking, and there were several motions to allow him to do so. Other congressmen intervened with more motions though, and in the end, the House voted not to let Giddings speak. "The champions of slavery were thus completely caught in the toils of their own violence," wrote historian George Julian, Giddings's son-in-law and a congressman himself, in 1892.[20]

As soon as the House vote ended, everybody realized what they had just done to themselves. They had tightened all the screws of parliamentary procedure so that Giddings was trapped, silent, in a corner. Representative Philip Triplett of Kentucky, seeing the unfairness of this, asked the speaker to suspend the rules to give Giddings a short time to defend himself. The speaker answered that, under House rules, that could not be done. Another representative asked for a second vote on the measure, but the speaker ruled that a second vote was not permitted. A suggestion by Adams to reopen the debate and at least read the resolutions again was similarly turned down. The slaveholding congressmen now had Giddings right where they wanted him.

While all this was going on, Giddings handed a note to a reporter from the *National Intelligencer* sitting in the chamber. It said what he was not allowed to say on the House floor:

> Mr. Speaker, I stand before the House in a peculiar position. It is proposed to pass a vote of censure upon me, substantially for the reason that I differ in opinion from a majority of the members. The vote is about to be taken, without giving me the opportunity to be heard. It was idle of me to say that I am ignorant of the disposition of a majority of the members to pass the resolution of censure. I have been violently assailed in a personal manner, but have had no opportunity of being heard in reply; nor do I now ask for any favor at the hands of gentlemen, but in the name of an insulted constituency, in behalf of one of the states in this Union, in behalf of the people of these states and our federal Constitution, I *demand* a hearing in the ordinary mode of proceeding. I accept no other privilege; I will receive no other courtesy.[21]

After the second vote, Giddings realized that he had lost and had been booted out of the House. He rose from his desk slowly and walked over to Adams. They shook hands warmly. "I hope we shall soon have you back again," Adams said softly. Giddings smiled wanly but was in too much shock to say anything. The Ohio congressman then walked over to the desk of another friend, and then another and another, to shake hands and say good-bye. To his surprise, he was met at the exit door to the chamber by Senators Henry Clay and John Crittenden, both of Kentucky, who along with many other senators had watched the House vote. Clay told Giddings that he had been wronged, that he should have had a chance to defend his resolutions and have the House vote on them. Clay said he admired the bravery of Giddings in speaking up for something he believed in. He said that Giddings should be able to denounce servitude just as Clay could defend it in the Senate and the president could defend it in the White House. Giddings left the hall all alone. That night, Adams wrote in his diary, "I can find no language to express my feelings at the consummation of this act."[22]

That night, Giddings boarded a train at Washington's busy station that took him back to his native Ohio. Amid all this American turmoil, the British had the last word. A London court had exonerated the mutineers on February 13, 1842. A Nassau court exonerated and released them on April 16.

AFTER GIDDINGS'S DEPARTURE, the angst over bondage grew every day. Senators and congressmen from the free and slave states bickered about forced labor continually, and men like Giddings became larger and larger targets. The hatred between the two sides became so heated that on the afternoon of May 7, following an argument over slavery at a racetrack, Henry Wise assaulted and beat Representative Edward Stanley with his cane. Adams shook his head mournfully. "Threats of lynching and assassination are the natural off spring of slave-breeders and slave-traders," he wrote in his diary a few days later. "Profanity and obscenity are their natural associates."[23]

Those opposed to servitude all over America were aghast at the ejection of Giddings for his antislavery stand. Abolitionist newspapers printed all the speeches from the censure debate and so, to the surprise of all, did some mainstream US papers and many leading newspapers in England. Throughout the country, thousands packed meetinghouses and churches to protest Giddings's censure. In his native Ohio, residents held dozens of public meetings to complain about the shabby treatment he had been put through in Congress. Antislavery leaders in that state insisted that Giddings run again for his seat, which an investigation revealed was legal. Ohio residents then began a campaign to restore him to the House, conducting a short but raucous campaign that involved leaflets, flyers, and posters hammered to the sides of building and neighborhood trees. A special election to fill Giddings's seat was set for May 5, 1842, and Giddings entered the race, an unusual step. He had little support from the Whig Party, whose leaders, as always, were afraid of repercussions, and none from the Democrats. Giddings was victorious in the special election, defeating his opponent 7,469 to 383, a resounding victory and a slap in the face to the US Congress and in particular the representatives of the southern states. His victory percentage was, and remains, the highest in contested congressional races in American history.[24]

On May 8, 1842, Giddings returned to a tumultuous welcome in the House, where he had been banished just five short weeks earlier:

I ARRIVED HERE ON WEDNESDAY EVENING and was soon surrounded by friends who certainly appeared glad to see me back. . . . Andrews, of Cleveland, introduced me to the House. Many looked up with smiling faces, while many appeared to be dumbfounded. I received many long and hearty greetings from those who had opposed my censure, and from some who voted against me. Governor David Wallace, of Indiana, in particular, seized me by the hand, and in the most feeling manner acknowledged his error in voting to censure me, and assured me of his most heartfelt satisfaction at seeing me again in my place. I cannot suppress the faith that a sure, though perhaps remote, triumph awaits it.[25]

GIDDINGS ALWAYS LOOKED FOR A WAY to talk about servitude without technically violating the gag rule. He found it on June 4, when several congressmen argued against a bill to reduce the size of the US Navy. The congressmen argued that the *Creole* incident showed that the United States had to have a large and strong sea force in case a war with Great Britain developed over incidents such as the slave ship mutiny. Giddings smiled broadly.

"We cannot honourably lend any encouragement or support to that essential commerce in human flesh. Every principal of morality, of national honor, forbids that we should lend any aid or assistance to those engaged in the traffic of the bodies of men, of women, of children. . . . I would not retain a single soldier in service to maintain this slave trade; on the contrary, I should rejoice if every slave shipped from our slave breeding states could regain his liberty, either by the strength of his own arms or by landing on some British island," Giddings said. He then denounced all government officials and southerners who demanded compensation for their labor loss.[26]

Giddings was unable to introduce his resolutions again thanks to parliamentary maneuvering by the southern Congressmen, but two years later, Adams launched a strong campaign to end the gag rule and was successful. The ability of representatives to discuss slavery on the floor of the house after 1844, thanks to the *Creole* mutiny, changed the entire nature of the national debates on bondage.

Giddings's efforts to upend the gag rule drew the attention of several young but notable politicians in the northern states. One was Salmon Chase, who would go on to be the governor of Ohio, secretary of the treasury, and chief justice of the US Supreme Court under Abraham Lincoln. Chase wrote Giddings in January 1842, just before his censure. In his long letter, Chase pointed out that the fierce opposition to Giddings showed that neither the Democratic or Whig Party really represented the people and that the party he had just cofounded, the Liberty Party, was needed. "[Unless the precise principles of American liberty] prevail, the country itself must perish," he said.

In a remarkable leap twenty years into the future, Chase then told Giddings that he thought Governor William Seward of New York would make an excellent president. (Seward ran for and lost the Republican nomination to Abraham Lincoln in 1860). Chase, the big Seward supporter, ran for the nomination himself.

A few days later Chase wrote again, this time urging Giddings to join Adams in the antislavery movement and urging both Giddings and Adams to join the Liberty Party. Giddings was opposed to the new party and urged Chase and others to simply increase the antislavery stand of the two major parties.[27]

A force again in Washington, Giddings continued to argue, off the floor of the House, that slavery was wrong. He based his arguments in the Declaration of Independence and the Constitution, charging that since the federal government had no power to eliminate slavery, it also had no power to support it, so its representatives had to cease and desist in any and all programs that aided the slave states. He charged, too, that the declaration was written to "secure the blessings of liberty" and said that meant all Americans, not just free and white Americans. He blamed southerners—and northerners too, because they were subservient to southern politicians. "When the day shall arrive when northern men will insist upon their rights, and refuse to contribute the substance acquired by their toil for the maintenance of southern slavery, that scourge of our land will cease."

These views were expressed in numerous antislavery essays he wrote for newspapers. They were reprinted as pamphlets and handed out and mailed all over the country in 1842 and 1843.[28] In all of them, he criticized both Tyler and Webster and said they were tools of the slavery movement in the southern states.

Giddings decided at some point that indeed there might be a chance to end slavery and that the slavers in Congress were vulnerable. He had seen that in his return to Congress after his censure. "At times I really apprehended that I would be trampled in the dust before the almost irresistible influence of slavery. Indeed, my life has been sought on account of my adherence to truth and justice. But I have been sustained and protected by that kind Providence which has always been round about me."[29]

He was cheered in the North and completely ignored in the South.

⚬⚬⚬⚬⚬⚬⚬

THE INTENSE DEBATES, public and private, the media coverage of the *Creole* mutiny, and the possibility of war with Great Britain smothered attention paid in Washington to a number of other issues going on in the United States, such as the lingering recession that had started in 1837, the expansion of banks in different states, and the expansion in the number of newspapers in small villages as well as big cities. One issue overwhelmed by the *Creole* obsession was the quiet drive of President Tyler and many southerners to have the United States annex the Republic of Texas. The Lone Star Republic, founded after the much publicized battle at the Alamo in 1836, stood out on the map of North America like a huge mountain. If it were annexed, it would account for about one-third of the land area of the United States. It would also add a major seaport, in Galveston, and continue the bridge of America into the West. It would be a stepping stone for other western territories to come into the Union too.

Tyler had long wanted to bring Texas into the Union as a state. A month prior to the seizure of the *Creole*, in October 1841, he talked to friends and cabinet officers about the issue. He told Henry Wise in the very first week of his "accidental presidency" that the addition of Texas was "an important part" of the new administration's plans.

The reasons for the proposed annexation were simple. It would enhance the size and power of the United States. It would increase shipping through Galveston, provide more open land for farming, and open the door to intercontinental railroads through the South. Cotton had been increasing dramatically as a crop, and there was no better place to grow it than on the warm and fertile plains of Texas.

Best of all, from Tyler's point of view, Texas would come into the Union as a slave state. That would enhance the power of the slaveholders and, at the same time, his own. Secretly, he saw the annexation of mammoth Texas as a jewel on his so far tarnished crown and believed it would catapult him to a presidential victory in the 1844 election.

He knew there would be northern opposition to his plans because of the slavery issue, but he did not care. There were too many baubles in Texas for him to worry about the slavery debate, which was never-ending anyway, he believed.

CHAPTER EIGHT

The Last Fight—Texas

April 25, 1844

SOUTHERNERS from Virginia to South Carolina to Louisiana were thrilled that President Tyler lusted after Texas. They would carry the banner of slavery to Galveston, San Antonio, and other places, make more money in the cotton industry, and create a whole new destination for people interested in moving west. Northerners were appalled because annexation would nearly double the size of slave territory in America.

Many northerners, led by Joshua Giddings, disagreed with Tyler, and loudly. "Where is the power to annex territory to the Union for the purpose of sustaining slavery in a foreign state? To open up new slave markets? To assume the war of a foreign state? To use the army and navy and violate our treaties with other governments for the purpose of perpetuating an institution which we detest?" Giddings said.

Giddings was jeered by some members of slave states and ignored by others, but a few minutes later he had the attention of all in the enormous congressional chamber when he played a rhetorical game about Texas and slavery.

Several congressmen had sneered when Giddings mentioned James Birney, a former third-party candidate for president, as a leading antislavery champion. Suddenly, Giddings said that he was not talking about Birney as America's number-one abolitionist, but another man.

"Who is it?" yelled one congressman.

"He is the author of the first abolition tract ever published in the United States, and in my opinion, the best ever put forth," smiled Giddings.

"Who is it? Name him!" shouted a congressman.

"I borrowed my own abolitionist sentiments from his writings, and have cherished them and shall continue to do so, from respect to his memory, if from no other motive," continued Giddings.

"Name him," yelled several congressman.

"His name was *Thomas Jefferson*," bellowed a triumphant Giddings.

Laughter.

"And his abolition tract was called the Declaration of Independence," Giddings roared. He then smiled in the sure knowledge that he had tricked them all.

He sat down to a long wave of laughter from both parties.[1]

Tyler disagreed with Giddings. He saw servitude as a benefit for Texas in future years. In 1850, long after he had left office, he wrote his son Robert that "the monopoly of the cotton plant was the great and important concern. That monopoly, now secure, places all other nations at our feet. An embargo of a single year would produce in Europe a greater amount of suffering than a fifty years war. I doubt whether Great Britain could avoid such convulsions." Ironically, that is exactly what the Confederacy thought at the start of the Civil War a decade later. It would withhold cotton from England unless it entered the war as an ally of the South. England refused and had no problems without southern cotton because it had so much of it in its warehouses from earlier trade.[2]

Tyler argued to Webster that some political deal might be reached, as it was with Missouri a generation earlier, to permit Texas to come into the Union as a slave state and some other territories as free states. They would balance each other out. Besides, he told Webster, Texas weather was perfect for forced labor. "Climate should be left to determine the question of slavery, as it would most assuredly. It has already abolished it as far as Delaware and if left to work out, its results would at a distant day produce similar effects in Delaware, Maryland and Virginia," he said.[3]

His interest in bringing Texas into the Union soared in the spring and summer of 1842, though, because he had lost the *Creole* battle with Great Britain and in the public eye looked like a weak leader. He wanted to be reelected president, and the chances of that were slim. He had already been disowned by his Whigs and ignored by his old party, the Democrats. That left little room in which to battle for the White House except some sort of third party. He needed a big success in the political arena, and that was Texas. If he could bring Texas into the constitutional fold, he would dramatically increase the size of the United States, as Jefferson had done with the Louisiana Purchase in 1803. This would make him enormously popular and enable him, even as a third-party candidate, to hold on to the White House.

"It is John Tyler's last card for a popular whirlwind to carry him through; and he has played it with equal intrepidity and address," said John Quincy Adams, who understood every move that Tyler was making and, although he loathed the president, quietly applauded him from the sidelines for his political dexterity.[4]

Presidential races between several strong candidates were not unusual in that era. In 1800 Thomas Jefferson's election had wound up in the House of Representatives, where he faced his own vice presidential running mate, Aaron Burr, and sitting president John Adams. In 1824 there had also been a race between several candidates, with John Quincy Adams victorious over William Crawford, Henry Clay, and Andrew Jackson. In 1836 Martin Van Buren defeated a field of three Whig candidates: William Henry Harrison, Hugh White, and Daniel Webster. Tyler could easily do the same thing, he believed.

The time was right for annexation. Flamboyant Sam Houston had been reelected president of the Republic of Texas in the fall of 1841. His Texan colleagues said that Houston was very much in favor of annexation, and as quickly as possible. He instructed the Texas minister to Washington to pursue annexation with Tyler and various senators and congressmen, but there was no strong feeling for it outside the White House. "All parties were satisfied that no treaty of annexation could be ratified by the Senate and there was not even a majority in favor of the policy in the lower House," wrote the ambassador.

The reaction of Congress appalled Tyler and he said so to his friend James Reilly. "I am anxious for it," he said, "and wish most sincerely I could conclude it at once."[5]

The president was careful in the way that he framed the Texas question. An example is this quote: "[Annexation] was neither local nor sectional, but made its appeal to the interests of the whole Union, and of every state in the Union." It was not a North and South issue, or a black and white issue, he continually told people, especially those who saw his advocacy of Texas as part of his policies.[6]

Ever since Texans had defeated Mexico's Antonio Santa Anna at San Jacinto, relations between the two countries had been frosty. To Mexican officials, the new Texans were just a motley crew of drunken cowboys with rifles. The editor of a Veracruz newspaper wrote in 1839 that "[Mexico] is not aware of the existence of a nation called the Republic of Texas, but only a horde of adventurers in rebellion against the laws of the government of the republic."[7]

Texas had enormous problems to overcome. Militarily, it had been accosted by Mexican forces in wars or skirmishes ever since the Alamo. One of the worst took place in 1841. The government sent a force of 321 soldiers and adventurers to Santa Fe, New Mexico, which it claimed was within Texas's borders. The force was attacked by the Mexican army, and what followed was a disaster. The Texan soldiers wilted in the heat, lost the battle, and were sent on a forced march all the way to Mexico City. Many died en route.

Texans demanded an attack on Mexico in retaliation, but the president of Texas at the time, Mirabeau Lamar, refused. Then Mexico invaded Texas in early 1842. President Santa Anna led an army of fourteen hundred men to San Antonio, scene of the Alamo battle six years earlier. They occupied and held San Antonio for several weeks before riding back to Mexico. Houston, who followed Lamar as president, was under enormous pressure from Texas's congress to invade Mexico. The congress ordered him to draft one-third of the men in Texas for the battle. Houston held off until the congress adjourned in July, and the invasion idea was discarded.

Texas was growing, and growing fast. In 1836 its population was thirty thousand whites and five thousand black slaves. Ten years later, there were 102,000 whites and 38,753 slaves. But this large population was dispersed throughout the state, making its thinly populated cities and villages vulnerable to Mexican attacks.[8]

As early as November 1842, northern politicians had attacked servitude in Texas and the idea that it would be allowed when Texas joined the Union. Abel Upshur, Tyler's close friend and at the time his secretary of the navy, reacted angrily to Adams's criticism in the Texas talks. "As to his attack upon Tyler and the rest of us, I do not care a farthing for it but he is determined, if possible, to get up a war against slavery, which must end either in the dissolution of the union or a surrender of that institution, the old man has nothing of his former strength left but his passions. His whole letter is a tissue of malignant representation, as he knows, but he has so framed them expressly that they may do as much mischief as possible," Upshur wrote.[9]

Another political leader who saw the acquisition of Texas an addition of a slave state was former secretary of state Daniel Webster, who left that office in May 1843. He wrote an antislavery/anti-Texas pamphlet and sent a copy to Tyler. "Mr. Webster has sent me his speech on the bondage question in pamphlet, with expressions of 'cordial friendship.' I have replied in a brief letter, putting him right on the subject of annexation. My view of that subject was not narrow, local or bigoted. It embraced the whole country and all of its interests," Tyler wrote later, in 1850.[10]

In both 1842 and 1843, Tyler friends Upshur and Gilmer wrote letters and made speeches supporting annexation, and their words brought upon the White House a torrent of abuse from leaders of the antislavery crusade, who saw in them yet another conspiracy, again backed by the White House, to permit servitude in the Lone Star State. At the same time, President Houston pressed even harder for annexation. An economic depression was battering Texas and the United States in the early 1840s. Houston told the Texas legislature that the republic was "without credit, without means, and millions of dollars in debt."

Annexation seemed logical, but Tyler's old nemesis, Great Britain, stood in the way.

The English had been playing a tricky game with Texas and Mexico at the same time they freed the mutineers from the *Creole*. Britain's interest in both Mexico and Texas seemed to be as a trading partner. There was no hard evidence that Britain hoped to gain control of either country at that time. If anything, the English had been belligerent, not appeasing, toward the Lone Star Republic. In 1839 Britain's foreign secretary, Lord Palmerston, warned Texas that if it did not pay a debt that Texans charged was not proper, "Her Majesty's government would be justifiable in sending a ship of war to Texas to get it." A year later, the British told Texan officials that they would step in to mediate peace talks between Mexico and Texas if Texas paid $1 million of what the British claimed they were owed by the Mexicans. The Texans refused.

Just after the *Creole* mutineers won their case in the British courts, and Tyler renewed his yearning for Texas, the British again offered to negotiate a treaty to end the acrimonious feelings between Texas and Mexico. The Texans at first agreed to the talks, but it backed off when the United States was not allowed to join.

Texas had been a plum dangling from a political tree for the United States since 1825. It had been sought eagerly by southern state leaders and fought against bitterly by anti-bondage leaders throughout the North. To them, a slave Texas meant forced labor in every other future territory that came into the Union as a state. Texas would set precedent for all of them. Abolitionists in the North traveled to England and won an extraordinary declaration from Lord Aberdeen, the linchpin in the *Creole* talks. He told the antislavery leaders that he would, by every proper means of influence, encourage the abolition of bondage in Texas, and he recommended that the Mexican government interest itself in the matter.

A month later, on the floor of Parliament, Lord Brougham, a leading British antislavery leader, said that "the importance of Texas cannot be overrated." He added that he "was irresistibly anxious for the abolition of slavery in Texas for if it was abolished there, that the consequence would be its abolition in the United States also."[11]

The British were fueled by a nationwide anti-bondage campaign launched in the United States in 1843 and 1844 to undercut the "annex Texas" movement. At the American Anti-Slavery Society national convention in 1844, members voted yes on a resolution stating that a primary objective was "to dissolve the American Union." Another resolution stated, "Secession from the present United States government is the duty of every abolitionist, since no one can take office or deposit a vote under its Constitution without violating his anti-slavery principles and rendering himself an abettor of the slave-holder in his sin."[12]

The threat of antislavery leaders to get states to secede from the Union was alarming to President Tyler. What would happen to America if that took place, if several states did indeed leave the Union? Could New England form its own country? Ohio? The irony was that it would be the southern states, not the northern ones, that would leave the Union in 1861, and the pro-America Tyler would end his career as a senator in the Confederate Congress, full of the seceding states that he abhorred.

John Quincy Adams scoffed at the British suggestion that servitude could be easily eliminated in Texas and in the United States. "I believe that their real policy, far from desiring the abolition of slavery, either in our southern states or in Texas is I suspect, on the contrary, that for a suitable equivalent they will readily acquiesce both in the annexation of Texas and the perpetuation of slavery here to weaken and ruin us," he said.[13]

Adams was petrified that meddling by the British would result in some sort of annexation of Texas by the Britain, with a handsome payoff to Mexico, or simply a renewal of Texas's determination to remain an independent republic. After all, Texas had been a free country for seven years now. It had developed an economy, culture, and self-sustaining government. Why not just continue along on that path?

Tyler was more worried than his nemesis Adams. He sat in the White House in the hot summer of 1843 and assessed the situation, all brought about by the *Creole*. The British were haughtily celebrating their success in freeing the mutineers of the *Creole* by now meddling in the Texan–Mexican–US negotiations with the goal of somehow annexing Texas themselves, he surmised. They had been reenergized in their grand plans to dominate the world by their victory in the *Creole* incident, Tyler told everybody.

"We can never admit of European interference in the affairs of this continent," one newspaper editor wrote, agreeing with the president.[14]

Now, Tyler cleverly turned the tables on the British. He argued to friends and colleagues, and through newspapers to all Americans, that the United States had just been humiliated by the haughty way in which the British had seized the *Creole* and freed the nineteen mutineers. Now they were back again, he said, ready to steal Texas from the United States and eliminate slavery there. This was not just talk. Tyler's emissary to England, Duff Green, was a prominent political figure in that era and an ally of John C. Calhoun. He wrote Tyler in the summer of 1843 that "Lord Aberdeen has agreed that the British government will guarantee the payment on the interest upon Texas loans upon condition that the Texas government will abolish slavery."[15]

The British would greatly interfere with the current Texas government and influence its actions or simply sail in and claim the entire republic for themselves, Tyler argued, citing their interference in slave ships on the high seas and the *Creole* especially. A lot of people in America agreed with him.

Senator Levi Woodbury of New Hampshire, a former member of Andrew Jackson's cabinet, framed the argument best: "Great Britain must not control

Texas; if such is the alternative, the United States must insist on immediate annexation. It is the last struggle for American independence, to be conducted peaceably if we may, but forcibly if we must. . . . The domination of the whole American continent will be seen to be at stake. Shall it rest in America, or in a small island on the coast of Europe? In us and our posterity or in our oppressor and rival? Texas must immediately become American or it will soon be British."[16]

It was a pivotal moment in American history.[17]

The president had to derail Great Britain's influence and Mexico's involvement in Texas affairs and get Texas to accept his offer of joining the Union. How to do it, though?

His answer: a secret mission.

He would find an American diplomat who could, through private back channels, get a deal for the annexation. It had to be accomplished in such a way that everyone, in each country, saw it as a national, patriotic maneuver and not tied to party politics or anyone's presidential aspirations. It would, of course, be tied to Tyler's reelection efforts, but his secret diplomat had to disguise that the best he could.

He needed a highly placed and respected government official, a Whig and a personal friend, someone he could trust completely. In the summer of 1843, he chose Abel Upshur, his new secretary of state. (He replaced Webster, who, fed up with politics both domestic and international, had recently resigned.)

Upshur had been at Tyler's side for decades and had served him ably during his presidential term. He was an ardent supporter of annexation. "If there existed a more enthusiastic advocate of annexation or one whose energies of body and mind were more unremittingly devoted to its accomplishment, I must say that I do not know the man," Tyler said a few years later.[18]

As secretary of state, Upshur wanted Texas to join the Union. As Tyler's friend, he wanted the president to be reelected and saw the annexation of Texas as a way to accomplish that.

Upshur's job was to secretly meet with Isaac Van Zandt, the Texas chargé d'affaires, to set up a secret negotiation for annexation and to meet with different members of Tyler's cabinet to make certain that he, and only he, had any discussion with Texas leaders. Finally, he was to meet with senators from both parties to gauge their feelings on the Texas issue and how the Senate could help the administration get Texas into the Union. Upshur never told anyone what he was doing, a real trick in diplomacy. "No intrigue has been set on foot to accomplish [annexation]," said Tyler as a cover for Upshur's clandestine work. "Texas herself wills it and the executive of the United States, concurring with her, has seen no sufficient reason to avoid the consummation of an act esteemed to be so desirable by both."[19]

Upshur did a fine job in his work with Texas officials. He talked to Van Zandt as often as he could that August and September and made a favorable impression on him. "Upshur brought up the subject in all of his official interviews, stating that it was the great measure of the administration; and that he was actively engaged, under the instructions of President Tyler, in preparing the minds of the people for it, and in learning the views of the Senators on the subject," wrote Van Zandt to a friend that autumn.[20]

Upshur did an even more admirable job with the senators. "Judge Upshur was very justly apprehensive that if it [annexation] should assume a party aspect, the zeal of editors of the respective parties would hurry them into that course which they might deem best subservient to the success of the party, forgetful, in their ardor for this, of permanent interest of the Union," said one senator.[21]

Secretary of State Upshur lobbied a number of senators and party officials but not the key men. He met with numerous friends of Henry Clay but not Clay. He met with numerous Van Buren associates but not Van Buren. By doing this, he spread a wide net of support but did not risk interference by powerful men who might be opposed to the idea. He did it slowly, too, day by day, state by state. He met senators in hallways, in restaurants, and under trees.[22]

Upshur made little headway at first because Texas and Mexico were still involved in discussions to end hostilities that had been simmering since the Battle of San Jacinto seven years earlier. In his December 1843 State of Texas speech, Houston never mentioned annexation. He also could not offer any assurances that everyone in the American government wanted Texas to join the Union. "[I] could not as [Van Zandt] could readily see, offer any positive assurance that the measure would be acceptable to all branches of government," he said.

At the same time, the negotiations between Texas and Mexico collapsed. Houston was annoyed. Tyler pounced upon the news of the end of the Mexico–Texas talks and told the world, in his annual message, that Mexico would declare war on the United States if it annexed Texas. Then, in what was probably his finest speech, he reminded Texans and Americans that the Mexican officials were the same ones who had "massacred" the defenders of the Alamo in 1836. (Any mention of Mexico and the Alamo infuriated Texans.) Tyler added that there was no difference between the Americans of 1776 and the Texans of 1843. "These United States threw off their colonial dependence, and established independent governments; and Great Britain, after having wasted her energies in the attempt to subdue them for a less period than Mexico has attempted to subjugate Texas, had the wisdom and justice to acknowledge their independence. Tyler added that he would "throw [himself] upon the patriotism of the people to sustain the government in its course of action."

By this time, Upshur had made considerable progress in his secret campaign to bring the Lone Star Republic into the Union. In his desk drawer, he had a list of names of senators in favor of annexation and those against. Slightly more than two-thirds, the necessary number for passage, were in favor.

The desire for annexation grew in Texas as its difficulties with Mexico rose. Texas did not want to be invaded by Mexico again. It did not need any more Alamos. Annexation would give Texas considerable, very official American protection against any invasion by Mexico or any other foreign power. By the end of 1843, the feelings for annexation were so great that the Texas legislature recalled its minister to Washington to apply political pressure to secure annexation.

What the Texas congressmen did not know, though, was that Houston had already entered into talks with Upshur and, through him, Tyler. Houston's reason for secrecy was different than Tyler's. Houston was terrified that if the annexation talks with the United States were made public and failed, the Mexican army would invade Texas and he would also lose the goodwill of both France and Great Britain, which had been wooing him for a year with no knowledge of the series of clandestine meetings and discussions with US officials.

Finally, on January 20, 1844, feeling pressure from all sides, Houston admitted the talks to the Texas congress in a secret message. "Hence, the utmost caution and secrecy on our part as to the true motives of our policy should be carefully observed," he said. Houston added that he had kept the upper hand in the discussions with the Americans. "If we evince too much anxiety it will be regarded as importunity and the voice of supplication seldom commands, in such cases, great respect."[23]

In his talks with the United States, Houston pushed hard on his friendly relationship with England, a country many Americans despised. "You would be amused to see their jealousy of England," wrote one of Houston's aides of the Americans in 1844. "Houston has played it off well and that is the secret of success if we do succeed."[24]

At the same time, Tyler was receiving a lot of false information: not only was Britain negotiating with Texas in public but dozens of British secret agents were in Texas or writing Houston from England.[25]

Back in Washington, Gilmer joined Upshur in his campaign and was just as successful. In January 1844, Upshur wrote William Murphy, the US chargé d'affaires to Texas, saying that the people of Texas wanted to join the Union just as fervently as, he now could show, the overwhelming majority of the US Senate. "No doubt can be entertained of the wishes of the people of Texas in regard to the annexation of that country to the United States. I have the most unequivocal proofs in a variety of forms that they are almost unanimous in favor of that measure," he said. He told Murphy that Houston was playing a game with the United States and England in seeking protection in Texas's feuds with Mexico.

Houston did not yet believe that Americans would welcome Texas. Upshur scoffed at that contention. "On that point," Upshur said, "I cannot of course speak with absolute certainty, but I feel a degree of confidence in regard to it which is little short of absolute certainty. The more the subject is discussed among our statesmen, the more clearly does it appear that the interests of both countries absolutely require that they should be united."

This was not just a hopeful letter, though. He had proof.

The proof was in his secret negotiations with the senators. "Measures have been taken to ascertain the opinions and views of senators upon the subject and it is found that a clear constitutional majority of two thirds are in favor of the measure. . . . There is not, in my opinion, the slightest doubt of the ratification of a treaty of annexation, should Texas agree to make one," he wrote.[26]

At the same time these negotiations were developing in secret, who began his own secret talks with both sides but former president Andrew Jackson, at the urging of Mississippi Democrat Robert Walker, who told Jackson, "I think the annexation of Texas depends on you." Walker told him to urge Tyler and Houston to conclude a ratification treaty. Different senators had been writing Jackson on the views of US government officials, and he had been in correspondence with Houston about the feelings of citizens of Texas regarding joining the Union. One senator told Jackson that on his count, forty Senators would vote for it and just thirty-five were necessary.[27]

Still, Houston hesitated. He told friends, yet again, that if Texas entered into negotiations with the United States, it would be attacked by Mexico and perhaps defeated. He asked the United States for military help to protect his country, which he assumed, rightly or wrongly, was in dire straits. "The exposed and defenseless situation of Texas did seem to require that the United States would not leave her defenseless or expose her to the invasions of Mexico pending such negotiations, to which the United States had invited her. Under these circumstances, and the protestations of President Houston, that he would not enter into such negotiations, which would inevitably induce the invasion of Texas the moment it was known if Mexico, without assurances from me, on behalf of my government, that such invasion would be checked by the United States," Houston wrote to Murphy, who then asked Tyler to order the US Navy into the Gulf of Mexico to protect Texas.[28]

Robert Walker penned one of the most comprehensive pamphlets on bondage, a publication that the men in Tyler's White House were certain would carry the vote for them. Walker's "manifesto" was odd but effective. To blunt criticism that Texas would come into the Union as a slave state, he wrote at length that this was true but that many slaves from border slave states would be taken to Texas by their masters, primarily to work in cotton fields, and that would dilute the number of African Americans in the border states, year by year, until there were none left. He argued too that all the southwestern territories were inhabited by "tainted" races of people, such as Hispanics, blacks, and Indians. Texas, as part of the Union, he said, would act as a huge "buffer" to keep all those people way from the whites in the North.[29]

Jackson, a shrewd politician, supported the annexation but carefully framed his approval on the idea that Texas would mean just as much to the northern states as it would to the South.

His lobbying for Texas was done quietly, as was the work of Upshur and Walker, all at the behest of Tyler. The president's political plan was to line up considerable support for the bill to annex Texas and then send the bill to Congress, certain that it would pass. By January 1844, Upshur was confident that could be done.[30]

Upshur finally did get in touch with Henry Clay, but Clay, who had enormous support for whatever he wanted to do in Congress, waffled for many months. Clay would write Giddings in September of 1844 that "whilst at the South I am represented as a Liberty man, at the North I am decried as an ultra-supporter of slavery, when in fact I am neither one. . . . The existence, maintenance and continuance of the institution of slavery depends exclusively on state power and authority," he said, restating his long-held approval of forced labor.

At that same time, Clay finally came out publicly in favor of the annexation of Texas as a slave state. "[I] would be glad to see it without dishonor, without war, with the common consent of the Union and upon just and fair terms," said Clay.[31]

JUST TWO WEEKS after Clay's alliance, the *Princeton*, a new naval warship with the country's largest cannons, was launched at Alexandria, just across the Potomac from the White House. President Tyler, members of his cabinet, numerous congressmen, and a dozen members of the diplomatic corps were on board for the ceremony on a chilly winter day. They were there for both the launch and a demonstration of the ship's guns, at ten tons the largest in the US Navy.

In the morning, Tyler and hundreds of others boarded a ship at Greenleaf Point that carried them to the *Princeton*. Also on the boat was former New York state senator David Gardiner and his attractive daughter Julia, age twenty-one. Dolley Madison, the venerated wife of the late president James Madison, stood nearby dressed in one of her signature turban hats. She cut a dazzling figure.

The large ship sailed into the Potomac, and the guns were fired several times to the approval of the elite crowd on board. Everyone went downstairs for lunch, but several dozen people pressed the captain to fire the guns again, and he reluctantly agreed. A circle of dignitaries surrounded the big guns as the captain prepared to fire them.

Chatting with others, Tyler was slow in finishing his lunch. Then, as he strode up the gangway to the guns, someone pressed a drink into his hand. Another offered a toast. The president stopped, lifted his glass, and listened to the toast. That last toast probably saved his life. The big guns did not fire properly. One exploded. The force of the explosion killed six, including Gardiner, Upshur, and Gilmer. A shaken Tyler ran to the scene on deck and did what he could to help. Julia Gardiner collapsed when she learned of her father's death, and Tyler carried her off the ship. The incident apparently sparked a romance. Two were married just four months later.

Tyler wrote, "A more heart-rending scene never occurred. What a loss I have sustained in Upshur and Gilmer. They were truly my friends and would have aided me for the next twelve months with great effect. But it is all over now and I must look out for new cabinet ministers. My great desire will be to bring [in] as many able men as the country can afford."[32]

The bodies of the dead were laid in state, first in the East Room of the White House and then at the Capitol on Friday. Thousands passed the coffins. "The East Room was crowded with the President and his Cabinet and sons, and women of his family, the two Houses of Congress, foreign ministers, the Mayors of Washington, George town and Alexandria, municipal officers and of the departments of the army and Navy and the relatives of the deceased," wrote Adams.[33]

Adams, the old liberal, was getting tired of the fight. His infirmities grew as the years went by. Exhausted, in 1844 he wrote, "I have now struggled nearly five years without the interval of a day while mind and body have been wearing away under the daily, silent but unremitting erosion of time. I rose this morning at four, and with a smarting, bloodshot eye and shivering hand, still at dawn and wrote. . . . Time is the race of a man with a wooden leg after a horse."[34]

On Saturday, the funerals were held, and the bodies buried at Congressional Cemetery. There, Tyler was nearly killed again when the horses pulling his carriage bolted and ran off. He was nearly thrown from the carriage.

Tyler did not let the tragedy slow the march toward the annexation of Texas. He named retired, veteran US senator John C. Calhoun, a slavery champion, as his new secretary of state. He asked his attorney general, John Nelson, to run the State Department on an interim basis until Calhoun's anticipated arrival in Washington a few weeks later.

Nelson stepped right into the Texas debate, firing off a letter to Texas officials. He said that while the president could not send a formal naval or army force to Texas since the nation was not at war, "he was not indisposed, as a measure of prudent precaution, and as preliminary to the proposed negotiations, to concentrate on the Gulf of Mexico, and upon the southern border of the United

States, a naval and military force, to be directed to the defense of the inhabitants and territory of Texas."[35]

Shortly afterward, Tyler did send warships to the Gulf of Mexico, off the shores of Texas. Prior to that, a Mexican minister wrote Washington that if the United States annexed Texas, Mexico would consider it an act of war. [36]

Upon his arrival in the capital, Calhoun found that he had many supporters, such as ambassador to England Edward Everett, who wrote the president that "considering the state of the country and the peculiar state of foreign relations, Mr. Calhoun will, to my judgement, bring to the public service a greater capacity of usefulness than any other individual could do; nor do I doubt that his disposition will fully second his ability."[37]

Calhoun also had numerous enemies, as he had for years. In 1839 a bitter George Gilmer, the governor of Georgia, wrote "[Calhoun] is too exclusively selfish, too ambitious and too grasping in all his efforts to be trusted by others to effect public purpose."[38]

Calhoun was completely behind the annexation of Texas. He wrote at the end of 1843, "The annexation of Texas to be necessary to the peace and security of both countries and will be beneficial to the rest of the civilized world. . . . As to the other portions of our Union, North and Northwest, her annexation would open a wide and valuable market for her products, while in a political point of view, it could not more than compensate for the fast extension opened to the now slaveholding states to the Pacific on the line of Oregon." Calhoun, a longtime defender of servitude, saw Texas as a wonderful new addition to the forced labor empire of the South.[39]

Calhoun was alarmed by the British, too, but over its international influence. He wrote British minister to the United States Richard Pakenham that the Texas question was a southern question. All Americans knew how bitterly the British hated slavery, so would they not try to liberate blacks in Texas and all the other southern states too? His letter garnered tremendous support in the South and sent northern antislavery people into a frenzy. It was really the first time that a southerner had advocated, boldly, something that drove government policy—that the overseers with the whips in the cotton fields had far more power than legislators with pens in the houses of Congress.

An influential promoter of bondage had been Upshur. Before his untimely death, he had carried on a letter and whispering campaign telling all that the annexation of Texas was good because it increased the size and power of the slaveholding South. It seemed to many that the advancement of servitude, not the advancement of the Union, was Upshur's goal. His remarks brought about a torrent of antislavery criticism in the North. Anti-bondage leaders and politicians castigated Upshur and Tyler in town meetings, letters, and newspaper editorials. The annexation slowly turned into a slave debate.

By the spring of 1844, Tyler was confident that he had the two-thirds vote needed in the Senate to pass the Texas treaty. Abel Upshur and Thomas Gilmer had assured him of that from their constant vote counts. Tyler paid little attention to the misgivings of many northern public officials and paid practically none to abolitionist leaders. He had it wrapped up and, votes in hand, was eager to get the treaty instantly passed and claim his prize.

Tyler also pleaded with everybody to annex Texas right away, before the treaty could be overturned by actions in Great Britain or Mexico. "If annexation is to be accomplished, it must, I am convinced, be done immediately. Texas is in no condition to delay. She will not stake her interests upon possible but remote, contingencies."[40]

When Tyler sent the treaty to Congress, he made an impassioned plea for its passage: "There exists no civilized government on earth having a voluntary tender made it of a domain so rich and fertile, so replete with all that can add to national greatness and wealth and necessary to its peace and safety that would reject the offer. . . . Under every view which I have been able to take of the subject I think that the interests of common constituents the people of all other states, and a lover of the Union left the executive no other alternative than to negotiate the treaty."[41]

Surprisingly, the treaty was defeated, and badly, in the first week of June 1844. The result had been apparent to everyone but Tyler for the several weeks prior to the vote. Why was it voted down? Didn't Upshur and Gilmer have its passage well in hand? First, both secret lobbyists had died in the *Princeton* explosion, and the president, told by both in late February that approval of the treaty was a sure thing, did not bother to replace them. The time between their deaths and the treaty vote was nearly four months, and opponents of the annexation were hard at work during that time. Tyler had no one keeping an eye on the senators pledged to approve the treaty during those four months.

Some changed their minds, slowly but surely, but the president did not know that. Second, Tyler paid no attention to severe criticism of the treaty during the month before the vote. Third, the antislavery leaders on their own could not defeat it, but the abolitionists' key congressmen and senators urged numerous other senators to vote no. Fourth, Gilmer and Upshur had simply believed the senators too strongly; many were not as firm in favor of annexation as the pair had thought. Fifth, the terms of the treaty were complicated. It required Texas to come into the Union as a territory, not a state, and then to beg the Congress to make it a state. No one knew when Congress would consider a vote on state-hood. Why not just let us in as a new state? the Texans asked.

The defeat stunned Tyler. It ended whatever last-minute hopes he had of winning either the Whig or Democratic presidential nomination or even gaining support from a third party. The president was finished politically. He would serve out nine more months of his term and then go home to Virginia.

He was bitter and showed his anger in a letter to a group of Democrats just before their 1844 convention. "In entering upon the office, I had to decide the question whether I would surrender honor, judgement, conscience , and the right of an independent mind, into the hands of a party majority, in whose views and opinions, it became very soon obvious I could not concur without such surrender or whether I should brave all consequences in the vindica-tion of the constitutional rights of the executive and in the discharge of the most sacred obligations of duty to the country," he said. He concluded that his "noble" nature had resulted in his political crucifixion. "Every harsh appellation was employed with my name, mobs assembled at midnight at the doors of the Presidential mansion, and the light of burning effigies threw its glare along the streets of some of the cities. . . . My reliance was placed upon the people." And the people, he said, supported him.[42]

In a grand and very whimsical gesture, he said he had risked his presidency for Texas and the good of the Union. "The question with me is between Texas and the Presidency. The latter, even if within my grasp, would not for a moment be permitted to stand in the way of the first," he said piously.[43]

Tyler was bitter about the defeat of the treaty because he saw it as a personal attack on him and because Congress had delayed ratification of a rewritten treaty in order to attempt to have it passed during the new Polk administration, letting the new president get all the glory.

But then the president had an epiphany. He had lost the vote and any chance at a presidential nomination, but there was still the glory of annexing Texas and a place in history. If he could still get Texas into the Union, somehow, someway, during the waning months of his term, he would leave office on a high note and go down in history as the man who brought Texas into the Union and forever change the course of the American story. He realized, looking at a calendar in his office, that the new president would not be sworn in for nine months, certainly more than enough time to rework the treaty and get it rammed through Congress by his men. So on June 10 the president, with a new spring in his step, was back at work on Texas.

Tyler immediately asked the House and Senate to work on a new joint resolution calling for statehood, which needed only a majority vote.[44] It was passed on March 1, 1845, and signed by Tyler on March 3, the day before his term ended.

On October 13, 1845, Texan voters approved the annexation by an overwhelming vote, 4,174 to 312. At the end of the year, Texas formally came into the Union, after much negotiation with Polk officials. Polk got all the credit, not Tyler. Tyler scoffed about Polk that "a greater victory was never achieved than that already accomplished."[45]

When the treaty had first passed on March 1, 1845, it did so to the cheers of supporters and the dismay of opponents. "[It is] preliminary to the equally fatal conspiracy of Julius Caesar!" wrote Adams. "The annexation of Texas is the first step to the conquest of all Mexico, of the West Indies islands, of a maritime, colonizing, bondsmen-tainted monarchy, and of extinguished freedom."[46]

Adams was not alone in his opinion. Congressman Daniel Barnard of New York agreed, telling fellow representatives, "As certain as truth and God exist, the admission of Texas into the Union will prove, sooner or later, an element of overwhelming ruin to the Republic."[47]

Some predicted a war with Mexico over Texas in just a few years. "We have adopted a war ready-made," wrote Horace Greeley, editor of the *New York Tribune*, "and taken upon ourselves its prosecution to the end."[48]

When the Lone Star Republic flag came down in Texas and the US flag was raised in its place, the Texas flag was folded up and handed to Sam Houston, who tapped it gently and lovingly. By that time, former president John Tyler was back home in Virginia, still without applause for the annexation, still without a party, and still without the nineteen mutineers from the *Creole*.

EPILOGUE

THE STORY OF THE *Creole* finally ended thirteen years later in the House of Representatives. In February 1855, Congress approved an agreement, arranged in London, that settled the claims of the American owners of the *Creole* as well as the owners of the *Hermosa*, *Enterprise*, and a number of other slave transport vessels that since 1814 had been seized at sea or arrived somehow on British islands.

The *Creole*'s ramifications were far-reaching, though, and extended well beyond the halls of Congress in America and Parliament in London.

What were the lessons of the *Creole*?

Lesson one: fear. No matter how much the mutineers on the transport wanted freedom, the overwhelming majority of bondsmen and bondswomen opted not to participate in the mutiny to get it, even when Washington threatened their lives. They wanted to avoid the tumultuous struggle on the deck of the ship and all the bloodshed. They did that because they were afraid the mutineers would lose and that anyone involved in the melee would be hanged alongside Washington and his colleagues. If the mutineers lost, those who had refused to participate would be left alone. If they sat back and did nothing and the mutineers won, then they won too, and without taking any risks. On that ship, at that moment, on that night, those men and women were scared and saw nonparticipation as the better part of valor. It was not a betrayal or even a disagreement, just a decision to remain on the sidelines.

There is an important point here, though. All nineteen men involved in the mutiny and all the others who knew about it but chose not to participate could not betray the group. Several large-scale revolts and mutinies and had failed because of betrayal. No one on the ship could say one word, offer one hint, about the upcoming revolt. They had to trust each other with the mutiny and with their lives. They may have disagreed with the men staging the revolt, but they were their brothers and sisters. Nothing could come between them.

Madison Washington has to be applauded for taking care of the captain and his family right after the mutiny. He had his men escort them to safety in the hold of the ship, out of the captain's cabin, which was jammed with angry men. He personally took care of Ensor. He kept him informed of where the ship was going and the leniency they planned to ask of the governor. Washington bound up the captain's wounds and assured him, continually, that no harm would come to him or his family members. Mrs. Ensor and the girls must have been frantic, and he calmed them down. He did that to help gain some sympathy from the governor of the Bahamas, to be sure, but he did not have to do it. It was an act of human kindness on his part, for which Ensor and his wife were grateful.

What about the small confines of the slave ship? At first, one might think that revolts would be easier on plantations or in cities than on ships. Slave ships were small, with few places to hide. Slaves were held in small compartments below decks, with locked doors. Tools that could be used as weapons were plentiful on land but not at sea. Secret communications worked far better on land. Yet it turned out that the ship served the mutineers far better than a plantation. The smallness of the arena helped them in the fight. All it took was inventiveness, an observant eye. and a few missteps by the captain and crew.

How did Washington, a cook, develop such leadership skills? We don't know. He had the advantage of size. He was almost five foot ten, taller than the average man of that era. He was muscular from years of slave labor on his old Virginia plantation. The men on the ship, and his fellow mutineers, saw his height and strength as power, and they saw power as leadership. He was an African American Samson

Lesson two: crowd power. The thousands of black Bahamians who jammed the piers around the *Creole* to cheer on the slaves, those who surrounded them when they were taken to the police station, and the men in small boats who continually sailed close to the Creole at anchor sent a very loud message: the men and women from the *Creole* had landed in the Bahamas, British territory, and were now free. All the other slaves who had wound up in the Bahamas over the years had been granted freedom and these people were too. Even the mutineers who had murdered a man were free, the crowd roared. All these people should go free.

Or else.

The never-spoken threat was clear. This was a country where the white British inhabitants were a very small minority of the population. British security was minimal. There would be no help from the British navy, which was far away. It would take an army a month to get there on transports. There was absolutely no protection for Governor Cockburn or his government if the crowd turned cruel. Could the masses become unruly? Of course.

Freedom for the mutineers was not a matter of maybe. British law had upheld the freedom of all their predecessors. A crowd's leaders could argue effectively that the decision had already been made in several cases and that the governor could not overturn it on whim. He had to free them. The British courts in London had to free them.

Or else.

The crowd believed there was nothing to be gained by discussing the *Creole* case with John Bacon, the US ambassador. He had to be dismissed or at least his claims had to be ignored. In the eyes of the crowd, there was to be no chance—none—that America could interfere in this matter just to help a few shipowners make money—money to be made at the expense of the black worker, the unpaid black worker, the enslaved black worker. To permit that was to insult all black Bahamians. Ambassador Bacon had to be ignored.

Or else.

Cockburn was more aware of that threatened violence than any other man on the island. He heard the crowd roar. He heard it roar every day, and he knew what it meant.

He would take care of the *Creole* matter.

Or else.

The final lesson of the slave ship story was the power of the African American grapevine. How did these men and women, seemingly unable to read and in bondage on plantations far away from books, newspapers, and public discussions, know so much about British law? The Underground Railroad was already running smoothly in 1841. It issued no magazines, brochures, or timetables, yet all slaves seeking freedom from plantations in the South, following a usually carefully planned escape route, knew all about it. They knew where the safe houses on the route to freedom were and how to get there, who lived there, and how long they'd be sheltered before their helpers would move them along to another secret safe house. How was that possible?[1]

It was possible because for years word had traveled across the South—across plantation fields and through riverfront warehouses, where workers loaded corn, wheat, tobacco, cotton, and other products. There is nothing as informative and forceful as the grapevine in any country in any era and in any color. African Americans used it and used it well, especially in the *Creole* saga.

THE SLAVES from the *Creole* were long gone by the time Congress settled the case. Some remained in the Bahamas, some settled in Jamaica, some traveled to other Caribbean islands, and some, like leader Madison Washington, simply vanished. It is unknown if any of the *Creole* travelers knew how the *Creole* helped get Texas into the Union, or if any of them cared.

The key figures in the *Creole* incident had different fates. Daniel Webster, who quit the cabinet in 1842, went back to the US Senate in 1845. He served most of one term before again becoming secretary of state, this time under President Millard Fillmore. He tried to run for president again, in 1851, but was in failing health. He lost and died shortly afterward.

Firebrand congressman Joshua Giddings, who eliminated the gag rule, led House antislavery activists for eighteen more years, until he lost an election in 1859. During that period he left the Whig Party and joined the antislavery Free Soil Party. In 1854 he became one of the founders of the Republican Party. In 1860 he smiled broadly when told that Virginians had offered $10,000 to anyone who captured him and brought him to Richmond. He finished his career as the US consul to Canada, where he died in 1864.

John C. Calhoun, Tyler's last secretary of state, returned to the Senate in 1848 but had little power there and backed the wrong party in major disputes. He was against the Compromise of 1850, which passed, and against US entry into the war with Mexico, which ended as he arrived back in the Senate. Calhoun died in 1850.

Henry Clay, the Senate's longtime power broker, left the Senate to run for president a third time in 1844. He lost and went back to the Senate in 1849. There, he returned to his former glory, introducing legislation that led to the

Compromise of 1850, which kept North and South out of a war, for the time being. He died in 1852.

John Quincy Adams luxuriated with Giddings in orchestrating the end of the gag rule in the House and continued to champion the cause of freedom until his death in 1848. He is best known as a president and a congressman, but he was also the driving force for creation of the Smithsonian Institution. A lifelong lover of science, he convinced Congress to provide a considerable sum of money to build the institution, which grew over the years into arguably the world's finest museum.

Lord Ashburton (Alexander Baring) returned to London after the signing of the Webster–Ashburton Treaty, in which the United Kingdom and the United States pledged to increase worldwide antislavery work, with both navies now chasing down ships loaded with captives on the Atlantic. He spent his life as a partner in his family's banking firm, Baring Brothers, and was a trustee of both the British Museum and the National Gallery.

Captain Robert Ensor recovered in the Bahamas and sailed back to Virginia with his family. He went right back to commanding transports making the Richmond-to-New Orleans run and did so for years.

History remembered all of them, but few remembered Madison Washington and his mutineers. History remembered that slavery ended, though, and the mutineers helped to bring that about in the winter of 1841 and 1842. For them, wherever they were, that was enough.

NOTES

Chapter One

1. Lee, "Madison Washington," 8; Frederick Douglass, *Heroic Slave*, 179; Hamilton, "Models of Agency," 96; Bernier, "Dusky Powder Magazines," 158n.

2. *Liberator*, January 7, 1842.

3. Washington stood close to five foot ten, average height today, but in the 1840s the average man was about five foot five. Washington towered over everyone on the slave ship. Slave manifest, National Archives, Fort Worth, Texas; Sales, *Slumbering Volcano*, 677–78.

4. . Washington's physical masculinity was seen as a necessity to the slaves. Slave ship builders were numerous; Frederick Douglass was one. Trivelli, "I Knew a Ship," 104.

5. Chapelle, *History of the American Sailing Navy*, 178.

6. Downey, *Creole Affair*, 10.

7. Sales, *Slumbering Volcano*, 121.

8. Douglass, *Heroic Slave*, 228.

9. Rediker, *Slave Ship*, 41–45.

10. Rupprecht, "All We Have Done," 255.

11. Jones, *Mutiny on the Amistad*, 14–30.

12. Frederick Douglass, quoted in Hyde, "The Climate of Liberty," 476.

13. Kettner, *Development of American Citizenship*, 56.

14. William Wells Brown, quoted in Ripley, *Black Abolitionist Papers*, 1:197.

15. That was Gifford's best guess in his New Orleans protest testimony. Others said the blacks made up anywhere from 80 to 90 percent of the population. Hendricks and Hendricks, *Creole Mutiny*, 100.

16. Hendricks and Hendricks, *Creole Mutiny*, 62–63.

17. Jacobs, "Incidents in the Life of a Slave Girl," 64.

18. Varon, *Disunion*, 76–77; Bacon, *But One Race*, 32–33.

19. *New Orleans Courier*, December 14, 1829.

20. Dass, *Black Rebellion*, 136.

21. Dass, *Black Rebellion*, 142.

22. Davis, *Problem of Slavery*, 32.

23. *Liberator*, June 10, 1842; Bernier, "Dusky Powder Magazines," 125; Hendricks and Henricks, *Creole Mutiny*, 42–43.

24. Cheek, *Black Resistance*, 22–23.

25. Higginson, *Black Rebellion*, 310–15.

26. *Alabama Free Press*, August 20, 1835; *Liberator*, September 19, 1935, September 16, 1935, October 3, 1835.

27. *Liberator*, September 5, 1835.

28. Aptheker, *American Negro Slave Revolts*, 327–30.

29. Donnan, *Documents Illustrative of the Slave Trade*, 132, 131.

30. Koch and Peden, *Life and Selected Writings of Thomas Jefferson*, 278–79.

31. Parrish, *Remarks on the Slavery of Black People*, 2, 4, 9.

32. Max Farrand, ed., *The Records of the Federal Convention, 1787* (New Haven: Yale University Press, 1937), 3:211.

33. Davis, *Problem of Slavery*, 270–71.

34. Davis, *Problem of Slavery*, 335.

35. Thomas Clarkson, *Abolition of the African Slave-Trade, by the British Parliament* (Augusta, GA: P. A. Brinsmade, 1830), 19, 33, 184.

36. Clarkson, *Abolition*, 342.

37. Hugh Thomas, *The Slave Trade* (New York: Simon and Schuster, 1999), 728.

38. Thomas, *Slave Trade*, 662.

39. Hart, *Slavery and Abolition*, 290–91.

40. Henry Wise to the US State Department, February 18, 1845, Hill, *Diplomatic Relations*, 114.

41. Crapol, *John Tyler*, 96.

42. Hyde, "Climate of Liberty," 480.

43. *Philadelphia Inquirer*, December 26, 1889.

44. Hamilton, "Models of Agency," 132.

45. Hundreds of slaves were kept in pens in Richmond before they were put on slave transports bound for New Orleans and other Gulf of Mexico ports, according to Solomon Northup. That is what happened to him. Northup, *Twelve Years a Slave*, 68–72.

46. Shipmates' joint testimony, New Orleans, December 14, 1841, Parliamentary Papers, 59:151–259.

47. Deposition of Zephaniah Gifford, Nassau, November 9, 1841, Parliamentary Papers, 59:138.

48. Sales, 124.

49. Gifford and several other members of the crew heard Washington yelling above the sound of the men clamoring up the wooden stairs to the deck of the ship. His description is from the New Orleans "protest," or hearing, of December 2, 1842, Parliamentary Papers, 59, 112–65. Washington's cry of "Liberty" was also recalled at a protest. Douglass, *Heroic Slave*, 177; Barnes, *Wolfsden*, 450.

50. Hendricks and Hendricks, 83–88.

51. Gifford's account is from his testimony at a New Orleans protest on December 2, 1842.

52. Hyde, "Climate of Liberty," 489; Douglass, *Heroic Slave*, 193.

53. New Orleans protests of Zephaniah Gifford, Lucius Stevens, Henry Speak, Blinn Curtis, John Silvy, Francis Foxwell, Jacque LaCombe, and William Devereux,

December 14, 1841, Parliamentary Papers, 59:151–59; S. Doc. No. 51, 27th Cong., 2d Sess., II, 1–46 (1842).

54. Rupprecht, "All We Have Done," 259.

55. The description of Blacksmith is based on a protest deposition by Robert Ensor in Nassau. Parliamentary Papers, 59:136–37; Barnes, *Wolfsden*, 440, 504.

56. Hendricks and Hendricks, 85; depositions of several crew members at the Nassau "protest," S. Doc. No. 51, 27th Cong., 2d Sess., II, 1–46 (1842).

57. Deposition of Jacob Leitner, Nassau, November 8, 1841, Parliamentary Papers, 59:144.

58. Shipmates' joint deposition, New Orleans, December 14, Parliamentary Papers, 59:151–59.

59. Merritt's testimony, S. Doc. No. 51, 27th Cong., 2d Sess., II, 1–46 (1842).

60. Deposition of Theophilus J. D. McCargo, Nassau, November 9, 1841, Parliamentary Papers, 59:143.

61. Deposition of Stevens, Nassau, November 10, 1841, Parliamentary Papers, 59:140.

62. Rupprecht, "All We Have Done," 259.

63. New Orleans protest documents, 1843, Parliamentary Papers, 59:112–65.

64. Testimony of Ensor, Gifford, Stevens, and Curtis at John Bacon's *Creole* incident inquiry in the Bahamas, November 12, 1841, S. Doc. No. 51, 27th Cong., 2d Sess. II, 1–46 (1842).

65. Deposition of Merritt, November 9, 1841, Parliamentary Papers, 59:142.

66. Jones, "The Peculiar Institution," 28–50; deposition of Ensor, Nassau, November 18, 1841, Parliamentary Papers, 59:137–38.

67. Deposition of Stevens, Nassau, November 10, 1841, Parliamentary Papers, 59:140.

68. Deposition of Stevens, Nassau, November 10, 1841, Parliamentary Papers, 59:140.

69. Protest testimony of Leitner and Gifford, Nassau, November 18, 1841, and 1843 hearing, Parliamentary Papers 59:138.

70. Downey, *Creole Affair*, 11–14; joint deposition of the shipmates, New Orleans, December 14, 1841, Parliamentary Papers, 59:151–59.

71. Douglass, *Heroic Slave*, 235; deposition of Gifford, Nassau, November 9, 1841, Parliamentary Papers, 59:139.

Chapter Two

1. Nineteenth-century map of Nassau, Mechanical Curator Collection, British Library.

2. Gifford, New Orleans protest, December 7, 1841, Parliamentary Papers, 59:117.

3. Testimony of Jacob Leitner, McCargo's New Orleans insurance company brochure, New Orleans Public Library.

4. Julian, *Life of Joshua R. Giddings*, 100–101.

5. The story of the *Creole*'s voyage and mutiny was told to Bacon and later to a hearing board in Nassau by Captain Ensor and crewmen Gifford, Curtis, and Stevens. Protests of the brig *Creole*, Nassau, November 17, 1841, Parliamentary Papers, 59:137.

6. Depositions of John Chattin, Stuart Lewis, William Lewis, and W. Y. Lewis, the crew of the *Hermosa*, Nassau, November 14, 1840, Parliamentary Papers, 59:199; separate deposition from the master of the *Hermosa*, Nassau, November, 14, 1840, Parliamentary Papers, 59:1.

7. Bacon to Webster, November 30, 1841, Parliamentary Papers, 59:125.

8. Sales, *Slumbering Volcano*, 81.

9. Edward Everett to the Earl of Aberdeen, March 1, 1842, Parliamentary Papers 59:118.

10. Rupprecht, "All We Have Done," 272.

11. Douglass, "Slumbering Volcano" speech, Papers of Frederick Douglass, series 1, 2:163, Library of Congress.

12. Cockburn to Bacon, November 12, 1841, Parliamentary Papers, 59:127; Sales, *Slumbering* Volcano, 82.

13. Shipmates' joint deposition, New Orleans, December 14, 1841, Parliamentary Papers, 59:151–59.

14. Fox to Lord Aberdeen, December 28, 1841, Parliamentary Papers, 59:112; Everett to Earl of Aberdeen, March 1, 1842, Parliamentary Papers, 52:115–17, 121.

15. Everett to Earl of Aberdeen, March 1, 1842, Parliamentary Papers, 59:118.

16. Everett to Earl of Aberdeen, March 1, 1842, Parliamentary Papers, 59:118.

17. Everett to Earl of Aberdeen, March 1, 1842, Parliamentary Papers, 59:120.

18. Bacon to Cockburn, November 14, 1841, Parliamentary Papers, 59:127–28.

19. Everett to Earl of Aberdeen, March 1, 1842, Parliamentary Papers 59:122; Fox to Earl of Aberdeen, February 25, 1842, Parliamentary Papers, 59:160.

20. Everett to Earl of Aberdeen, March 1, 1842, Parliamentary Papers, 59:123.

21. Everett to Earl of Aberdeen, March 1, 1842, Parliamentary Papers, 59:122.

22. Deposition of Merritt, Nassau, November 13, 1841, Parliamentary Papers, 59:132.

23. Deposition of Merritt, Nassau, November 13, 1841, Parliamentary Papers, 59:132.

24. Everett to Earl of Aberdeen, March 1, 1842, Parliamentary Papers, 59:116.

25. Everett to Earl of Aberdeen, March 1, 1842, Parliamentary Papers, 59:115–16; Rupprecht, "All We Have Done," 272.

26. Deposition of Woodside, November 13, 1841, Parliamentary Papers, 59:131–32.

27. Deposition of Gifford, November 9, 1841, Parliamentary Papers 59:133; John Bacon, S. Doc. No. 51, 27th Cong., 2d Sess. II, 1–46 (1842); shipmates' joint deposition, New Orleans, December 14, 1841, Parliamentary Papers, 59:151–59.

28. Depositions of Stevens, Gifford, Ensor, and Curtis, November 13, 1841, November 17, 1841, Parliamentary Papers, 59:130.

29. Everett to Earl of Aberdeen, March 1, 1842, Parliamentary Papers 59:115–16.

30. Everett to Earl of Aberdeen, March 1, 1842, Parliamentary Papers, 59:115–16; Rupprecht, "All We Have Done," 273.

31. Anderson to Cockburn, November 18, 1841, Parliamentary Papers, 59:129.

32. Woodside deposition, Nassau, November 13, 1841, Parliamentary Papers, 59:132.

33. Anderson to Cockburn, November 18, 1841, Parliamentary Papers, 59:130.

34. Merritt's testimony at Bacon's inquiry into the *Creole* incident, Bahamas, November 12, 1841, Parliamentary Papers, 59:132–33.

35. Robinson, *Reports of Cases*, 10:203–54.

36. Shipmates' joint deposition, New Orleans, December 14, 1841, Parliamentary Papers, 59:151–59.

37. Deposition of Stevens, Nassau, November 13, 1841, Parliamentary Papers, 59:130.

38. Protest deposition of Stevens, Ensor, Curtis, and Gifford, November 17, 1841, Parliamentary Papers, 59:136.

39. Bacon to Webster, November 30, 1841, Parliamentary Papers, 59:125.

40. Everett to Earl of Aberdeen, March 1, 1842, Parliamentary Papers, 59:114–15, 117.

41. Anderson to Cockburn, November 18, 1841, Parliamentary Papers, 59:129.

42. John Killens, ed., *The Trial Record of Denmark Vesey* (Boston: Beacon Press, 1970), 46, 58.

43. Bacon to Webster, November 17, 1841, Parliamentary Papers, 59:123–24.

44. Sales, *Slumbering Volcano*, 84; Bacon statement at deposition in Nassau, November 18, 1841, Parliamentary Papers, 59:137.

45. Sales, *Slumbering Volcano*, 120.

46. Bacon to Webster, November 30, 1841, Parliamentary Papers, 59:123. Cockburn's heated denial was mentioned in a note from Bacon, who did not give a deposition on this issue, on November 15 1841, Parliamentary Papers, 59:128.

47. Luther, *Writings and Speeches*, 193; *Liberator*, February 19, 1858.

48. Harrold, "Romanticizing Slave Revolt," 101.

49. Henry Highland Garnet in an 1843 speech to the National Convention of Colored Citizens, Buffalo, New York, quoted in Ripley, *Black Abolitionist Papers*, 3:410.

50. Dass, *Black Rebellion*, 172; *Liberator*, 1842.

51. *New York Evangelist*, December 25, 1841; Frederick Douglass, West India emancipation speech, delivered at Canandaigua, New York, August 4, 1857. Papers of Frederick Douglass, Library of Congress.

52. Frederick Douglass, "American Prejudice against Color," Papers of Frederick Douglass, Series 1, 3:193–94, Library of Congress.

Chapter Three

1. *National Intelligencer*, June 2, 1840.

2. Giddings diary, letter to a friend, January 15, 1840, Julian, *Life of Joshua R. Giddings*, 88; Clay to a Mr. Porter, December 8, 1840, Hopkins, *Papers*, 9:458–59; Tyler, *Letters*, 2:9.

3. December 4, 1841, April 2, 1841, Nevins, *Diary of John Quincy Adams*, 514, 519.

4. Monroe, *Republican Vision*, 95; *New York Herald*, July 30, 1841.

5. A. O. P. Nicholson to James K. Polk, June 14, 1841, James. K. Polk, *Correspondence of James K. Polk*, 14 vols. (Knoxville: University of Tennessee Press, 1972–2001), 5:698.

6. *New York Herald*, quoted in George Rawlings Poage, *Henry Clay and the Whig Party* (New York: Peter Smith, 1965), 56n.

7. Wise to Tucker, May 29, 1841, Tyler, *Letters*, 2:34.

8. Wise to Tucker, June 5, 1841, Tyler, *Letters*, 2:37–38.

9. Tyler, *Letters*, 2:4-5.

10. Peterson, *Presidencies*, 42; April 6, 1841, Nevins, *Diary of John Quincy Adams*, 522.

11. Clay to Daniel Ullman, May 12, 1847; Remini, *Revolutionary Age*, 687–88.

12. Tyler to C. A. Wickliffe, August 24, 1845, Preston Davis Papers, Virginia Historical Society.

13. Peterson, *Presidencies*, 50; Morgan, *American Slavery, American Freedom*, 5.

14. April 9, 1841, Tyler, *Letters*, 2:20.

15. Tyler to William Rives, April 9, 1841, Tyler, *Letters*, 2:21; speech of Rives, *Cong. Globe*, 27th Cong, 1st Sess., appendix, 368 (1841).

16. Tyler recalled the humiliating letters from the State Department in a letter to his son Robert, October 16, 1848, Tyler, *Letters*, 3:13.

17. *Richmond Whig*, April 30, 1841.

18. Tyler to Tazewell, October 11, 1841, Tyler, *Letters*, 2:127.

19. Monroe, *Republican Vision*, 108, 114.

20. Tyler, *Letters* 2:92.

21. Hopkins, *Papers*, 1:588.

22. Wise to Tucker, July 11, 1841; Tyler *Letters*, 2:52.

23. Giddings diary, 1838, Julian, *Life of Joshua R. Giddings*, 54.

24. Tyler to Anne Tyler, December 28, 1831, Tyler, *Letters*, 1:426.

25. Tyler to John Cunningham, July 15, 1852, Tyler, *Letters* 2:499–500.

26. *National Intelligencer*, March 9, 1842; Monroe, *Republican Vision*, 119.

27. Tyler to Clay, April 30, 1841, Hopkins, *Papers of Henry Clay*, 9:527–29.

28. Tyler to Tucker, July 26, 1841, Tyler, *Letters* 2:51–52.

29. Schurz, *Henry Clay*, 200.

30. Richardson, *Compilation*, 3:1892.

31. Richardson, *Compilation*, 3:1892; Tyler, *Letters*, 2:frontispiece.

32. *Charleston Courier*, May 5, 1841.

33. Webster to Harrison, December 11, 1840, in Baxter, *One and Inseparable*, 274; Remini, *Revolutionary* Age, 568.

34. Clay to John Clayton, February 12, 1841, Hopkins, *Papers*, 9:499.

35. Tyler, *Letters*, 2:115.

36. Brugger, *Beverley Tucker*, 1–10.

37. Monroe, *Republican Vision*, 88.

38. Baxter, *One and Inseparable*, 187.

39. Baxter, *One and Inseparable*, 191.

40. Thomas Gilmer to Frank Minor, January 1, 1841, Papers of John Tyler, College of William and Mary.

41. Baxter, *One and Inseparable*, 228.

42. Baxter, *One and Inseparable*, 260.

43. Baxter, *One and Inseparable*, 283–86.

44. Jones, *Mutiny on the Amistad*, 39.

45. Webster to Graham, April 12, 1842, in Hamilton and Williams, *Papers of William*

Alexander Graham, 3:186–87; John Bell to R. P. Lechter, May 2, 1841, *Tyler's Quarterly and Genealogical Magazine* 8 (1927):178.

46. Schurz, *Henry Clay*, 203.

47. *Richmond Enquirer*, June 4, 1841.

48. Tyler to Alexander Gardiner, May 6, 1845, Tyler, *Letters* 2:97–102.

49. Thomas Ewing to John Crittenden, December 29, 1842, Tyler, *Letters* 2:25–26.

50. Adams, *Memoirs*, 10:456–57; April 16, 1842, Nevins, *Diary of John Quincy Adams*, 521–22.

51. Peterson, *Presidencies*, 54; William Preston to Willie Mangum, May 3, 1841, Shanks, *Papers*, 3:155–57; S. Jones to Tyler, April 14, 1841, Papers of John Tyler, College of William and Mary.

52. Tyler, *Letters*, 2:135.

53. Tyler, *Letters*, 2:cover page, 191.

54. January 1, 1842, Nevins, *Diary of John Quincy Adams*, 532.

55. Clay to Tucker, April 15, 1841, Tyler, *Letters*, 2:30.

56. James Lyons, letter to the *New York World*, August 31, 1880.

57. Various letters to friends, December 1840, Hopkins, *Papers*, 9:457–65.

58. Clay to N. B. Tucker, April 15, 1841, Tyler, *Letters*, 2:30; Colton, *Private Conversations*, 453–54; Remini, *Daniel Webster*, 524; Remini, *Revolutionary Age*, 181.

Chapter Four

1. Nickolas Carroll to Willie Mangum, April 7, 1841, Shanks, *Papers*, 3:132–35.

2. Rozwenc, *Meaning of Jacksonian Democracy*, 75.

3. Colton, *Private Conversations*, 453–54.

4. Colton, *Works*, 3:206–13

5. Remini, *Revolutionary Age*, 177.

6. Tyler, *Letters* 2:39.

7. Tyler to a Mrs. Waller, September 13, 1844, Tyler, *Letters*, 3:155.

8. Clay to the Whig caucus, September 13, 1841, Hopkins, *Papers*, 9:608–9.

9. Schurz, *Henry Clay*, 207.

10. *Tallahassee Floridian*, September 18, 1841; Botts to Richmond Coffee House, August 16, 1841, Tyler, *Letters*, 2:112.

11. Wise to John B. Coles and others, November 5, 1841, Tyler, *Letters* 2:113–14.

12. *Cong. Globe*, 27th Cong., 2d Sess., appendix, 257 (1841–1842).

13. Remini, *Revolutionary Age*, 182.

14. Schurz, *Henry Clay*, 229–30.

15. Tyler, *Letters* 2:57.

16. Henry Clay to his wife, Lucretia, August 16, 1840, Hopkins, *Papers*, 9:439.

17. Remini, *Daniel Webster*, 622, 626.

18. *Frankfort Commonwealth*, May 7, 1844.

19. Giddings diary, December 24, 1838, Julian, *Life of Joshua R. Giddings*, 54; Allan

Nevins, *The Diary of Philip Hone*, 2 vols. (New York: Dodd, Mead, 1927), 2:53; Remini, *Daniel Webster*, 579.

20. *New York Tribune*, September 29, 1841.

21. Remini, *Daniel Webster*, 616.

22. Remini, *Daniel Webster*, 616.

23. Daniel Webster, "Memorandum on the Banking Bills and the Vetoes, 1841," in Wiltse and Moser, *Papers of Daniel Webster*, 5:177–79.

24. Tyler, *Letters*, 2:33–34.

25. Tyler, *Letters*, 160.

26. Tyler, *Letters*, 219.

27. John Tyler to the Norfolk (Virginia) Democratic Association, December 2, 1844, Tyler, *Letters*, 2:95.

28. Tyler to Robert Tyler, March 12, 1848, Tyler, *Letters* 2:107.

29. *Intelligencer*, September 10, 1841.

30. Henry Wise, speech to the House of Representatives, Tyler, *Letters* 2:60.

31. Tyler, *Letters* 2:65.

32. Schurz, *Henry Clay*, 215–16; Remini, *Daniel Webster*, 574.

33. Remini, *Daniel Webster*, 574.

34. Tyler, *Letters* 2:85.

35. Clay to a Mr. Porter, January 16, 1842, Hopkins, *Papers* 9:632.

36. Schurz, *Henry Clay*, 218.

37. Julia Tyler, *Cincinnati Graphic News*, June 25, 1887.

38. Tyler, *Letters*, 2:39.

39. Upshur to Tucker, September 7, 1841, Tyler, *Letters*, 2:46–47; Clay on Whig principles, in Congress, Colton, *Works*, 3:216.

40. Julia Tyler, *Graphic News*, June 25, 1887.

41. Cumming, *Secret History*, 24.

42. Colton, *Works*, 3:279.

43. Upshur to Tucker, August 7, 1841, in Frederick Merck, *Slavery and the Annexation of Texas* (New York: Alfred Knopf, 1972).

44. Schurz, *Henry Clay*, 227.

45. Daniel Webster, *Mr. Webster's Address at Andover* (Boston: Press of T. R. Martin, 1843), 35.

46. John Tyler Jr. to Lyon Tyler, 1883, Tyler, *Letters* 2:121–22.

47. Upshur to Tucker, March 6, 1842, Tyler, *Letters* 2:156–57.

48. Remini, *Daniel Webster*, 529; Baxter, *One and Inseparable*, 193.

49. *National Intelligencer*, September 13, 1841.

50. Tyler to Norfolk Democratic Organization, September 2, 1844, Tyler, *Letters* 2:95–96.

51. *National Intelligencer*, September 15, 1841.

52. Peterson, *Presidencies*, 95.

53. Tyler to Norfolk Democratic Organization, September 2, 1844, Tyler, *Letters* 2:95–96.

54. Tyler to Thomas Cooper, October 8, 1841, Tyler, *Letters* 2:125–26.

55. Remini, *Daniel Webster*, 532.

56. Peterson, *Presidencies*, 95.

57. Webster, *Mr. Webster's Address*, 35.

58. Schurz, *Henry Clay*, 212.

59. Tyler to Thomas Jefferson, May 12, 1810, Tyler, *Letters* 2:104.

60. Heidler and Heidler, *Henry Clay*, 358.

61. *Tallahassee Floridian*, September 18, 1841; letter to John Crittenden, September 8, 1841, Tyler, *Letters* 2:92.

62. *New York Herald*, May 10, 1843.

63. *New York Herald*, June 10, 1842.

64. Peterson, *Presidencies*, 90–91.

65. Crapol, *John Tyler*, 106.

66. *Madisonian*, August 21, 1841.

67. Upshur to Tucker, March 13, 1842, Tyler, *Letters*, 2:158.

68. Tyler, *Letters* 2:105.

69. Tyler to his son Robert, June 3, 1858, Tyler, *Letters* 2:19.

70. Upshur, 1842, Tyler, *Letters* 2:135.

71. Upshur to Tucker, December 23, 1841, Tyler, *Letters* 2:154.

72. *New York Herald*, September of 1841, in Tyler, *Letters* 2:115–16.

73. Richardson, *Papers and Messages*, 4:190–93.

74. Monroe, *Republican Vision*, 138.

75. Tyler to John Rutherford, June 23, 1841, Tyler, *Letters* 2:50.

76. Upshur to Tucker, March 28, 1842, Tyler, *Letters* 2:165

77. Webster to a friend, September 11, 1841, in Webster, *Mr. Webster's Address*, 37.

78. George Badger's letter of resignation, Tyler, *Letters* 2:110.

79. Willie Mangum to Priestly Mangum, August 10, 1842, Shanks, *Papers*, 3:376–77; Monroe, *Republican Vision*, 142.

80. Monroe, *Republican Vision*, 112.

81. *New York Herald*, November 22, 1842.

82. *Madisonian* of early October quoted in the *Washington Globe*, October 19, 1841.

83. Webster to Everett, August 25, 1842, Wiltse and Moser, *Papers of Daniel Webster*, 5:232–33, 238.

84. Hopkins, *Papers*, 9:631.

85. Downey, *Creole Affair*, 93.

Chapter Five

1. Higginson, "Story of Denmark Vesey," 740, 744.

2. New Orleans depositions by William Merritt, Zephaniah Gifford, and others, November 17, 1841, S. Doc. No. 51, 27th Cong., 2d Sess. II, 1–46 (1842).

3. Jones, "Peculiar Institution," 35.

4. Carroll, *Slave Insurrections*, 215.

5. *New Orleans Commercial Bulletin*, quoted in the *Richmond Enquirer*, December 16, 1841; Jones, "Peculiar Institution," 34.

6. *Niles Weekly Register*, October 1, 1825; *New York Evening Post*, May 18, May 20, May 23, May 26, December 14, and December 15, 1826.

7. Jones, "Peculiar Institution," 35.

8. William Ogilby to Fox, April 29, 1842, Parliamentary Papers, 59:280.

9. Theodore Ward, *Madison Washington*, a never-performed four-act musical, Hatch-Billops Archive, New York, New York.

10. *Anti-Slavery National Standard*, January 13, 1842.

11. Jones, "Peculiar Institution," 33; Lord Aberdeen to Lord Ashburton, May 26, 1842, BM 43123, private letters, Papers of George William Gordon, University of Edinburgh.

12. Gifford's New Orleans testimony, S. Doc. No. 51, 27th Cong., 2d Sess. II, 1–46 (1842); Jervey and Huber, "Creole Affair," 204.

13. Jervey and Huber, "Creole Affair," 205; Richardson, *Compilation*, 3:278.

14. Franklin and Schweninger, *Runaway Slaves*, 186.

15. Downey, *Creole Affair*, 86.

16. *New Orleans Courier*, December 10, 1841; *New Orleans Bulletin*, early December 1841; Jervey and Huber, "Creole Affair," 205.

17. *Washington Globe*, quoted in Sales, *Slumbering* Volcano, 135.

18. Carol Bleser, ed., *Secret and Sacred: The Diaries of James Henry Hammond a Southern Slaveholder* (New York: Oxford University Press, 1988), 88–89; *Cong. Globe*, 27th Cong., 2d Sess., 333–34 (1842).

19. May, *John Tyler*, 84.

20. Moore, *History and Digest*, 410–11, 417.

21. Tyler, *Letters* 2:205.

22. Webster to Everett, January 29, 1842, Wiltse, *Papers of Daniel Webster*, 1:177–85; *Cong. Globe*, 27th Cong., 2d Sess., 256 (1842).

23. Lord Aberdeen to Everett, April 18, 1841, Parliamentary Papers, 59:195.

24. Lord Aberdeen to Everett, April 18, 1841, Parliamentary Papers, 59:195.

25. Lord Aberdeen to Everett, April 18, 1841, Parliamentary Papers, 59:195.

26. Remini, *Daniel Webster*, 618.

27. Clay to a Mr. Porter, January 16, 1842, Hopkins, *Papers*, 9:632.

28. Remini, *Daniel Webster*, 542; Jervey and Huber, "Creole Affair," 205.

29. May, *John Tyler*, 85.

30. Davis, *Problem of Slavery*, 671.

31. Remini, *Daniel Webster*, 542; Chitwood, *John Tyler*, 308–9.

32. Everett to Webster, Wiltse, *Papers of Daniel Webster*, 1, 488.

33. Everett to Webster, December 31, 1841, Webster, *Diplomatic and Official Papers*, 33.

34. Everett to Webster, December 31, 1841, Webster, *Diplomatic and Official Papers*, 544.

35. Jones, *Webster-Ashburton Treaty*, 113–14.

36. Downey, *Creole Affair*, 123.

37. Downey, *Creole Affair*, 122.

38. Downey, *Creole Affair*, 124.

39. September 5 and 6, 1842, Nevins, *Diary of John Quincy Adams*, 542–43.

40. Jones, *Webster-Ashburton Treaty*, 43.

41. Tyler, *Letters* 2:216.

42. May, *John Tyler*, 88.

43. Crapol, *John Tyler*, 103–4.

44. Lord Ashburton to Lord Aberdeen, April 26, 1842, May 29, 1842, Jones, *Webster-Ashburton Treaty*, 118.

45. Tyler to Robert McCandlish, July 10, 1842, Tyler, *Letters*, 2:172–73.

46. Tyler to Robert McCandlish, July 10, 1842, Tyler, *Letters* 2:108.

47. Tyler, *Letters*, 2:219.

48. Chitwood, *John Tyler*, 305–6.

49. Howe, *What Hath God Wrought*, 673.

50. Peterson, *Presidencies*, 126.

51. Log of HMS *Termagant*, October 21, 1839, Parliamentary Papers, 59:245.

52. Seagram to Elliott, October 30, 1839, Parliamentary Papers, 59:246.

53. Seagram to Elliott, October 30, 1839, Parliamentary Papers, 59:127.

54. Hendricks and Henricks, *Creole Mutiny*, 100.

55. *Liberator*, February 11, 1842.

56. James McDowell, *Speech of James McDowell, Jr. (of Rockbridge) in the House of Delegates of Virginia, on the Slave Question: Delivered Saturday, January 21, 1832* (Richmond, VA: Thomas W. White, 1832).

57. *Richmond Enquirer*, December 2, 1831.

58. *Acts Passed by the General Assembly of the State of North Carolina (1830–1831)* (Raleigh: Lawrence and LeMay, 1831); Carroll, *Slave Insurrections*, 168.

59. Sinha, *Slave's Cause*, 412–13.

60. *Cong. Globe*, 27th Cong, 2d Sess., 110, 203–4 (1842).

61. Phillips, *American Negro Slavery*, 487–88.

62. Oakes, *Ruling Race*, 180.

63. Blumrosen and Blumrosen, *Slave Nation*, 34–35.

64. Chitwood, *John Tyler*; Mayer, *Son of Thunder*, 168–69.

65. Aptheker, *American Negro Slave Revolts*, introduction; Dass, *Black* Rebellion, 134–35; *Virginia Gazette*, September 12, 1800.

Chapter Six

1. David Birney to Lewis Tappan, February 2, 1835, Dumond, *Letters of James Gillespie Birney*, 1:179.

2. *Liberator*, December 13, 1839.

3. July 24, 1841, Nevins, *Diary of John Quincy Adams*, 528.

4. Ralph Waldo Emerson, *The Complete Works of Ralph Waldo Emerson*, 12 vols. (Boston: Houghton, Mifflin, 1803–1882), 10:371–77.

5. Ronald Walters, *The Anti-Slavery Appeal: American Abolitionism after 1830* (Baltimore: Johns Hopkins University Press, 1976), 129.

6. Lowance, *Against Slavery*, 135.

7. Thomas, *Liberator*, 281.

8. Kraditor, *Means and Ends*, 123; Lowance, *Against Slavery*, 54–55.

9. Lowance, *Against Slavery*, 224–27; Ruchames, *Abolitionists*, 164.

10. Leavitt to Giddings, October 29, 1841, Papers of Joshua Giddings, Library of Congress; Weld to J. F. Robinson, May 1, 1836, Barnes and Dumond, *Letters*, 1:197.

11. Theodore Weld to Lewis Tappan, December 14, 1841, Barnes and Dumond, *Letters*.

12. Hart, *Slavery and Abolitionism*, 168–69.

13. Theodore Weld to his wife, January 1, 1842, Barnes and Dumond, *Letters*.

14. Giddings diary, 1838, Julian, *Life of Joshua R. Giddings*, 48; Hecht, *John Quincy Adams*, 595; Herbert Aptheker, *Abolitionism: A Revolutionary Movement* (Boston: Twayne, 1929), 52.

15. Dillon, *Abolitionists*, 102.

16. March 29, 1841, Nevins, *Diary of John Quincy Adams*, 519.

17. Weld to his wife, January 25, 1842, Barnes and Dumond, *Letters*.

18. Gerda Lerner, *The Grimke Sisters from South Carolina: Rebels against Slavery* (Boston: Houghton-Mifflin, 1967), 221–22.

19. Barnes and Dumond, *Letters*, 2:577–78; description from Henry Brewster Stanton, Weld MSS, Angelina Grimke to J. Smith, November 19, 1837, Barnes and Dumond, *Letters*.

20. Elkins, *Slavery*, 181; Ceplair, *Public* Years, 6.

21. Lowance, *Against* Slavery, 56–57.

22. Lowance, *Against Slavery*, 223–24; Dillon, *Abolitionists*, 84.

23. James Oates, *The Scorpion's Sting: Anti-Slavery and the Coming of the Civil War* (New York: W. W. Norton, 2014), 67–68.

24. Elkins, *Slavery*, 192.

25. *Emancipator*, July 28, 1836.

26. Weld to his wife, January 25, 1842, Barnes and Dumond, *Letters*.

27. Weld to Lewis Tappan, February 3, 1843, Barnes and Dumond, *Letters*, 2:974.

28. Ceplair, *Public Years*, 138; Kraditor, *Means and Ends*, 119.

29. Weld to Sarah Grimke, March 27, 1837, Barnes and Dumond, *Letters*, 2:605.

30. David Potter, *The Impending Crisis* (New York: Harper and Row 1976), 40.

31. Dillon, *Abolitionists*, 122.

32. Thomas, *Liberator*, 178; Kraditor, *Means and Ends*, 122.

33. Barnes and Dumond, *Letters*, 2:93.

34. Dumond, *Letters of James Gillespie Birney*, 2:662.

35. Barnes, *Anti-Slavery Impulse*, 180–81.

36. Register of Debates, 24th Cong., 1st Sess., 79–80, 2d Sess., 714–15.

37. Thomas, *Liberator*, 346–47.

38. Thomas, *Liberator*, 188–190

39. Varon, *Disunion*, 102.

40. Sinha, *Slave's Cause*, 451.

41. Gerrit Smith, "Gerrit Smith Defends the Right of the Abolitionist to Discuss Slavery," in Ruchames, *Abolitionists*, 113.

42. December 21, 1837, Nevins, *Diary of John Quincy Adams*, 491.

43. January 11, 1807, Waldstreicher and Mason, *John Quincy Adams*, 19.

44. March 12, 1819, Waldstreicher and Mason, *John Quincy Adams*, 55–56.

45. March 12, 1819, Waldstreicher and Mason, *John Quincy Adams*, 55–56.

46. April 29, 1819, Waldstreicher and Mason, *John Quincy Adams*, 61.

47. July 5, 1819, Waldstreicher and Mason, *John Quincy Adams*, 63.

48. July 15, 1820, Waldstreicher and Mason, *John Quincy Adams*, 69.

49. February 11, 1820, Waldstreicher and Mason, *John Quincy Adams*, 71.

50. February 28, 1820, Waldstreicher and Mason, *John Quincy Adams*, 77.

51. February 28, 1820, Waldstreicher and Mason, *John Quincy Adams*, 77.

52. August 11, 1835, Nevins, *Diary of John Quincy Adams*, 462.

53. August 14, 1835, Nevins, *Diary of John Quincy Adams*, 463.

54. March 3, 1842, Waldstreicher and Mason, *John Quincy Adams*, 265.

55. Jesse Macy, *The Anti-Slavery Crusade: A Chronicle of the Gathering* Storm (New Haven, CT: Yale University Press, 1919), 80–86.

56. December 20, 1837, Nevins, *Diary of John Quincy Adams*, 490–91.

57. November 22, 1837, Nevins, *Diary of John Quincy Adams*, 488–89.

58. January 28, 1842, Waldstreicher and Mason, *John Quincy Adams*, 535.

59. *National Intelligencer* June 2, June 16, June 19, 1841; *New York Herald*, June 21, 1841; *Charleston Courier*, June 15, 1841.

60. Barnes and Dumond, *Letters*, 911.

61. Julia Tyler, "Reminiscences of Mrs. Julia Tyler," *Cincinnati Graphic News*, June 25, 1887.

62. Adams's quotes are from a letter from Weld to his wife in the spring of 1842, Barnes and Dumond, *Letters*.

63. January 31, 1842, Nevins, *Diary of John Quincy Adams*, 536.

64. Hecht, *John Quincy Adams*, 595.

65. February 3, 1842, Nevins, *Diary of John Quincy Adams*, 536.

66. Julian, *Life of Joshua R. Giddings*, 107.

67. June 14, 1841, Waldstreicher and Mason, *John Quincy Adams*, 257.

68. February 6, 1842, Waldstreicher and Mason, *John Quincy Adams*, 261.

69. Giddings diary, Traub, *John Quincy Adams*, 489.

70. Julian, *Life of Joshua R. Giddings*, 107.

71. Weld to his wife, January 25, 1842, Barnes and Dumond, *Letters*.

72. Julian, *Life of Joshua R. Giddings*, 108.

73. February 5, 1842, Nevins, *Diary of John Quincy Adams*, 537.

74. Julian, *Life of Joshua R. Giddings*, 109.

75. February 4, 1842, Nevins, *Diary of John Quincy Adams*, 536–37.

76. February 7, 1842, Nevins, *Diary of John Quincy Adams*, 538.

77. Traub, *John Quincy Adams*, 492.

78. Traub, *John Quincy Adams*, 488–94.

79. Albert Hart, *Slavery and Abolitionism, 1831–1861* (New York: Harper and Row, 1906), 294; Edward Pierce, *Memoir and Letters of Charles Sumner*, 4 vols. (Boston: Roberts Brothers, 1877–1893), 2:200.

80. November 19, 1841, Waldstreicher and Mason, *John Quincy Adams*, 259.

81. Thomas, *Liberator*, 160; Fred Kaplan, *John Quincy Adams: American Visionary* (New York: Harper and Row 2014), 523.

82. Davis, *Problem of Slavery*, 660.

83. Peterson, *Presidencies*, 125.

84. Sales, *Slumbering Volcano*, 130.

Chapter Seven

1. Julian, *Life of Joshua R. Giddings*, 47–48.

2. Julian, *Life of Joshua R. Giddings*, 38, 50.

3. Julian, *Life of Joshua R. Giddings*, 51.

4. Giddings diary, January 21, 1839, Julian, *Life of Joshua R. Giddings*, 63–64.

5. Julian, *Life of Joshua R. Giddings*, 52.

6. Giddings diary, December 16, 1838, Julian, *Life of Joshua R. Giddings*, 53.

7. Giddings diary, December 27, 1838, Julian, *Life of Joshua R. Giddings*, 56.

8. Giddings diary, January 7, 1839, Julian, *Life of Joshua R. Giddings*, 60.

9. Giddings diary, January 30, 1839, Julian, *Life of Joshua R. Giddings*, 64.

10. Julian, *Life of Joshua R. Giddings*, 65.

11. Giddings diary, February 12, 1839, Julian, *Life of Joshua R. Giddings*, 67.

12. Julian, *Life of Joshua R. Giddings*, 67–68.

13. Julian, *Life of Joshua R. Giddings*, 70.

14. Julian, *Life of Joshua R. Giddings*, 98.

15. Julian, *Life of Joshua R. Giddings*, 76–77.

16. September 2, 1841, Waldstreicher and Mason, *John Quincy Adams*, 270.

17. Waldstreicher and Mason, *John Quincy Adams*, 120–22.

18. February 28, 1821, Waldstreicher and Mason, *John Quincy Adams*, 97.

19. Waldstreicher and Mason, *John Quincy Adams*, 281.

20. Julian, *Life of Joshua R. Giddings*, 123.

21. Julian, *Life of Joshua R. Giddings*, 125.

22. March 22, 1841, Waldstreicher and Mason, *John Quincy Adams*, 539.

23. May 21, 1842, Waldstreicher and Mason, *John Quincy Adams*, 540.

24. Gerald Home, *Negro Comrades of the Crown: African-Americans and the British Empire Fight the United States before Emancipation* (New York: New York University Press, 2012), 137.

25. Giddings diary, Julian, *Life of Joshua R. Giddings*, 128.

26. Downey, *Creole Affair*, 102.

27. Samuel Chase to Giddings, January 22, 1842, and February 1842, Julian, *Life of Joshua R. Giddings*, 132–33.

28. Essays printed in Julian, *Life of Joshua R. Giddings*, 136.

29. Letter to Henry Fassett, Julian, *Life of Joshua R. Giddings*, 138.

Chapter Eight

1. Julian, *Life of Joshua R. Giddings*, 156–57.

2. Tyler, *Letters*, 2:483.

3. Tyler, *Letters*, 2:483.

4. May 4, 1844, Nevins, *Diary of John Quincy Adams*, 569–70.

5. Yoakum, *History of Texas*, 2:347.

6. Silbey, *Storm Over Texas*, 32.

7. Campbell, *Gone to Texas*, 173.

8. Campbell, *Gone to Texas*, 159.

9. Tyler, *Letters*, 2:268.

10. Tyler to Webster, 1850, Papers of John Tyler, College of William and Mary.

11. Julian, *Life of Joshua R. Giddings*, 276.

12. Julian, *Life of Joshua R. Giddings*, 274.

13. Adams, *Memoirs*, XI:374

14. Silbey, *Storm Over Texas*, 38.

15. Duff Green to John Tyler, July 3, 1843, Papers of Duff Green, University of North Carolina.

16. Silbey, *Storm Over Texas*, 38.

17. Silbey, *Storm Over Texas*, 41; John C. Calhoun to Richard Pakenham, April 18, 1844, Meriwether, *John C. Calhoun*, 18:273–81.

18. Papers of John Tyler, 4:6901–2, College of William and Mary.

19. Tyler, *Letters*, 2:323.

20. Yoakum, *History of Texas*, 2:422–23.

21. William Penn, *Madisonian*, April, 25, 1844.

22. William Penn, *Madisonian*, April, 25, 1844.

23. Campbell, *Gone to* Texas, 184.

24. James Henderson to Thomas Jefferson Rusk, February 1844, Campbell, *Gone to Texas*, 184.

25. William Murphy to Tyler, March 10, 1844, National Archives, Washington, DC.

26. Tyler, *Letters*, 2:283–84.

27. Yoakum, *History of Texas*, 2:435.

28. William Murphy to John Tyler, February 17, 1844, Tyler, *Letters*, 2:287–88.

29. Silbey, *Storm Over Texas*, 35.

30. Chitwood, *John Tyler*, 348.

31. Clay to Giddings, September 11, 1844, Julian, *Life of Joshua R. Giddings*, 164–65.

32. Julian, *Life of Joshua R. Giddings*, 289.

33. February 28, 1844, Nevins, *Diary of John Quincy Adams*, 567.

34. March 25, 1844, Nevins, *Diary of John Quincy Adams*, 568.

35. S. Doc. No. 349, 28th Cong., 1st Sess., 10 (1843–1844).

36. Calhoun to Van Zandt, April 11, 1844, J. Franklin Jameson, ed., *Correspondence of John C. Calhoun*, 2 vols. (Washington, DC: Government Printing Office, 1900), 2:41; José Maria De Bocanegra, Mexican minister of foreign affairs, to Waddy Thompson, August 23, 1843, *Niles Register* 45:264.

37. Edward Everett to John Tyler, April 8, 1844, Tyler, *Letters*, 2:301.

38. George Gilmer to Thomas Gilmer, January 28, 1839, Tyler, *Letters*, 2:295.

39. Julian, *Life of Joshua R. Giddings*, 296.

40. John Tyler to delegates to the 1844 Democratic National Convention, May 30, 1844, Tyler, *Letters*, 2:319–21.

41. Richardson, *Compilation of Papers and Messages*, 4:307–13.

42. Tyler, *Letters*, 2:319–21.

43. Tyler, *Letters*, 2:319–21.

44. *Cong. Globe*, 28th Cong., 2d Sess., 127–28 (1844–1845).

45. Tyler, *Letters*, 2:330.

46. June 10, 1844, Nevins *Diary of John Quincy Adams*, 570–71.

47. Silbey, *Storm Over Texas*, xiii.

48. *New York Tribune*, March 1, 1845.

Epilogue

1. Walter Johnson, "White Lies: Human Property and Domestic Slavery aboard the Slave Ship Creole," *Atlantic Studies* 5, no. 2 (2008):237–63.

BIBLIOGRAPHY

Historical Papers

Creole slave manifest, National Archives, Fort Worth, Texas.
Papers of Duff Green, University of North Carolina, Chapel Hill.
Papers of Frederick Douglass, Library of Congress, Washington, DC.
Papers of George William Gordon, Fourth Lord of Aberdeen, University of Edinburgh.
Papers of John C. Calhoun, University of South Carolina, Columbia.
Papers of John Tyler, College of William and Mary, Williamsburg, Virginia.
Papers of Joshua Giddings, Library of Congress, Washington, DC.
Papers of Preston Davis, Virginia Historical Society, Richmond.
Parliamentary Papers, 1843, British House of Commons and Lords, London.

Journal Articles, Pamphlets, and Book Chapters

Bernier, Celeste-Marie. "'Dusky Powder Magazines': The Creole Revolt (1841) in Nineteenth Century American Literature." PhD dissertation, University of Nottingham, 2002.

Hamilton, Cynthia. "Models of Agency: Frederick Douglass and the 'Heroic Slave.'" *Proceedings of the American Antiquarian Society* 114, no. 1 (2005):87–136.

Harrold, Stanley. "Romanticizing Slave Revolt: Madison Washington, the Creole Mutiny and Abolitionist Celebration of Violent Means." In *Anti-Slavery Violence: Sectional, Racial and Cultural Conflict in Antebellum America*, edited by John McKivigan and Stanley Harrold, pp. 89–107. Knoxville: University of Tennessee Press, 1999.

Higginson, Thomas. "The Story of Denmark Vesey." *Atlantic*, June 1861.

Hyde, Carrie. "The Climates of Liberty and 'The Heroic Slave': Natural Rights for the Creole Case." *American Literature* 85, no. 3 (September 2013):475–504.

Jacobs, Harriet. "Incidents in the Life of a Slave Girl." In *The Abolitionist Sisterhood: Women's Political Culture in Antebellum America*, edited by Jean Fagin Yellin and John C. Van Horne (Ithaca: Cornell Paperbacks, 1994).

Jervey, Edward, and Harold Huber. "The Creole Affair." *Journal of Negro History* 65, no. 3 (Summer 1980):196–211.

Jones, Howard. "The Peculiar Institution and National Honor: The Case of the Creole Slave Revolt." *Civil War History* 21, no. 1 (March 1975):28–50.

Lee, Edward. "Madison Washington: Slave Mutineer" *Black Fox Literary Magazine* 8, no. 36 (Winter/Spring 1988).

Rupprecht, Anita. "'All We Have Done, We Have Done for Freedom.' The Creole Slave-Ship Revolt (1841) and the Revolutionary Atlantic." *International Review of Social History* 58, special issue 21 (2013):253–77.

Smith, Gerrit. "Gerrit Smith Defends the Right of the Abolitionist to Discuss Slavery." In *The Abolitionists' Collection of Their Writings*, edited by Louis Buchames. New York: G. P. Putnam's Sons, 1963.

Trivelli, Marifrances. "I Knew a Ship from Stern to Stern." *Log of Mystic Seaport* 46, no. 4. (1995):1955.

Play

Ward, Theodore. *Madison Washington*. New York: Hatch-Billops Archive.

Books

Adams, Charles Francis. *Memoirs of John Quincy Adams*, 12 vols. Philadelphia: J. B. Lippincott, 1876.

Aptheker, Herbert. *American Negro Slave Revolts*. New York: International Publishers, 1943.

Bacon, Margaret. *But One Race: The Life of Robert Purvis*. Albany: State University of New York Press, 2007.

Barnes, Gilbert. *The Anti-Slavery Impulse, 1830–1844*. New York: Harcourt, Brace and World, 1933.

Barnes, Gilbert, and Dwight Dumond, eds. *Letters of Theodore Weld, Angelina Grimke Weld and Sarah Grimke, 1822–1844*, 2 vols. New York: D. Appleton-Century, 1934.

Barnes, Josiah. *Wolfsden: An Authentic Account of Things There and Thereunto Pertaining as They Are and Have Been*. Boston: Phillips, Sampson and Co., 1856.

Baxter, Maurice. *One and Inseparable: Daniel Webster and the Union*. Cambridge, MA: Harvard University Press, 1984.

Bleser, Carol, ed. *Secret and Sacred: The Diaries of James Henry Hammond, a Southern Slaveholder*. New York: Oxford University Press, 1988.

Blumrosen, Alfred, and Ruth Blumrosen. *Slave Nation: How Slavery United the Colonies and Sparked the American Revolution*. Naperville, IL: Sourcebooks, 2005.

Brugger, Robert. *Beverley Tucker: Heart Over Head in the Old South*. Baltimore: Johns Hopkins University Press, 1978.

Campbell, Randolph B. *Gone to Texas: A History of the Lone Star State*. New York: Oxford University Press, 2003.

Carroll, Joseph. *Slave Insurrections in the United States, 1800–1865*. New York: Negro Universities Press, 1938.

Ceplair, Larry. *The Public Years of Sarah and Angelina Grimke, Selected Writings 1835–1839*. New York: Columbia University Press, 1989.

Chappele, Howard. *The History of the American Sailing Navy: The Ships and Their Development*. New York: Bonanza Books, 1949.

Cheek, William. *Black Resistance before the Civil War*. Beverley Hills: Glencoe Press, 1970.

Chitwood, Oliver. *John Tyler: Champion of the Old South*. Newtown, CT: American Political Biography Press, 1939.

Colton, Calvin, ed. *The Private Conversations of Henry Clay*. New York: A. S. Barnes, 1855.

———. *The Works of Henry Clay*, 10 vols. London: G. P. Putnam's Sons, 1904.

Crapol, Edward. *John Tyler: The Accidental President*. Chapel Hill: University of North Carolina Press, 2006.

Cumming, Hiram. *Secret History of the Perfidies, Intrigues and Corruption of the Tyler Dynasty, with the Mysteries of Washington City Connected with that Vile Administration in a Series of Letters to the ex-Acting President by One Familiar with the Subject*. Washington, DC: Hiram Cumming, 1845.

Dass, Sujan, ed. *Black Rebellion: Eyewitness Accounts of Major Slave Revolts*. Atlanta: Two Horizons Press, 2010.

Davis, David. *The Problem of Slavery in the Age of Revolution, 1770–1823*. Ithaca: Cornell University Press, 1975.

Dillon, Merton. *The Abolitionists: The Growth of a Dissenting Minority*. DeKalb: Northern Illinois University Press, 1971.

Donnan, Elizabeth. *Documents Illustrative of the Slave Trade to America*, 4 vols. Washington, DC: Carnegie Institute, 1951.

Douglass, Frederick. *The Heroic Slave: Autographs for Freedom*. London: Sampson, Low, Son, and Co., and John Cassell, 1853.

Downey, Arthur. *The Creole Affair: The Slave Rebellion That Led the US and Great Britain to the Brink of War*. New York: Rowman and Littlefield, 2014.

Dumond, Dwight. *Letters of James Gillespie Birney 1831–1857*, 2 vols. New York: D. Appleton-Century Co. 1938.

Elkins, Stanley, ed. *Slavery: A Problem in American Institutional and Intellectual Life*. 3rd ed. Chicago: UniversityMayof Chicago Press, 1959.

Franklin, John Hope, and Loren Schweninger. *Runaway Slaves: Rebels on the Plantation*. New York: Oxford University Press, 1999.

Hamilton, J. G., and Max Williams, eds. *The Papers of William Alexander Graham*, 6 vols. Raleigh: North Carolina State Department of Archives and History, 1957.

Hart, Albert. *Slavery and Abolitionism, 1831–1861*. New York: Harper and Bros., 1906.

Hecht, Marie. *John Quincy Adams: History of an Independent Man*. New York: Macmillan, 1972.

Heidler, David, and Jeanne Heidler. *Henry Clay: The Essential American*. New York: Random House, 2010.

Hendricks, George, and Willene Hendricks. *The Creole Mutiny: A Tale of Revolt aboard a Slave Ship*. Chicago: Ivan R. Dee, 2003.

Higginson, Thomas. *Black Rebellion: A Selection from Travelers and Outlaws*. New York: Arno Press, 1969.

Hill, L. F. *Diplomatic Relations between the United States and Brazil*. Durham, NC: Duke University Press, 1932.

Hopkins, James, ed. *The Papers of Henry Clay*, 11 vols. Lexington: University Press of Kentucky, 1956–1990.

Howe, Daniel. *What Hath God Wrought: The Transformation of America, 1815–1848*. New York: Oxford University Press, 2007.

Jones, Howard. *Mutiny on the Amistad: The Saga of a Slave Revolt and Its Impact on American Abolitionism, Law and Diplomacy*. New York: Oxford University Press, 1987.

———. *To the Webster-Ashburton Treaty: A Study in Anglo-American Relations*. Chapel Hill: University of North Carolina Press, 1977.

Julian, George. *The Life of Joshua R. Giddings*. Chicago: A. C. McClurg, 1892.

Kettner, James. *The Development of American Citizenship 1608–1870*. Chapel Hill: University of North Carolina Press, 1978.

Koch, Adrienne, and William Pedin, eds. *The Life and Selected Writings of Thomas Jefferson*. New York: Modern Library, 1953.

Kraditor, Aileen. *Means and Ends in American Abolitionism: Garrison and His Critics in Strategy and Tactics, 1834–1850*. New York: Pantheon Books, 1967.

Lowance, Mason, ed. *Against Slavery: An Abolitionist Reader*. New York: Penguin, 2000.

Macy, Jesse. *The Anti-Slavery Crusade: A Chronicle of the Gathering Storm*. New Haven, CT: Yale University Press, 1919.

Marsh, Luther, ed. *The Writings and Speeches of Alvin Stewart*. New York: Negro University Press, 1959.

May, Gary. *John Tyler*. New York: Henry Holt, 2008.

Mayer, Henry. *Son of Thunder: Patrick Henry and the American Republic*. Charlottesville: University Press of Virginia, 1991.

Meriwether, Robert, ed. *John C. Calhoun Papers*, 28 vols. Columbia: University of South Carolina Press, 1959–2003.

Monroe, R. Daniel. *The Republican Vision of John Tyler*. College Station: Texas A&M University Press, 2003.

Moore, J. B. *History and Digest of the International Arbitrations to Which the United States Had Been a Party*, 6 vols. Washington, DC: Government Printing Office, 1898.

Morgan, Edmund. *American Slavery, American Freedom*. New York: W. W. Norton, 1975.

Nevins, Allan. *The Diary of John Quincy Adams, 1794–1845*. New York: Frederick Ungar Publishing, 1953.

Northup, Solomon. *Twelve Years a Slave*. New York: Miller, Orton & Mulligan, 1855.

Oakes, James. *Ruling Race: A History of American Slaveholders*. New York: W. W. Norton, 1998.

Parrish, John. *Remarks on the Slavery of Black People: Addressed to the Citizens of the United States*. Philadelphia: Parrish, Kimber Conrad & Co., 1806.

Peterson, Norma Louise. *The Presidencies of William Henry Harrison and John Tyler*. Lawrence: University Press of Kansas, 1989.

Phillips, Ulrich. *American Negro Slavery*. New York: Appleton, 1928.

Rediker, Marcus. *The Slave Ship: A Human History*. London: Penguin, 2002.

Remini, Robert. *The Revolutionary Age of Andrew Jackson*. New York: Harper and Row, 1976.

———. *Daniel Webster: The Man and His Times*. New York: W. W. Norton, 1997.

Richardson, James. *Compilation of Papers and Messages of the Presidents, 1789–1897*, 11 vols. Washington, DC: Government Printing Offices, 1899.

Ripley, Peter, ed. *The Black Abolitionist Papers*, 5 vols. Chapel Hill: University of North Carolina Press, 2015.

Robinson, Merritt. *Reports of Cases Argued and Determined in the Supreme Court of Louisiana, from October 1841 to March 1846*, 12 vols. New Orleans: E. Johns, 1842–1847.

Rozwenc, Edwin, ed. *The Meaning of Jacksonian Democracy: Problems in American Civilization*. Boston: D. C. Heath, 1963.

Ruchames, Louis. *The Abolitionists: Collections of Their Writings*. New York: G. P. Putnam's Sons, 1963.

Sales, Maggie Montesinos. *The Slumbering Volcano: American Slave Ship Revolts and the Production of Rebellious Masculinity*. Durham, NC: Duke University Press, 1997.

Schurz, Carl. *Henry Clay*. New York: Frederick Ungar, 1968.

Shanks, Henry, ed. *The Papers of Willie Person Mangum*, 5 vols. Raleigh: North Carolina Department of Archives and History, 1950.

Silbey, Joel. *Storm Over Texas: The Annexation Controversy and the Road to Civil War*. New York: Oxford University Press, 2005.

Sinha, Manisha. *The Slave's Cause: A History of Abolition*. New Haven, CT: Yale University Press, 2016.

Thomas, John. *The Liberator: William Lloyd Garrison*. Boston, Little Brown, 1963.

Traub, James. *John Quincy Adams: Militant Spirit*. New York: Basic Books, 2016.

Tyler, Lyon. *The Letters and Times of the Tylers*, 3 vols. New York: DeCapo Press, 1970.

Varon, Elizabeth. *Disunion: The Coming of the American Civil War, 1789–1859*. Chapel Hill: University of North Carolina Press, 2008.

Waldstreicher, David, and Matthew Mason. *John Quincy Adams and the Politics of Slavery: Selections from the Diary*. New York: Oxford University Press, 2017.

Webster, Daniel. *The Diplomatic and Official Papers of Daniel Webster, while Secretary of State*. New York: Harper and Brothers, 1848.

Wiltse, Charles, and Harold D. Moser, eds. *The Papers of Daniel Webster*, 7 vols. Hanover, NH: University Press of New England, 1974–1986.

Yoakum, Henderson. *History of Texas from Its First Settlement in 1685 to Its Annexation to the United States in 1846*, 2 vols. New York: Redfield, 1856

Newspapers

Alabama Free Press
Anti-Slavery National Standard
Charleston Courier

Cincinnati Graphic News
Congressional Globe
Liberator
Madisonian
National Intelligencer
New Orleans Courier
New York Evangelist
New York Evening Post
New York Herald
Niles Register
Philadelphia Inquirer
Richmond Enquirer
Tallahassee Floridian
Washington Globe

INDEX

Aberdeen, Lord, 37, 99, 109–110, 114, 121, 184, 185

Abolition House, 140, 141, 151, 169

abolitionists: attacks on, 146; Britain and, 98, 119, 128; courts and, 131; *Creole* and, xiii, 46, 48, 118–19, 128, 169; slave rebellions and, 11, 12, 46; secession and, 184; third parties and, 140; US government and, 98. *See also specific individuals*

Adams, John Quincy, 131, 134–35, 138, 140–58, 162, 171–76, 192; *Amistad* trial and, 49, 117, 134, 157–58, 168; civil war and, 146; *Creole* crisis and, 142, 147, 151, 154, 157–58, 169; gag rule and, 142–43, 145–47, 149–50, 167, 169, 175; Harrison and, 51; Missouri Compromise and, 144–45; Select Committee and, 140–42; Smithsonian Institution and, 201; Texas and, 182–85, 196; Tyler and, 69–70, 77, 181, 182; Wise and, 59

Adams, Louisa, 151

Ajax, 7

Alvord, John, 141

American Anti-Slavery Society, 137, 184

American Revolution, 5

Amistad: overview of, ix; abolitionists and, xiii; Adams and, 49, 117, 134, 157–58, 168; Supreme Court and, 3–4, 48, 111, 158, 168; Washington, M. and, 15

Anderson, G. C., 39, 41–43, 45, 99

Andros Island, 6, 7

Anti-Masons, 54

anti-slavery law (1807), xiv, 6, 13, 122

anti-slavery law (1833), xiv, 6, 102–3, 122, 128

anti-slavery movement: backlash against, 129; civil war and, 131; decline of, 129–32; feuds within, 129–30, 138–39; origins of, 127–28; revitalization of, 48. *See also* abolitionists

Apteker, Herbert, 126

Arnold, Thomas, 156

arson, 8

Ashburton, Lord, 92, 103–4, 112–23, 158–59, 201

Augusta, 97

Bacon, John, 30–34, 37, 39–40, 45–47, 99, 102, 104–5, 199

Badger, George, 83, 91

Bahamas: overview of, 5–7; diplomatic corps and, 104; invasion of, 47–48, 93, 111; slave ships and, 33–34, 198. *See also* Nassau

Barbour, James, 144

Baring, Alexander (Lord Ashburton), 92, 103–4, 112–23, 158–59, 201

Barrow, Alexander, 93

Bell, John, 67

Bennett, James Gordon, 92

Benton, Thomas Hart, 89

Birney, James G., 129–30, 137, 179

Black, Edward, 168

Black Lives Matter, xiv

Blacksmith, Ben, 20, 22, 24, 25, 27

Blake, Ruel, 10

Botts, John Minor, 58, 74, 79, 87–89, 156, 171–72

Brazil, 14

Britain: abolitionists and, 119, 128; anti-slavery law of, xiv, 6, 102–3, 122, 128; Bahamas and, 5–7; boundary dispute and, 103; cotton and, 159, 180; military power of, 121; piracy and, 96; Quintuple Treaty and, 123; Somerset decision and, 126; southern states and, 159; Texas and, 183, 185–86; War of 1812 and, 103, 122

Brougham, Henry Peter (Lord Brougham), 184

Brown, John, 14

Brown, William Wells, 5

Burr, Aaron, 181

Byrd, William, 11

Calhoun, John C., 58, 76, 93, 101, 126, 185, 192, 193, 200

Canada: anti-slavery laws in, 9; British loyalists and, 5; boundary disputes and, 103, 120–21; extradition and, 110; free black community in, 2

Caroline, 103, 121

Carroll, Nickolas, 72

Cass, Lewis, 122

census, falsification of, 172

Channing, William, 111

Chase, Salmon, 176

Cilley, Jonathan, 154–55

Civil War, 180

Clay, Henry, 51–55, 70–77, 79–88; bank bill and, 58, 60, 67–68, 71, 73–74, 77, 173; Compromise of 1850 and, 200–201; *Creole* crisis and, 55, 108, 111; dispute with William King, 79–80; Harrison and, 51, 52, 63, 70–73; impeachment efforts of, 90; kitchen cabinet and, 79; political style of, 52–53, 67, 73; popularity of, 75–77; pursuit of presidency, 55, 58, 85, 88, 165, 200; resignation conspiracy and, 83–86; slavery and, 81, 110, 165, 191; term limits and, 74; Texas and, 191; Tyler's war against, 93

Clay's Compromise, 82

Clayton, John, 63

Cockburn, Francis, 34, 44, 48, 199; overview of, 31–32, 102; legal proceedings and, 47, 98–101, 104–5; slaves liberated by, 33, 39, 45–46

Cockburn, George, xi, 32–33

Colonization Society, 143

Comet, 98

Confederacy, 180, 184

Congress (ship), 39

Congressional Globe, 108

Constitution: gag rule and, 143; impeachment and, 90; presidency and, 54, 56, 62, 87; slavery and, 69, 81, 102, 146, 170, 176, 184

cotton: anti-slavery law and, 101–3; Bahamas and, 6; Britain and, 159, 180; cotton gin and, 12; illegal slave trade and, 14; monopoly of, 180; Texas and, 14, 177–78, 190

Cranch, William, 56

Creole: overview of, 1–3; crew of, 16; exoneration of mutineers, 174; Giddings's nine resolutions, 169–71; lessons of, 197–200; New Orleans and, 100–101, 105; slaves released from, 41–43, 99; Southerners and, 48, 96, 101, 115, 118, 125–27; testimony of crew, 95–96; US Navy and, 175. *See also specific topics*

Crescent City. *See* New Orleans

Crittenden, John, 64, 83, 86, 88, 90, 91, 173

Crockett, Davy, Jr., 160–61

Cumming, Hiram, 81

Curtis, Blinn, 18–19

Cushing, Caleb, 171

Cuthbert, Alfred, 141

Decatur, 97

Declaration of Independence, 110, 152, 153, 176, 180

Democratic Party, 53, 66, 172

Weld, Theodore, 135: overview of, 136–39; anti-abolitionist attack on, 141; Bible and, 132; congressional debates and, 138, 140, 147–49, 151, 153, 155–56; *Creole* case and, 142, 147, 151, 157–58; gag rule and, 147; petition campaign and, 134; Select Committee and, 142; writings of, 132–33, 137

Whig Party: anti-Tyler manifesto, 86–88; authority of, 53; collapse of, 54, 82; criticism of, 58; divisions within, 149; Harrison and, 63; slavery and, 61, 82, 132–33

Whitney, Eli, 12

Wilson, Hiram, 9

Wise, Henry: overview of, 14, 59; Adams and, 150; Clay and, 53, 58; congressional debates and, 154, 156, 157; Harrison and, 51; kitchen cabinet and, 78–80; states' rights and, 61; violence and, 155, 174; Webster and, 65, 80

Woodbury, Levi, 185

Woodside, William, 39–40

Wright, James, 9